STEINHARDT

A Time to Speak

A TIME TO SPEAK

by

Seymour J. Cohen

JONATHAN DAVID, Publishers
New York

Contents

CONTENTS—*continued*

CONTENTS—*continued*

CONTENTS—*continued*

Introduction

The sermons in this volume, which follow the order of the weekly Torah cycle, were first heard from the pulpit of The Anshe Emet Synagogue. Many of them appeared in the congregational Bulletin, in a revised form. I attempted, through them, to help the worshipper get a better understanding and keener appreciation of the weekly biblical text.

This publication might never have seen the light of day were it not for the helpfulness of Mr. and Mrs. Morrie Chaitlen, in reestablishing the Anshe Emet Publication Fund. I am indebted to this wonderful couple for their thoughtfulness and generosity. Other friends have joined in strengthening the publication effort. I include among them, Mr. and Mrs. Joseph M. Levine and Mr. and Mrs. Irving Crown.

My heartfelt thanks goes forth to Mrs. Priscilla Fishman, who was kind enough to read the entire text. A gifted editor, Mrs. Fishman made many valuable suggestions for the improvement of style. Dov Prombaum, and my elder son, Marc David, read the proofs.

Through all of these years, my dear wife, Naomi, has been my most candid critic. Her encouragement, in a myriad of ways, is surely evident in each line of this publication. To her, and to our children, Grace, Marc and Leeber, I express my thankfulness for the joys of maintaining a home where the love of our tradition is ever manifest.

Montaigne compared authors (and this is surely true of preachers), to "bees who pillage here and there among the flowers, but who succeed in producing honey which is entirely their own." It is my hope and prayer that this volume will be pleasant to the taste of all.

SEYMOUR J. COHEN

8th Day of Hanukkah, 5728
January 2, 1968

Genesis

At Last I Can See

"And God opened her eyes and she saw a well of water." (Genesis 21:19)

NORMALLY, OUR ATTENTION is focused on the principal personalities in the great Biblical epics. We attempt to understand the lives of these great men and women, and illuminate our own existence through an appreciation of their deeds. On Rosh Hashanah we concern ourselves with faithful Abraham, we re-examine the testing of Isaac, we hear the lament of Rachel, and we are torn by the trials of Hannah. But it is good to remember that along with the great there were also Biblical men and women who were splendid in small roles. Let us spend a few moments on one of the supporting characters in the drama which unfolds these days.

The center of our attention is forsaken and forlorn Hagar, Abraham's concubine who bore him Ishmael. Later when the aged Sarah was blessed with Isaac, familial strife developed. At Sarah's request Hagar and her child were banished. They wandered in the wilderness until Hagar's water supply ran out. Not knowing what to do, and unable to watch her son's suffering, she left the child under one of the bushes to shield him from the sun, and sat down at a distance. Terrified at the fate which faced her and her child, she burst into tears. The Bible reports that God then opened her eyes and she saw a well. The well was there all the time, but Hagar was so immersed in her anxiety that she was unable to see the solution to her problem. How often in life, what we are looking for is right in front of us, but we do not open our eyes to find it.

This summer I read a remarkable book called *The Phenomenon of Man*. Its author, Pierre Tielhard de Chardin, was

3

a French Jesuit, a priest-scientist, who was concerned with man's becoming more truly human, realizing his potential, completing and fulfilling himself. De Chardin saw his work, which was published posthumously, as an attempt to see and to make others see, what happens to man. He argued quite cogently that the whole of life lies in the process of seeing.

The history of the world, he held, is a constant attempt of man to develop more perfect sight. It is through clear sight that we understand the wonderful world about us. "To see or to perish," is the very condition laid upon everything that makes up the universe. This is the great either-or which man must respond to.

As I read Pierre Tielhard de Chardin, I recalled a story by John Griffin, an Air Force Sergeant who had suffered a concussion during World War II when his bomb-laden plane exploded. His vision faded away slowly until he was totally blind. He married subsequently, was blessed with two children, and began to earn a living as an author. Then, twelve years after his accident, as he was walking from his home to his workshop, he suddenly began to regain his vision; a blockage of the circulation to his optic nerve had been broken. He saw his wife and beheld his young children for the first time. "You don't know what it is for a father to see his children for the first time; they are much more beautiful than I ever expected."

Griffin's entire body and mind were shaken by this most traumatic shock. The doctors recommended that he go to a quiet monastery, until he adjusted to his miraculous recovery. In a diary he described how he waited for the blessings of sight to be restored; he describes the intense experience of joy for which sight served as the instrument.

He delights in his ability to read his morning prayers; he is moved to be able to read the words of the 19th Psalm, "The law of the Lord is perfect, restoring the soul . . . " "The commandment of the Lord is pure, enlightening the eyes." As his soul was nourished, as these words of Scripture sank in, he felt an awakening of tenderness and love for all creation. He had but one prayer at that moment: "If only these clari-

4

ties could remain always, to erase the numbness of the end-less pettinesses." Now he understood God's reason for re-storing his sight.

All of us in a sense are blind, and there will be no greater moment for us than when we are able to see clearly again, to use Pierre Tielhard de Chardin's words. "I doubt," he wrote, "whether there is a more decisive moment for a think-ing being than when the scales have fallen from his eyes." In that moment a man realizes or discovers that he is not alone in this world; he discovers that he is not an isolated being lost in the cosmic solitudes. When man is able to see and appreciate and understand, he realizes his place in the context of the great world about him. "When there is no vision, the people perish," Proverbs tells us. We might add, when there is true vision a people lives, creates.

This is, perhaps, the meaning of our prayers on Rosh Ha-shanah. Like Hagar we are wanderers in the wilderness of life. Each of us is a *Homo viator*, the "itinerant man," to borrow Gabriel Marcel's phrase. Each of us is a pilgrim. "Perhaps," this French philosopher wrote, "a stable order can only be established on earth if man always remains conscious that his condition is that of a traveler."

In our lonely passage through this world we are terrified, we are anxious, we burst into tears. Yet God's will, which can sustain us, is so near. We have only to open our eyes to find it. There is an eternal source of meaningful faith near us. It can provide us with life-giving sustenance to nourish us in our wanderings. This holy day is an invitation to each one of us to open our eyes, to begin to see, and find renewal in life.

5

Sight and Insight

"When the woman saw that the tree was good
for eating and a delight to the eyes ..."
(Genesis 3:6)

MANY MODERNS pride themselves on their sophistication and dismiss the opening chapters of Genesis as stories that only a child can believe. They forget that the Bible was, and is, primarily an adult book that has a host of profound messages.

In the spirit of seeking for the message of the Bible, we ought to re-examine the accounts of Adam and Eve. You know the story well. The first couple was told that they were not to eat of certain trees of the Garden. The woman, after a conversation with the serpent, looked at the tree of knowledge. She saw that the tree was good for eating and "a delight to the eyes ... She took of it fruits and ate; and she gave some to her husband also and he ate."

Eve made her judgment, as so many of us do, based upon one consideration. If something is pleasant to our eyes we find it acceptable. There is nothing intrinsically wrong in admiring and appreciating appearances of beauty, provided that we go a little further in our examinations. We judge by eye-appeal, and much talent and money is invested to make things acceptable to our sight.

A charming story, told of a first century rabbi, concerns a delegation which went to Rome after the destruction of the Temple, to petition the emperor for a more lenient treatment of the subjugated people of Judea. Among the petitioners was Rabbi Joshua ben Hananiah. A man of great wisdom, talented in speech, logical in argument, he was physically most unattractive. The emperor's daughter met him and was taken aback by him. She exclaimed, "What brilliant wisdom in such an ugly vessel!"

The emperor's daughter made her judgment based upon what her eyes beheld. Judging people by our modern standards of beauty, a philosopher like Moses Mendelssohn, or a mathematician like General Electric's researcher, Charles Steinmetz, would rarely expect to be invited to participate in a telecast. Their physical appearances would rule them out.

The rabbis tell that the eyes see, the heart covets and the hands attain. The moment we behold something which appears atractive to us we want it. Our evaluations are superficial.

During these last few weeks I have been rereading the life of Samuel. Samuel anointed Saul as the first king of Israel, but it soon became apparent to the old leader that Saul was not the man to lead Israel. God commanded Samuel to anoint another monarch to replace Saul, and to go to the city of Bethlehem to consecrate Jesse's son. Which son was never designated.

When Samuel beheld Eliab, the eldest son, he said to himself, "Surely the Lord's anointed is before me." Eliab was handsome and of imposing height. His stature was regal, his bearing correct, and it appeared that he would be a natural successor to Saul, who was massive in build. The Lord said to Samuel, "Look not at his appearance or the height of his stature; I have passed him by; for the Eternal does not see as man sees. Man looks at the outward appearance, but the Lord looks at the heart" (I Samuel 16:7).

Little David, the young shepherd boy, was then selected. "Man looks at the outward appearance, but the Lord looks at the heart" is a most striking teaching.

In most cases, imitation is not a good thing. The British historian Arnold Toynbee, speaks of the "Nemesis of mimesis." It is dangerous to copy. We lose all hope of originality of personality when we ape and mimic. There is one great quality of imitation, however, which we ought to develop—that

7

which the philosophers called *imitatio dei,* imitating the example of God. As He is gracious, we are to be gracious; as He is generous, we are to be generous. Let us learn to judge as He judges, not merely by sight but by insight.

What Is Man?

"WHAT IS MAN that Thou art mindful of him?" is the question of the Psalmist. It has been repeated in every generation.

MAN IS EVERYTHING

Poetry is one of the best gauges of the spirit of an age. When the poet speaks forth he articulates what sensitive people are thinking. At the beginning of the 20th century the answer to our question, "What is man?" could be found in the typical response of Saul Tchernihovsky:

> *"Laugh at all my dreams, my dearest;*
> *Laugh and I repeat anew*
> *That I still believe in man—*
> *As I believe in you."*

Tchernihovsky, who ranked among the greatest of our Hebrew poets, could be classified as a secular humanist. His was a belief in the inevitable perfectability of man. For him the world was getting better and better. Man was the master of all creation, responsible to no Creator. When men turned to God and called Him king, it was a sign of their weakness. When individual man related himself to a moral God, he underestimated his own power and denigrated his own capabilities. Tchernihovsky's "I still believe in man and the spirit born in him" was a strident note typical of the optimism of the pre-World War I era. Tchernihovsky went on to speak of his optimistic hope in a universalistic society. Men, he felt, would no longer hate, "love at last shall bind the peoples in an ever-lasting bond."

9

MAN IS NOTHING

In a classic account we learn that after Plato defined man to be a two-legged animal without feathers, Diogenes plucked a cock and brought it into the academy. Plato then added to his definition that man was an animal with flat nails, emphasizing that man was no different from the rest of the animal kingdom.

There are others who have reduced the worth of individual man to almost nothing. Over and over again there are those who remind us that man is insignificant. The paradox of our own age is that the higher man soars, the smaller he becomes in individual stature. Though a man might live for even a thousand years, what is the length of his life but a butterfly existence when measured in terms of the age of the universe. Man's greatness and potentiality cannot be minimized, yet we are ever mindful of his weakness and impermanence.

Pascal once spoke of "La grandeur et la misere de l'homme"—man's greatness and his wretchedness.

It is told that the saintly Rabbi Mendel of Kotzk taught his disciples that a Jew ought to carry two pieces of paper in each of his pants pockets. One ought to read, "Behold, who am I but dust and ashes;" the other, "For my sake the world was created."

MAN IS SOMETHING

Man becomes important when his life attains supreme significance, when it relates to God. In the words of Professor Heschel, "Humanity without divinity is a torso." Man unrelated to God is devoid of the qualities by which he is spiritually distinguished from the rest of the natural order.

I think that we have traveled a long way from the time when it was said of a distinguished jurist, "The needle of his compass has never pointed steadily to anything in the sky, to anything transcendent or to anything absolute."

Two world wars, the brutality of man to man, have compelled us to reject the notion "Man is the maker of all deities

. . . builder of all laws and first to last . . . the measure of all things."

Modern man has reached the point where he realizes the impossibility of life without faith. Man is important. Judaism has always emphasized this. His life attains supreme significance, however, when it relates to God. In an age when the poor were held in no esteem, the Bible rang out, "Who so mocketh the poor blasphemeth his Maker. The rich and the poor meet together—the Lord is the Maker of them all."

Modern literature is filled with numerous tragic examples of man who strives to build his world, relying only upon himself. A modern Hebrew poet cries out,

"But woe to Man,
Woe if his eyes are opened
Woe to him from the abyss beneath his feet
The bridge to which he trustingly bent—it is straw!"

A Frenchman writes, "Face to face with the universe man would be the sole evidence of his audacious dreams of divinity, since the God he vainly sought was himself."

Our answer to the question, "What is Man?" is a simple one. Man assumes dignity and his life becomes important when he learns to relate to God in faith. So many of us are afraid to retrace our steps and to find our way back to Him. Perhaps we need the courage of a young Israeli soldier who was brought up in a most irreligious background. When taunted by a girl friend who dismissed religion and the possibility of a cultured person becoming a person of faith, this young man wrote, "What is faith, whence does it arrive? Man stands before a mystery which he cannot resolve. What is creation all about? This is a question concerning the very essence of the universe and man's place in it. Is there a goal, a purpose to the world? Is it rooted on an ethical foundation? A man of faith can indeed be a cultured person . . . indeed the greatest among them are people of faith."

11

Legend and Life

SHABBAT BERESHIT is marked by the reading of the opening chapters of Genesis. In a sense, this Sabbath serves as the culmination of the High Holy Day season. The recurring theme of the entire festival season is our constant plea for life. The Biblical account of Adam and Eve in the Garden of Eden teaches us the attitude of Judaism toward the real essence of life, differentiating life from mere existence.

Professor Louis Ginzberg once quoted a legend which asked, "Why did Adam, who was very wise, act so foolishly as to eat first of the tree of knowledge, thus bringing upon himself mortality and ultimate death. Could he not first have eaten of the tree of life and gained immortality? Guaranteed everlasting life, he could have then eaten of the tree of knowledge."

The legend answered its own question by stating that there was something unusual about the two trees. The tree of life was encased and concealed in the tree of knowledge. The tree of knowledge had grown its bark completely about the other's trunk. Adam was compelled to eat of the tree of knowledge in order to reach the tree of life.

Life is meaningful only when it is based upon understanding and appreciation. Through knowledge, the distillation of the collective wisdom of man, we touch the very core of our being.

We Jews always gave a top priority to religious education. Historically, the first stages of a new area of Jewish settlement were marked by the establishment of a school. In his studies, Dr. Solomon Schechter pointed out that when our ancestors fled to Amsterdam in the 16th century, their first task was to build a school. The community of Cracow, in the same century, after passing through terrible epidemics, reorganized

12

its schools at the earliest opportunity. This action was taken at a time when the community was experiencing great distress and had to undergo many sacrifices.

The early builders of modern Israel also appreciated the significance of schools. At the very moment that the foundation stone of the Hebrew University was laid, artillery fire could still be heard from a battle thirty miles to the north. The wisdom of preparing a proper educational foundation was demonstrated in Israel's recent history. A beleaguered land was able to repel her enemies and to absorb a million immigrants. Only an alert, knowledgeable community could have undertaken so tremendous a task.

What meaning does all this have for the American Jewish community? Professor Louis Finkelstein related that the saintly Israel Salanter converted synagogues into hospitals during an epidemic in Kovno, and observed that "The commandment to heal the sick and save life is so urgent that if a community were confronted with the choice of maintaining, for a time, its synagogues and religious schools or its hospitals, we should all have to agree that the sick come first."

We may now ask ourselves what happens if we are faced with the question of choosing between hospitals, or religious worship and education for an entire generation. What should our attitude be? Judaism cherishes the life of man, but long life is not an end in itself. Life has meaning when there is knowledge. Life has purpose when there is understanding.

The American Jewish community would do well to grant a high priority to Jewish and general education, commensurate with the great concern we have for the raising of our medical standards. Medicine adds years to our lives; religious knowledge adds life to our years. We have demonstrated that the Jews of this generation are master builders of magnificent hospitals and wonderful medical schools. May history also regard our age as one which was concerned with knowledge, wisdom and understanding.

Brothers All

SCRIPTURE IS FILLED with instance after instance of the bitter conflict between brothers. The opening chapters of the Bible tell us of Abel's murder. When asked "Where is your brother Abel?" Cain responded, "I do not know. Am I my brother's keeper?" Elsewhere in the book of Genesis, we have the accounts of Isaac and Ishmael, Jacob and Esau. Finally, a goodly part of the first book of the Bible is given over to the tragedy of Joseph and his brothers.

Professor Abraham Heschel holds that the bitterness that arises between brothers is part of our human situation. Human beings have a brother-to-brother relationship, and therein is our grief and our glory. Conflict between brothers arises from our very humanity. During the incident of Abraham's separation from his relative Lot, the patriarch said, "Let there be no strife, I pray you, between you and me, between my herdsmen and yours, for we are men who are brothers" (anashim ahim anahnu). The very fact that men are brothers seems to set the stage for potential conflict.

What is at the heart of this painful struggle between brothers? It begins perhaps as a rivalry between siblings. Each child wants to maintain his unique unchallenged place in the family constellation. The frustration in not getting what one wants leads to ultimate controversy.

What does the conflict between brothers bring about? Our Biblical record uses this penetrating expression "They hated him (Joseph) so they could not speak a friendly word to him." They reached a nadir in their relationships which led to a break in human understanding and in communication. Someone wisely observed that if you hate a man you cannot understand him, and if you understand him, you cannot hate him.

14

When Joseph's brothers brought a blood-stained garment to Jacob they said, "Please examine it, is it your son's tunic or not?" Picture the situation. Their hatred for Joseph was so intense that they could not even pronounce his name! How true this is. When someone hates another human being, he cannot bring himself to mention his name. King Saul's hatred for David was so bitter that he inquired about him in these words: "Wherefore comes not the son of Jesse to the meal neither yesterday nor today?" Prince Jonathan, on the other hand, loved the young shepherd and answered, "David requested leave of me."

There is an old legend which tells that King Solomon was in doubt as to where to build the Temple. Upon the instruction of a heavenly voice, he went to Mt. Zion at harvest time under cover of night. He came upon a field owned by two brothers. One was a bachelor and poor—the other was blessed with wealth and many children. The monarch saw the poor brother adding to the other's heap of grain, reasoning that his brother, with many children, needed more than he did. At the same time the rich brother was adding to the poor brother's store, remembering that his brother was without means. On the very night of Solomon's visit, each brother, a grain sack upon his back, came upon the other. Realizing each other's motivations, they tearfully embraced. Solomon determined that this very spot was to be the future site of the Temple. Any ground which had witnessed so remarkable a manifestation of brotherly love was the proper locale for God's House. Where brothers meet in love and mutual understanding, there is God's sanctuary.

When the prophet Ezekiel spoke of the ultimate reunion of the two Jewish kingdoms which had been divided, he used the symbolism of two sticks. Upon one, at the command of God, he wrote "Judah," and on the other, he wrote "Joseph." He then put them together to make them appear as one stick.

There are many interpretations of this symbolism. The prophet could have used two scrolls or any other objects. May I suggest that the reason why the stick was selected was that a piece of wood can be either a bludgeon or a staff on which to lean. It can be used either to hurt or to help. The struggle between brothers can be a source of strife. Hopefully, however, through deeper understanding, that struggle can be transformed into harmonious living.

Moral "Loners"

"The Lord God said, 'It is not good for a man to be alone, I will make a fitting helper for him.'" (Genesis 2:18)

AFTER GOD MADE MAN he found it necessary to create his mate. Our verse is a most familiar one. A recurring theme in contemporary literature is the loneliness of modern man in our complex society. We appear unrelated to others and are unable to communicate with those about us. As part of "The Lonely Crowd," we are spiritually and emotionally isolated, adrift in the swirling sea of life, lacking the warmth of the companionship of other human beings. Our modern society, with its undeniable blessings, deepens the incidence of loneliness.

In many cases, however, people choose to be alone. They guide their lives by self-determined moral principles. Their values are related only to themselves. They reject collective morality. These moral "loners" make decisions which affect themselves and, more important, the lives of others, based upon what has been called a "privatist" ethic. If a pattern of behavior meets their private, personal standards and appears to be good for them, that is all that counts.

A serious moral crisis in French society hit the world's press several years ago. All over France cheating on examinations was becoming a widespread practice. In one city, 80% of the students who took a special qualifying examination knew in advance what questions would be asked. Copies of the baccalaureate test were being sold on an open black market. French parents, when questioned as to their reaction, were unmoved. Observers felt that in many cases the parents themselves were implicated. They knew about their chil-

17

dren's actions and, in some instances, even made the cash available for the purchases. The excuse that was offered condoning their children's behavior was that the examination meant life or death for the student. A student in France cannot go on to higher education without successfully passing the baccalaureate examination. The children who cheated realized that they were cheating and decided to save themselves and not the system.

To get back to our own nation, a dean of women in a southern college reported that there was not only an increase in cheating in all phases of American education, but what was worse, a shift in attitude towards acceptance of cheating.

The basic assumption of those who act alone in decision-making is that individual misconduct is of no social consequence, especially if no one gets hurt. Tragically, we must confess that this "privatist" ethic is repeated in all walks of life, in hundreds of different situations.

The basic point of departure of religion is that man cannot fulfill himself in a lonely life and in making moral decisions in isolation. "It is not good for man to be alone" means, among other things, that only by responsible participation in society do we really grow. In response to other men we ourselves become men. Broadening our concern from ourselves to other men enriches our lives. The more expansive our concern, the more normal we become.

There is a wonderful story about two disciples of a teacher who asked him, "We are taught that we must bless God for the bad as well as the good. How is that possible?" "Go to Reb Zusya," replied the sage, "he will give you the answer." They sought out Reb Zusya and found him at study. His face was furrowed by the sorrows of a tragic life. His coat was clean, but patched. As he gazed at the two students, he asked, inquiringly, "You came to see me?" "Yes," they answered, "we came to find out how it is possible for a Jew to praise God for the troubles that come upon him as well as the joys." Reb Zusya, who hardly knew a good day in his life, who rarely had a full meal to eat—yet reflected a spiritual radiance, smiled and said, "You came to ask me—how would I

18

know? I never had any trouble in all of my life." Zusya's life had been meaningful, for it was not confined within an egotistic framework. People who think only of themselves find that their problems loom extremely large. When an object is held too close to the eye, optically it appears out of its real proportions.

When men think only of themselves, when they chart the course of their lives with their own private star as the only fixed point in their personal heavens, they lead lives which are psychologically destructive. Their ethical system is based upon their own self-made standards. They cannot fulfill themselves. Man is a being who realizes himself in society.

When we attempt to utilize a "privatist" ethic as our chief device for self-fulfillment, we fail. When we cut ourselves off from other men in making our decisions we convert the very knife, an otherwise useful tool, into a dangerous weapon. When we cut away the bond which binds us to other men, we are in danger of inflicting mortal wounds not only upon our flesh, but upon our minds. A "privatist" ethic is psychologically destructive. "It is not good for man to be alone." Man can only fulfill himself in the fellowship of others.

What of Our Generation?

*"And Noah was a righteous and wholehearted
man in his generation. Noah walked with God."*
(Genesis 6:9)

IN READING THIS VERSE, the phrase, "in his generations," invited comment by our sages. There was considerable
discussion in the interpretive literature on the meaning and
intent of the words. Some observers said that Noah was a good
man for his age, but that in a better time, amidst truly righteous people, he would not have been so outstanding.

A regard for our surroundings is all important. Long
before sociologist David Riesman spoke of our generation as
being "outer-directed," influenced by our fellow men, Maimonides observed, "The nature of man is that his ideas and
actions are influenced by his friends and associates." In the
12th century, Maimonides said boldly, "Men conform to the
practice of other men in their community" (Hilchot De'ot
VI, I). What is the spirit of our environment which shapes
the thinking of our generation?

Arthur Miller, the playwright, published a perceptive
analysis of our contemporary scene called "The Bored and
the Violent." He observed that brutality is present in our
civilization, manifesting itself most sharply in the cruel ado-
lescent gangs to be found in both our impoverished slums
and our sophisticated suburbs. This unfortunate fact reveals
a world-wide crisis of the spirit; the phenomenon of youthful
delinquency is found on both sides of the Iron Curtain.

Miller seeks out the underlying cause for this unhappy
circumstance. He believes that the essential problem of our
time is boredom. Life is pointless. "People no longer seem
to know why they are alive."

There was a time when we thought that the solution to
the problems of the slums was a purely physical matter. All
that was needed to change the character of society was to clear

our blighted areas and build better housing. However, even in our most opulent communities there have been tragic incidents which reflect man's boredom and the hunt for thrills, and we came to realize that the problem of the modern youth and the modern man will not be solved by physical means alone.

The problem of boredom is not limited to our young alone. Our present prosperous environment has brought mixed blessings. Our generation is sated; the men and women of our times are self-satisfied. On the whole, our lives are uninspiring, and we seek out the physical and tactile thrill. Rather than the experience which dulls our senses though, the thrill which we need is one which deepens our understanding of our role as human beings. Modern man must consciously reach out for inspiration.

In ancient times it was customary to visit one's teacher on the eve of a festival. Why did men travel many miles to see their teacher? It was more than a gracious social call. They went to be inspired.

We can help ourselves rise above our boredom if we consciously seek out the inspiring personalities of our time. We need the encounter with the men and women who can encourage us to become more than what we are. We need the confrontation with those spiritually stimulating individuals whose very presence will give us not only information but also inspiration. They may not always be available to us in person, but we can alleviate our boredom by reading their inspiring works which reflect the permanent values of life.

As Jews there is another exciting dimension to our experience as human beings. Our ancestors visited the Temple three times during the year. We ought to seek the stimulation of a visit to the land of Israel. It is refreshing for an individual who lives a smug life to go out and see a pioneering society, to witness Jewish idealism in action.

We can also seek for the inspiration which comes to any Jew when he appears in a house of worship, finding the emotional excitement of prayer and the spiritual stimulation of the service. We need not be victims of the boredom of our age. Paths of inspiration remain open to us.

21

Spacemen Then and Now

"Come, let us build us a city with a tower whose top shall be in the sky—and make a name for ourselves." (Genesis 11:4)

THEN

WE ALL REMEMBER the story of the Tower of Babel from our childhood days. An early generation of men was unhappy that they were earth-bound. They built a tower and hoped to reach heaven. In the end, their attempt failed. The people of the world who had been united were scattered. In place of one common language, mankind developed many tongues.

The ancients thought that the sky was the floor of heaven, not far above the earth. All that man had to do to get to heaven was to add brick upon brick, pierce the sky, and when the tower was high enough, he would be there. This was mankind's first attempt to reach outer space.

Jewish legend makers embellished the Biblical account. They said that three different groups joined together in this monumental undertaking. The first school of thought said, "Let us ascend into the heavens and wage war with God." Another school spoke, "Let us get to heaven, set up our idols, and worship them there." The third group urged, "Let us ascend into heaven and ruin it with our weapons." The legend goes on to say that years were spent in the building of the tower. The builders became more concerned with the work than with the workmen. As it took a full year to mount to the top, a brick became more precious in the eyes of the builders than a human being. If a man fell down and met his death, no one noticed it. But if a brick dropped, everyone wept, because it took a year to replace it.

22

There is a deeper meaning to this account. Let us consider it as a parable, a narrative which may or may not be literally true. Its purpose is to teach us a meaning beyond itself. Beyond the words which our eyes see, there is a meaning which only our spiritual sight can detect. The Tower of Babel account is the Biblical judgment on any civilization that either refuses to reckon with God or seeks to dominate either the earth or the heavens. It points out the consequences of what famed theologian Paul Tillich called "spiritual capitalism," wherein man develops the notion that everything can be achieved by the human race and that which is achieved is due entirely to man's own efforts.

NOW

There is a similarity between the efforts of this generation and ourselves. We are part of a space age. Our imagination is captivated by the thought of man, who had for thousands of years been earth-bound, being borne aloft into the furthermost reaches of space. Is there not a danger, one might ask, that in such space flight, man might get an inflated impression of his own worth? Certainly man's flight into space gives our generation a surpassing sense of technical achievement. However, a fundamental truth remains: the more our knowledge is expanded the more we realize that we are only on the fringe of complete understanding. Each discovery, each insight, brings man to a new plateau. With every new finding that unveils a hitherto hidden truth about the universe, we discover that other veils still remain. The wonder of the universe, the miracle of our very existence, is still with us.

Religion welcomes the advance of science, but warns that man must recognize his limits, see himself in the perspective of all of creation. He is finite, mortal and limited. You remember the warning that is implicit in the fable of the little frog who blew itself up to vast proportions and boasted of its size. Finally, the frog puffed so much that it exploded. Our own rocket-minded generation can heed the promise of God to Noah after the flood: "I will maintain My convenant with

23

you, that never again shall all flesh be cut off . . . and never again shall there be a flood to destroy the earth" (Genesis 9:11). God will not destroy man, but man has to make certain that he does not destroy himself.

Let man soar into outer space, search deep into the secrets of the atom. Let these discoveries not be used to conquer the heavens, to dominate God, or to make gods out of ourselves. May our discoveries be used for the betterment of mankind and for the well-being of the human race.

In Search of a Name

*"And they said, Come build us a city, and a
tower with its top in the sky, to make a name
for ourselves . . ."* (Genesis 11:4).

THE BIBLE is a many-faceted jewel. Its lustre shines on, un-
dimmed, throughout the ages. The Bible is many things. Essentially it judges man—his aspirations and actions, his
thoughts and deeds. The Bible represents the verdict of
religion concerning the yearnings of man.

Most men share a common hunger. We want to make a
name for ourselves. If one rereads the opening chapters of
Genesis, one notes an ambivalence towards this search for
reputation. The account of the Tower of Babel appears to
condemn the generation of men who sought honor and
glory for themselves. On the other hand, when it came to the
great promise made to Abraham, the first Jew, the Bible
reports God saying, "And I will make your name great"
(Genesis 12:2). This was to encourage the patriarch as he
was about to uproot himself from his father's house and cut
himself off from his native land.

The universal hunger for a name is reflected in world
culture. The almost insatiable appetite for reputation is
stimulated by various factors. Among them is the hope for
an immortality of name. The Greek, Plato, wrote about "The
desire to become famous and not lie in the end without a
name." Ben Sira spoke about those who leave children
behind, "Their bodies were buried in peace, but their name
liveth unto all generations" (44:13-14).

Some men seek for the good name in their own time.

25

Ecclesiastes evaluates life and says, "Better a good name than precious oil."

To understand the dilemma regarding our opening passage, which seems to disparage seeking for a name, and the passages which justify the hunger for reputation, one must understand the significance of the name in ancient man's thought. Martin Buber, in his effort to make the Bible more meaningful, has written about the implications of certain Biblical phrases. He explains that when Moses inquired of God concerning His name—"When I come to the Israelites and say to them 'The God of your fathers has sent me to you,' and they ask me, 'What is His name?' what shall I say to them?" (Exodus 3:13), it was more than a title which Moses was seeking. Moses was asking, "What is Your nature?" When the Bible refers to a person's name, it speaks about his essence or nature.

When Jacob, after 20 years of exile, was returning to his homeland, he had an encounter with a mysterious stranger. The nocturnal visitor blocked his way to the Promised Land. Jacob wrestled with his adversary until the break of dawn, when the stranger pleaded with Jacob to let him go, for the light was coming. Jacob answered, "I will not let you go unless you bless me." The stranger said, "What is your name?" Jacob gave his name, and at that point, Jacob's name was changed to Israel. Jacob, in turn, said, "Tell me your name," but his adversary answered, "You must not ask my name." The name of a person, for the rabbis, was likened to his very being.

If we are willing to grant that a man's name is his nature or his essence, then we can understand why tradition praised those who sought a good name. Man, being true to himself, permits his real personality to flourish and grow. He has a right to seek a good name and reveal his essence to the world. On the other hand, if man tries to develop a reputation based upon artificiality, if he attempts to expand his name based upon notoriety, then his search for reputation is not to be commended.

26

In this context of self-seeking, we can understand the teaching of Hillel: "A name made great is a name destroyed" when it is a case of "vaulting ambition which overleaps itself." If you are true to yourself, to your real essence and nature, the reputation which you have acquired is one which the community should respect.

Best—Not Second Best

"Terah took his son Abram, his grandson Lot, the son of Haran, and his daughter-in-law Sarai, the wife of his son Abram, and they set out together from Ur of the Chaldees for the land of Canaan; but when they had come as far as Haran, they settled there." (Genesis 11:31)

THE FIRST CHAPTERS of the book of Genesis move at a rapid pace. The spotlight of our attention swings quickly from the account of the first man to the trials of Noah. Shortly thereafter, we are already introduced to the patriarch, Abraham. The lesser personalities are carried along in the tide of narrative, and we rarely take time to understand them. It would be worthwhile for us to pause for a meditative moment and consider Terah, the father of Abraham.

Normally, we think of Terah as an idolator. Our school children lampoon him for placing too much faith in his idols. But in all fairness, some credit must properly be given to him. If you look at your text carefully you will see that it was Terah's decision to start the trek to the land of Canaan. An old Rabbinic text pays tribute to him and says, "He arose and went from there (Ur of the Chaldees) for the sake of heaven" (Seder Eliahu Rabba, Chapter 5).

Terah was dissatisfied with Mesopotamian civilization with all its glitter and material wealth. He felt an emptiness in his life. He was determined, though far advanced in years, to make a decisive break, to start a new spiritual adventure, and he took his family with him.

Frequently, ordinary men and women are stirred to extraordinary action. They are attracted by a great cause and

28

commit themselves to a most difficult goal. Then something happens to them. In the midst of the road they give up, they fall by the wayside, and move on no longer. Terah also had good intentions. Originally he planned to go all the way ("they set out together ... for the land of Canaan"). Somehow in the midst of his trek he lost heart ("when they had come as far as Haran they settled there"). The strong Hebrew words "settled there" dismisses the argument of those who say that it was only a temporary stop. Somehow, in the midst of his odyssey, Terah lost heart and tired of his journey. We can speculate on the reasons for his action; perhaps he was too tired to move on for he was an old man; perhaps he was afraid of the uncharted route that lay before him and the wastelands through which he would have to pass; perhaps the surroundings at Haran appeared to be more inviting than he could ever expect to find in barren, far-off Canaan.

Terah's actions are repeated in the lives of many people. These individuals want to change the order of things, and they begin their efforts with resolve. Yet in the midst of the road they accept an inconsequential modification rather than continue to work for a real substantive change. They compromise too soon! So many men have lofty visions and settle for paltry gains.

Abraham, Terah's son, was made of sterner stuff, and he deserved to be the father of all who believe in the one God. He understood the great lesson of life that when one is in search of a great and worthy goal, there is only one way to go, and that is to continue to move on towards that goal. One can never give up, one can never content oneself with the compromise, "Well, I have come far enough; I do not have to move on any farther." For this courageous faith, Abraham was worthy of receiving the Divine summons, "Go forth from your native land and from your father's house to the land that I will show you."

Abraham merited the best because he did not settle for second best.

29

"Who Cares?"

"The earth became corrupt before God; the earth was filled with injustice." (Genesis 6:11)

OUR LEGENDS have expanded the story of the generation of the flood. Sinfulness and depravity became so prevalent that corrupt living was accepted as the norm of behavior. Crimes, ranging from petty thievery to the grossest immorality, were disregarded by a community which was apathetic, self-satisfied and complacent. The generation of the flood lived in an age of abundance. The wantonness of the time was due to the ideal conditions which mankind enjoyed. They knew neither labor nor worry, and as a consequence of their extraordinary prosperity, they grew insolent. In their arrogance, they rose up against God.

They were scoundrels who lived within the letter of the law. What did they do? When a man brought a basket of vegetables to the marketplace, his neighbors would edge up to it. One after the other, they would steal a little, making certain that which they took was worth less than a penny's worth. As the law does not concern itself with trifles, the farmer would have no redress, as each theft was in itself of petty value. With the accumulated thefts, however, the farmer was left with no ware, and no opportunity for justice. "The earth was corrupt before God." Men became so sinful that they were unashamed when they sinned before God Himself.

The generation of the flood suffered from what has been labeled "indifferentism." Their philosophy of life was summed up in the phrase, "Who cares?" Who cares if there is

30

corruption in the world? Who cares if there is evil? Everyone is doing it, and I might as well be like everyone else.

Professor Hugo S. Bergman of the Hebrew University once described the logical outcome of the "Who cares" philosophy. In time, he argued, the philosophy of "Who cares" leads to a philosophy of no choice, of fatalism. This theory of life argues that there is no free choice, that all has been fixed and preordained since the time of creation; that the good man is good of necessity, and the evil man, evil of necessity. We are faced with predetermined facts of existence that we cannot alter. This philosophy of no choice was summed up by Bergman in this simple phrase—"We do not do; everything is being done." This approach to life presents man in a frozen posture. He must accept things as they are. Man does not have to try to change the world in which he lives.

Pathetically, too many people slip into the mood of "Who cares?" Too many accept the evils of our society as the norm. They adopt the attitude of a passive, indifferent onlooker. As long as their own lives are unaffected, as long as their own flesh is not pained, why worry about others? Why worry about the community?

The rabbis warned against the individual who saw his fellow men agonizing in distress and who said selfishly, "I will go home, eat and drink, and peace will be upon my soul" (Taanit 11a). The approach of indifferentism reveals the moral helplessness of these individuals. They have no real ground beneath them and no lofty ideal above them. Any aspiration is limited to personal satisfaction.

Some time ago, a famous actress, Patricia Neal, suffered a massive stroke. Her husband described the ambulance ride to the hospital at the time of collapse. The faces of the onlookers were impassive. As they watched the ambulance and the prone figure, they were unemotional and relaxed. "It's all right," each one of them was saying, "It's not me." How frequently this experience of "Who cares" is repeated. "Who cares" what happens as long as it touches someone else and doesn't affect me?

The story is told of an angry poet who sat in his study and

31

complained bitterly, "The world is selfish." Every man cares only for himself. A person might fall on a public street and no one would stop to help him. Passersby would stare, pause for a moment, and walk by. The poet wrote on and suddenly his peace was shattered. He heard the sound of a child crying outside. Deeply disturbed, with pen still in his hand, he rushed out of his room. Then a moment of genuine joy overcame him. He realized that it was only a strange child crying. The story ends on the note—Only a *strange child!*

A currently popular folk song asks:

> *"How many roads must a man walk down*
> *Before you call him a man?*
> *Yes, 'n how many times can a man turn his head*
> *And pretend that he just doesn't see?*
>
> *Yes, 'n how many ears must one man have*
> *Before he can hear people cry?*
> *Yes, 'n how many deaths will it take till he knows*
> *That too many people have died?"*

The spirit of the generation of the flood has not left mankind. Whenever we choose to wrap the mantle of the innocent and uninvolved bystander around ourselves; whenever we maintain our imagined innocence in the face of evil, pain and corruption in this world—the generation of the flood is still within us.

Abraham, Exemplar of Faith

*"And he believed in the Lord; and He counted
it to him for righteousness."* (Genesis 15:6)

YOU WILL NOTE that the word "He," referring to the
Lord, has been capitalized. Abraham put his trust in the
Lord and God reckoned it to his merit.

A hassidic interpreter gave a most unusual turn to our
text. He said that Abraham felt that his ability to believe
was an act of righteousness and kindness from God; that the
Lord helped him to believe. This teacher would have us read
the verse with the sense that Abraham believed in the Lord
and Abraham counted it for righteousness. To be sure, this
interpretation takes great liberty with the text, yet it does
have more than homiletic meaning. How wonderful it is to
be able to believe! Not all men attain that status.

In interpreting "And thou shalt love the Lord thy God
with all thy heart, and with all thy soul and with all thy
might . . ." a commentator noticed that the Hebrew letters for
"And thou shalt love" are the very same letters which spell
out "the patriarchs." "And thou shalt love the Lord thy God
with all thy heart" reflects the spirit of Abraham, the first
man of faith. "With all thy soul" mirrors the temperament of
Isaac, who was ready to be sacrificed upon the altar. "With
all thy might" typifies Jacob, whose life was one of constant
service to God.

What does faith mean? Faith in Hebrew has the meaning
"steady, firm, dependable." In a most critical hour in Jewish
history, Moses prayed. His hands were heavy, and Aaron
and Hur, one on each side, steadied them, and the Bible
reports, "His hands remained steady until the sun set." The

33

man who places his faith or trust in God believes that there is this element of steadiness in the universe, the world is dependable, there is order to life, man's existence is not subject to the caprice or the whims of the gods. Faith implies confidence in God.

Abraham was the first to teach mankind the essence of real religion. Man's life, interpreted by belief, motivated by faith, is glorious. When life is stripped of faith, existence loses its profoundest meaning and sublimest aspirations.

When the subject of faith is discussed, an oft-present attitude is that "Some people may find it easy to have faith. They have had an adequate religious education, they have been exposed to study and reading, they have met great and inspiring religious spirits." For the average individual, though, the life of faith is almost impossible. One is reminded of the story of the 17th century French writer, Pascal, who was met by a man who said, "I wish I had your faith. Then I would live your life." Pascal responded, softly, "Live my life and you will soon have my faith." Professor Abraham J. Heschel once wrote, "Faith is sensitivity, understanding, engagement and attachment; not something achieved once and for all, but an attitude which one may gain or lose." Faith must be renewed by each generation; recaptured and relearned in each stage in the life of man.

The Psalmist proclaimed, "For the Lord is good; His mercy endureth for ever; And His faithfulness unto all generations." Paraphrased, this may surely mean that God's righteousness, kindness and goodness is eternal, but our faith in Him must be renewed from generation to generation. An ancient source spoke of the reward which comes to a man who has faith and confidence in God. "We find that our father, Abraham, inherited both this world and the world to come only as a reward for the faith with which he believed."

Life in this world takes on its fullest meaning and we receive the promise of a destiny in the future eternity only when we believe. Did not the prophet Habbakuk teach (2:4), "But the righteous shall live by his faith." The righteous is grateful for God's righteousness in endowing him with the ability to believe and to trust.

34

The Courage to Break One's Ties

"The Lord said to Abram, Go forth from your native land and from your father's house to the land that I will show you." (Genesis 12:1)

SEVERAL YEARS AGO an unusual exhibit of tropical birds was presented at the Brussels World's Fair. As visitors passed along a line of brightly lighted boxes, they viewed magnificently colored birds. Amazingly, these birds were not in cages; they were flying around in boxes without bars, netting or glass. Why didn't the birds fly out? Why did they remain confined? Was there some invisible glass or some electrical current which kept them in? To such recurrent questions, the keeper would respond, "No, there is nothing between you and the birds. The only thing that keeps them in is the light."

The explanation turned out to be quite simple. The passage through which the Fair visitors walked was in total darkness. The only light in the building was in the birds' box. The birds were contented to be warm, they were delighted to be well fed, and they could not muster up enough bird courage to fly out into the darkness. They would not venture into the unknown. They were prisoners, not confined by bars which shut them in, but rather prisoners of the light.

As I reread God's command to Abram to leave Mesopotamia, and Abram's courageous decision to go, I thought of this incident of the birds. Abram was told to venture forth from the extremely comfortable, materially affluent, well-lit surroundings of Mesopotamia, and to move forth into the darkness and the unknown. The late Professor E. A. Speiser once entitled the twelfth chapter of Genesis as "The Most

35

Fateful Commencement in History." For the Jew, Biblical history starts with this chapter.

Abram's bravery in setting out on a journey to an as yet unnamed destination, sets the tone of the religious experience of Israel. The words "Go forth from your native land and from your father's house to the land that I will show you" are the true keynote of the entire biblical experience. In commenting on this verse, Speiser paraphrased the medieval commentator Ibn Ezra, "If you understand the secret of this single statement, you will understand the rest."

In the command to "go forth," there is no reference to the past. There is only the insistence that a new beginning for mankind was necessary. The old record had to be wiped clean. This event in the life of the patriarch was to be one of the most decisive in all human affairs. Throughout the history of our people Israel, they would recall and remember this event over and over again.

Abram might have chosen to bask in the strong light of Mesopotamia, but somehow he sensed that there was a better answer to the larger questions of human destiny somewhere else in the world. Abram's decision to leave his native land was a protest against the barrenness and sterility of the Babylonian religion. The validity of his choice has been demonstrated through the history of our people, "a small but dedicated society in one of the remoter areas of the world which managed long ago to maintain itself, and outlast the richest and most powerful civilizations of that age."

Abram had to be courageous to rebel against the religion of the greatest ruling power of his time. He also gave up much material comfort when he left Mesopotamia, but he was aware of an ever growing spiritual deficit in the civilization which he was leaving.

Abram was willing to break with comfort to get a glimpse of a different way of human existence. He left the brightness of Mesopotamia for the darkness of the land of Canaan. There he would behold a spiritual vision which, in the long run, was far brighter than any he had ever experienced in his homeland.

From Abram's life there is a lesson which each of us can learn. Too often we are like the birds of Brussels; we are prisoners of our comforts, chained by the so-called pleasures of the society in which we live. We need the courage of Abram to move forth into a questing life of unseen dangers, but with a bright reward of spiritual freedom.

To Know Him Is to Love Him

"For I have known him, to the end that he may command his children and his household after him, that they may keep the way of the Lord, to do righteousness and justice..." (Genesis 18:19)

WE FREQUENTLY turn to a dictionary to check the meaning of a word or the nuance of a phrase. In some instances we discover that there are alternate meanings. In Hebrew, the verb root "to know" can mean several things—to see, to be acquainted with, to experience.

In commenting upon our verse, which quotes God's words, "For I have known him ..." the medieval exegete, Rashi, interprets "know" as the language of love or of affection. In amplifying his definition that "to know is to cherish," Rashi continues by saying, in effect, that whoever loves a person and is concerned with the intensification of the relationship, brings him closer so that he knows him better and is more familiar with him.

This observation seems to be quite sound. In modern life, because of improved communication and transportation, we are brought into contact with many more people than were our ancestors. Their associations were limited in scope and circumscribed by geography. On the other hand, you and I can span the world in the course of a day or two. We can pick up a phone and talk to someone in any part of the world. A very perceptive sociologist, Ernst van Der Haag, observed that we moderns are acquainted with more people and know fewer persons.

Yes, we nod and greet hundreds and hundreds of people.

38

We may even call them, most familiarly, by their first names. But how well do we know them in the sense of really caring for their well-being?

The only way a person can really get to know and love another human being, to rise above the level of mere acquaintanceship, is by the enhancement of interpersonal relationships. We can only say "to know him is to love him" when we really know and appreciate the next human being. The acid test of the linkage is, "How much have we tried to bring him closer?"

As we think of a deepened bond between men, we can hope for an improved relationship between the Creator and the created, between God and men. In this instance, we need only to capitalize the letter H in our familiar expression— "To know Him is to love Him."

To know God, to know His tradition, is to love Him. I believe that emotion is a powerful element in developing an adherence to religion, but that tie remains loose unless it is strengthened by intellectual attainment. Emotional religion remains superficial unless it is buttressed by study. To know God is to know His tradition, to know the manner in which our ancestors encountered Him. The love for God which comes out of a knowledge of His ways is really a two-way process—the more one knows God the more one loves Him, the more intensely does one search to find out what God desires of man.

"And these words which I command thee this day shall be upon your hearts . . ." was interpreted to mean "place these words upon your heart; thus you will recognize God and cling to His ways" (Sifre).

Will Your Children Be Called
By Your Name?

IN THE ROSH HASHANAH TORAH reading, Abraham is told by God, "It is through Isaac that your name will be carried on" (Genesis 21:13). This was the best assurance that the aged patriarch could receive; his faith would be continued by his son.

Whether dealing with physical possessions or spiritual heritage, we all share a common hope. We wish that what we have and enjoy will some day be bequeathed to our children.

Often, when the peace of night has returned to my household and my children rest in their beds, I wonder whether the promise given to a father in ancient times—that through his child his name would be carried on—might also be granted to me. Simply, I ask, "Will my children be called by my name?" Surely, they will bear the family name, for that is required by law. But, more importantly, I challenge myself by questioning, "Will they bear my spiritual name? Will they be the heirs to the tradition which I love, the way of life which I adore?" Candidly, each of us can question, "Will my child be called by my name?"

The rabbis tell us that a thing is called by a man's name for several reasons. "Everything for which a man suffers is called by his name." Thus, we call our Torah the Torah of Moses. Why? It was Moses who, according to tradition, remained for 40 days and 40 nights on the bleak Sinai peak to receive God's revelation. Moses suffered much to bring Heaven's truth to man's earth. Similarly our children will be called by our name because of the *tzaar gidul banim,* the anguish which is attendant to the process of rearing children;

the pains of childbirth are compounded by the anxieties of puberty and the disturbances of adolescence. Parents continue to experience concern for their children, even when their young have families of their own.

The rabbis offered a second reason for having a thing called by one's name: "That on which a man expends great effort is called by his name." If one expends energy, exerts effort in any good cause, the cause is identified with him. A poet's lines are called by the writer's name because he authored the verse and summoned it into being. He is creatively akin to the sculptor who takes raw materials, fashions them, and causes an object of beauty to emerge. We say of a painting, "This is a Picasso" or "This is a Chagall." The artist's work is known by his name. Your children will be called by your name not only because of the anguish which you felt for them over the years, but because of the many efforts which you have invested in them to assure their physical well-being.

Yet, it is not enough to feel anguish and expend effort. There is another factor which must be taken into account before one's children are truly his own. "Anything for which a man gives of his soul is called by his name." In Hebrew, these words are *noten nafsho alav,* prepared to give, in a figurative sense, of his very soul. This third reason seems most significant.

If one wishes to ensure a successful transmission of a heritage, one must be ready to have whole-hearted devotion, to give of one's very soul and self. If we really want to have our children called by our name we must follow that course of action which gives to our young people the best of the Jewish spirit. We ought to enhance their knowledge of our way of life and enrich their life's experience by having them study together with other Jews. We ought not limit their Jewish knowledge to the minimum that a child should know, but busy ourselves with giving them more and more of our religious heritage.

The passionate hope of a child being called by the name of a parent or grandparent was keenly felt by father Jacob. In his final encounter with his grandchildren, Manasseh and

41

Ephraim, he prayed that, "the God before whom my fathers Abraham and Isaac walked, the God who has been my shepherd from birth until this day, the angel who has redeemed me from all evil, bless the lads. In them may my name be recalled." That our children will carry on our name is among the most precious of all human expectations. May that hope be fulfilled for each of us.

Wholeness and Holiness

"And when Abram was ninety-nine years old, the Lord appeared to Abram and said to him, I am God Almighty; walk before Me and be wholehearted." (Genesis 17:1)

ABRAM IS SUMMONED to a life of spiritual greatness and personal fulfillment. He is asked by God to walk before Him, to accept completely the faith in the One God.

The Hebrew word for whole-hearted has the meaning of completeness. If man is to realize the spiritual dimension of life, he has to be complete and whole before God.

Much of our contemporary anxiety is due to the fact that we are incomplete and our lives are not whole. We are often guided by split standards of values. We live in moral schizophrenia. We believe one thing and act completely differently. Modern man must learn to bind himself together and to become whole by achieving moral consistency and inner integrity. Just as God is One, our way of thinking and our mode of doing must become one.

If we are torn by conflicting emotions and religious feelings, if we feel one way when we are in the synagogue and act another way while we are in the arena of life, we reject the Oneness of God. We must learn from father Abram of old to hear this great call of faith, "Walk before the Lord and be whole-hearted." A splendid story is told of the man who wanted to make a "golem," an image that could be brought to life. To animate this golem, the golem maker would write the first, the middle and the last letters of the alphabet, *"aleph, mem, tof,"* across the forehead of the robot. When the golem came to life, he was fearful lest he become a sinner and, through his deeds, menace the world. The golem pleaded with his maker, "Destroy me before I destroy life." The wonder-worker looked at the inscription of the three letters, *aleph, mem* and *tof*. They spelled *"emet,"* truth. He rubbed out the *aleph,* and all that was left were the last two characters which spelled the word *"met"* dead, whereupon the robot crumbled into the dust.

Once the *aleph,* the "One" is taken out of our lives, once we lose that which makes us wholehearted, there is only void and emptiness. We can lead happy and holy lives by becoming whole men, by leading careers that are integrated and consistent, reflecting God's Oneness and His Unity.

The Divine Encounter

OUR WORLD IS STRANGE and its people are baffling. Persons from the same background, brothers from a common family, relatives who have long lived together, react in varying ways to a similar situation.

Abraham and Lot were kinsmen. They had shared many an experience. Together they had made the long pilgrimage from Ur of Chaldees to Canaan. Abraham, the uncle, had been Lot's great master in the art of religion. He had taught Lot that one of the great manifestations of the good life lies in the proper receiving of people. Both Abraham and Lot received unusual visitors, angels in the guise of men. Of Lot the Bible tells, "And he rose to meet them." Concerning Abraham, it is reported, "And he ran from the entrance of his tent to greet them." How different the conduct of the two hosts. Lot waited, while Abraham went out to meet his guests half way.

This conduct could be expected of Abraham. He actively sought encounters with men in the same spirit in which he sought and found God. A sage once taught that Abraham may be compared to a man who was traveling from place to place on a desolate road. He suddenly came upon a palace that was filled with light. "Is it possible that so beautiful a place has no owner?" Then, the master appeared and identified himself, "I am the owner." So Abraham traveled along the road of life and asked, "Is it conceivable that this world is without a guide, without a ruler?" And God answered, "I am the guide, the master of the universe."

Implicit in this account is the thought that, at first, man must seek God, and when he does, God will meet him half way. "The Lord is near unto all who call to Him, to all those who call upon him in truth." Man must begin the search. He must ask the question and then God will respond to him.

A delightful story is told of a little boy, Yehiel, the grandson of a hasidic teacher, Rabbi Barukh. Once he was playing hide-and-seek with another youngster. Yehiel hid himself well and waited for his playmate to find him. He waited and waited, and finally came out of his hiding place. The other lad was nowhere to be seen. It suddenly dawned upon Yehiel that his friend had not looked for him from the very start of the game. In tears, he ran to his grandfather and complained bitterly of his faithless friend. Tears welled up in Rabbi Barukh's eyes, and he said, "God says the same thing: 'I hide, but no one wants to seek Me.' "

Man must, like Abraham of old, be prepared to meet God half way. The initiation of an occasion which will ultimately lead to divine encounter was caught in the words of Judah Halevi:

> *"I have sought Thy nearness.*
> *With all my heart have I called Thee.*
> *And going out to meet Thee*
> *I found Thee coming toward me."*

For the Sake of One Look

"Flee for your life. Do not look behind you, nor stop in the Plain; flee to the hills, lest you be swept away." (Genesis 19:17)

"Lot's wife, behind him, looked back, and she thereupon turned into a pillar of salt." (Genesis 19:26)

SURELY YOU HAVE had this experience. You obtain a new mechanical device or electrical appliance. Prominently on the package these words appear—"Do not use before reading the instructions."

My interest is focused on a woman who did not listen to instructions. You remember the familiar story of how two messengers came to Lot and his family. They told Lot about the fate which lay in store for his adopted city of Sodom and warned him to leave the city in time, as it was on the brink of destruction.

Lot tarried and delayed his departure. Finally the two messengers seized his hand, the hands of his wife and his two daughters, and forced them to evacuate the city. At that very moment one of the men issued instructions to the entire family to be sure to keep moving on, and added one specific detail of warning, "Do not look behind you."

Lot's wife did look behind and the Bible records that she turned into a pillar of salt. This unusual account made a deep impression on the ancient mind. More than 1500 years after the incident, authoritative Jewish and Christian historians reported that it was still possible to see the pillar of salt that was once Lot's wife.

I am amazed every time I reread the Rabbinic comments on

47

Lot's wife's action. Most commentators speak of her transformation as a punishment for not heeding the specific directions of the men who were the messengers of God. But there are those who condone her action instead of condemning it. What made her turn around, they ask. Her motherly instincts compelled her to look around. Apparently this school of thought believed that she felt pity for her married daughters, who were still in Sodom and she looked behind to see if they were following her. (In addition to the two daughters identified in the Bible, this midrash speaks of two married daughters.) Lot's wife could not control herself; her feminine compassion forced her action.

This sympathetic understanding of Lot's wife was also expressed in a Russian poem written by Anna Akhmatova (1889-1965). Akhmatova started her literary career as a poetess of passion concerned essentially with self, but the tragic events of the First World War and the Russian Revolution "turned the languorous self-centered woman into a Sibyl of old." From a poetess of passion she became a poetess of compassion. Amidst the cataclysmic events that shook her native land, the poetess could not forget her past, and though it appeared, by 1923, that the past had disappeared forever, and would never be restored, its recollection haunted her. Using the image of Lot's wife she expressed the ambiguous character of her grief. She understood that Lot had been led out of Sodom by God, but she could not help but have a deep sympathy for his wife, who wanted one last look at the place where she had been a bride, borne her daughters, and known happy days.

> She turned her back to look but was frozen by anguish
> Of death, and her eyes could no longer see;
> Her body was turned to salt, and imprisoned
> By earth were her feet, as she sought to go free.
> Is there nobody who will shed tears for this woman?
> Or feel for her loss and the choice that she took?
> In my heart alone she shall not be forgotten,
> Who gave up her life for the sake of one look.

The writer's compassion for the woman who gave up her life "for the sake of one look" raises a fundamental question. When is it good to look back? When, on the other hand, is it improper and wrong to look back?

ON LOOKING BACK

Various observers have suggested that people look back because they are afraid to look forward. We live in a world of rapid change. For many people any change in the status quo, any altering of the familiar, stirs up anxiety. They face terror at every turn in the road, suffer a morbid fear of what the future has in store for them. There are some who look back because of the almost hypnotic power of their past. They are obsessed by their old failures and their attention is riveted upon the shortcomings of their past. This looking back is unhealthy, for it immobilizes and freezes the observer into inaction.

Some men come to this point of life as they pass an eventful birthday, and then with a sigh say, "If I could only turn back and live my life over again." But it is impossible to turn back.

S. I. Agnon, Nobel Prize winner for literature, wrote in *A Guest for the Night* of a man who returns to the town of his youth. He had been away for many years and he finds his town in ruins. "He seeks solace in the locale of his tranquil childhood, in nostalgia, but discovers that the world of childhood, of home, of the *shtetel* is no more." Arnold Band, Agnon's narrator in this story, discovered that which Thomas Wolfe found and used as the title of his last novel, *You Can't Go Home Again*. One cannot look back in vain regret and self pity. One ought not look back, if that which we will behold will not enrich our future.

Perhaps the answer to the question, "When is it good to look back?" can be stated simply. It is good to look back when our hindsight judgment will commit us to work for a healthier future.

Important and Urgent

"The Lord appeared to him by the terebinths of Mamre; he was sitting at the entrance of the tent as the day grew hot. Looking up, he saw three men standing near him. As soon as he saw them, he ran from the entrance of the tent to greet them . . ." (Genesis 18:1)

IN THE POPULAR MIND, there are national types. When one thinks of a Frenchman, one imagines him to be a lover. The Englishman is depicted as a staid and dignified gentleman. The Jew is typified as a frenzied, rushing individual. We seem, to some observers, to be a people who are always in a hurry.

There are times when being in a hurry, rushing and running, is the proper response to the demands of life. In the biblical account of Abraham's confrontation with three visitors, we see Abraham agitated and excited. "He *ran* from the entrance of the tent to greet them . . ." "He *hastened* into the tent to Sarah and said, Quick . . . knead and make cakes." Then, "Abraham *ran* to the herd, took a calf . . . and gave it to a servant boy, who *hastened* to prepare it."

Our commentators explain that Abraham was not well when the three men approached him. At an advanced age, he had just gone through the covenant of circumcision. Despite his temporary physical disability, he sat at the entrance of his tent hoping that he would find some wayfarers upon whom he could lavish his most gracious hospitality. The patriarch could have used every type of excuse to absolve himself from fulfilling this mitzvah. Yet the Bible describes Abraham as *running* and *hastening*.

50

Abraham was a remarkable teacher; he was demonstrating that what is important to you must become urgent. In life, there are many important things which await our action. Only when we consider them to be urgent do we manage to deal with them. To the Jewish mind, the giving of charity was an important and urgent activity. Helping another man was regarded as being so urgent that we must rush to do it. Unlike other commandments for which there is a prescribed blessing before doing the deed, when we give charity, there is to be no interruption between the need for the deed and our carrying out that responsibility. We do not recite a blessing before practicing *zedekah*.

In the area of race relations, Americans have long recognized the importance of a constant improvement in the lot of those who are the victims of racial discrimination. The pressure of the civil rights movement has made this amelioration an urgent matter. What was important for 100 years since the end of the Civil War, has now become urgent.

Searching for peace has always been important. This quest has preoccupied the attention of American statesmen for a long time. But the importance of restoring peace to Southeast Asia has been escalated to an urgent issue.

The need for self-government among the emerging African nations is considered as an important need of our time. The precipitous action of the Rhodesian Prime Minister, Ian Smith, has converted this question into an urgent one.

In Jewish life, every intelligent observer has recognized the importance of maintaining the loyalty of our young people to our faith. One did not have to be a highly perceptive observer to realize that inter-marriage was mounting. A year ago, one magazine article in *Look*, "The Vanishing American Jew," took the important issue of Jewish survival and made it an urgent one.

In all of these illustrations, swift action is of the essence. We must act upon what is important and urgent before it is too late.

When a man learns to respond quickly, to become involved in human service, something happens to his soul. His stature

51

as a human being seems to grow. Observe the sequence of the verse which describes Abraham's meeting with the three men. As the story unfolds, *three men stood over him*. Abraham rises to the situation. "He ran to meet them." At that moment, *he was face to face with them*. After Abraham carried out the good deed of hospitality, the account reads, *"He stood over them."* When we have the courage to face life's challenges; when we have the good sense of dealing with that which is important and placing it in the category of "urgent"; when we rush to do that which has to be done before it is too late, we grow a little taller and we add inches to our spiritual height.

Unfinished Man

WHEN ISAAC WAS BOUND upon the altar, he asked a fundamental question that had long troubled him. He inquired of God, "King of the world, when You made the light, You said in the Torah that the light was good. When You made the heaven and earth, You said in the Torah that they were very good. When you made every herb and every creature, You said that they were good. But when You made man in Your own image, You did not say in the Torah that man was good. Wherefore, Lord?" The answer came down from heaven on high to the earth below. God responded, "Because man, I have not yet perfected. Through the Torah, man is to perfect himself and to perfect the world."

This remarkable legend teaches a most profound lesson. Man is incomplete. Man must strive to complete himself. He is the partner with God in the creation of the whole man.

Albert Camus in *The Rebel* emphasizes this point: "Man ... is not a finished creation but an experiment of which he is partly the creator ..." Many important modern thinkers of the 19th and 20th centuries have written in a similar vein. Though these great minds did not agree on what man must ultimately become, they all stressed that "man is not complete, that he is in the process of being created, that he must be further transformed before he can attain his definitive nature." (Henry Nelson Wieman in *Man's Ultimate Commitment.*)

Some time ago, a distinguished anthropologist, tracing the development of man, made the point that it is dangerous for man to crystallize his final conception of himself. The human race, he argued, has the possibility of improvement and betterment. Man has been on the face of this globe for a long period of time. Throughout history, at many critical junctures in human development, it would have been possible to say, "This is man!" But these words would have been mind-freezing. They would have immobilized the development of man at every step of his long odyssey through time. Each time that man thought that he was complete, that he had reached a barrier to further development, somehow this barrier was surmounted. Man was able to maintain an even higher degree of perfection.

Man is always *becoming*. He must continue the struggle to perfect himself.

There are students who constantly look back to man's past and accent the inadequacies of his nature. But the great thrust of human life is in the future. The Jewish philosopher Ahad Haam observed that man is a combination of memory and will. Memory reflects the past, and will is part of our hope for the future.

The dynamic of futurity has been one of the most powerful factors in Jewish life. We revere the past, persevere in the present, but we pray and work for the better future. As we read the Torah, we are strengthened by the memories of how man attempted to perfect himself. We are not disheartened by the realization that in our own lifespan we personally will not be able to attain the level of the complete man. We know that only part of this task can be completed by any human being. Though we cannot finish the task, we do not permit ourselves to stand by idle. When the Torah reports the completion of the first stage of creation, we read, "God blessed the seventh day and hallowed it; because in it He rested from all his work, *asher bara Elohim la'asot.*" This last phrase is grammatically difficult, and is literally translated as "which God created to make." The verb form, *la'asot*, is in the infinitive, "to make." From this we may learn that the world is still being made. Our personal world, our personal being, is still being perfected. The best is yet to come.

Who Was He?

THE BIBLE DOES NOT supply us with the names of all the characters on its vast stage. Frequently only an allusion is supplied, as in the case of Abraham, "He saw three men standing near him." The Bible tells us that "Jacob was left alone; a nocturnal visitor came upon him, and the man wrestled with him." The stranger and the patriarch were locked in battle. As the antagonist attempted to prevail, he injured Jacob's hip. Despite the pain Jacob held on to him tenaciously. The opponent pleaded, "Let me go for dawn is breaking." Who the man was, his true identity, is not disclosed.

Years later, Jacob sent his favorite son, Joseph, to find out how his other children were faring. Joseph met a man as he was wandering in the fields. The man asked him, "How can I help you? What are you looking for?" Here again the Bible gives us no clue.

Legend has it that both of these encounters took place not with men but with angels. In the case of the first experience, Jacob's adversary-angel was anxious to run, for he had duties in heaven. At dawn, together with the other members of the celestial chorus, he would sing praises to God. Joseph's angel on the other hand wanted to be helpful to men.

An old preacher Rabbi Leib, who, I am sure, never missed an opportunity for required prayer and voluntary blessing, said, "See the difference." One angel wanted to run away. He used his practice of the ritual as an excuse to escape from his ethical responsibilities. On the other hand Joseph's angel realized the importance of the ethical act of giving direction to the wanderer and guidance to the troubled in heart. Rabbi Leib, who was a very devout Jew and kept both the ritual and ethical law, was emphasizing that some seemingly pious men use ritual to help them avoid direct confrontation with life.

It is not altogether easy for a rabbi to translate the ethical teachings of Judaism and make them part of our people's day to day affairs. Most individuals live by the notion that it is hard to keep the ritual law. They think of the restrictions and remember the limitations. Yet ritual is easier to live with than ethics. If you probe just a little you will see that the discipline of ritual is easy for the committed Jew to follow. The ritual law is precise, specific and carefully spelled out. One can dramatize the beauty of our observances and develop a moving rationale for their symbols. When it comes, however, to carrying out the ethical imperatives of Judaism we face a far more difficult task. It is much easier to live with a code than to wrestle with your conscience. Ethical decisions are not simple matters of black on white, comparable to looking up a law as to the correct time for the lighting of candles or the number of months that a child ought to say *kaddish*. The ethical life is made up of many shades of gray. When we are faced with an ethical dilemma we are confronted with alternatives, and a choice must be made between conflicting values.

A case in point may be the problem of an aged mother and her middle-aged daughter who debate in the rabbi's study the proposition that an aged person should not live with a grown child and her grandchildren, but ought rather go to a home for the elderly. The apartment is small and there is tension between the generations. The middle generation is caught on the horns of an ethical dilemma. We must honor our parents. On the other hand, we have a responsibility to our offspring. Ethical decisions are hard to make, for they deal with emotions which are psychologically painful. How easy it is to talk about human rights and human dignity when they are in the abstract. How difficult is it to realize our lofty ideals when we are faced with a concrete situation. "Wholesale arrangements," a wise American once

56

observed, "are different than retail ones" (Oliver Wendell Holmes).

We must always remember the ethical demand that "As in water face answers face, so the heart of man must be ready to respond to the heart of his fellow" (Proverbs 27:19).

An Extra Phrase

"And these are the days of the years of Abraham's life which he lived, a hundred three score and fifteen years." (Genesis 25:7)

BIBLICAL CHRONOLOGIES are most uninviting to the average reader. When we see a listing of names and years, we are usually tempted to skim or skip over them. Our commentators, however, as keen students of Scripture, approached the Bible differently. They saw a significant lesson in every word and even in each letter. May I cite an example of their method in interpreting the verse read in the synagogue this week? At first glance, the description of the passing of Abraham attracts little attention. We learn the bare facts that the patriarch lived to a ripe old age. Upon closer examination, however, we observe that although Biblical Hebrew is usually quite terse and to the point, there is a redundancy in language in this verse.

"These are the days of the years of Abraham's life which he lived." It is obvious that when a man has had so many days and lived for so many years that he lived. The expression "which he lived" appears to be superfluous. A commentator reflected, "What is the meaning of the extra words 'which he lived'?" He answers his query, "This is to tell you that all his days were full of life and there was no death in them." This is an exciting thought. Abraham lived an affirmative existence: nothing in his day-to-day activity smacked of negativism, of destructiveness and of death. Everything that he did was positive, creative, and lifegiving.

We may, at this point, ask, "What gives life to the living?" Men answered this question by their thoughts and through their deeds. In the grey dawn of consciousness in ancient

58

times, men's great concern was with immortality, survival after death. The landscape of the ancient world is filled with man's attempt to live on after his passing. Pharaoh's pyramids are perhaps the best case in point. The ancients' greatest concern about life was projected into the future. Their constant preoccupation with immortal life gave life to the living. Medieval man was busy with thoughts which were largely heavenly-bound. His thinking was filled with celestial notions. The hopeful expectation to participate in God's Heavenly Kingdom affected literature and dominated the pictorial arts. Go to any museum and study the paintings of the Middle Ages. A goodly number of them deal with Heaven, the Throne of God, His angels. Constant thought of heavenly life gave life to the medieval man.

In modern times, when we ask, "What gives life to the living," the answer usually revolves about the idea of meaning.

For modern man, the basic building block in the structure of his personal existence bears the label, "meaning." Men want to feel that what they do, when they pour out their energies, apply their talents, and give wholly of themselves, stirs the moment, that all their activity has meaning. We feel alive and are assured of our vitality when we sense that our contribution, our effort, our participation is significant. We feel alive when we believe that what we are doing is relevant and that as human beings we are understood.

A second important factor in giving life to the living is the sense of assurance that what we are doing is not a transitory act that will be dissipated by the passage of time. We hope that our actions are blessed with permanence, that they possess lasting qualities. We measure our efforts constantly. "Will it survive for the ages?"

In Hebrew, the phrase *sh'nay haye Abraham* (the years of the life of Abraham) is the same as the expression for the "two lives of Abraham." This is the twin hope of modern man, that what he does, stirs the moment and survives for the ages. May we be blessed with that contentment which comes from the knowledge that our life is full of living, that it has meaning for today and eternity.

59

Three Ways

"And Isaac went out walking in the field toward evening..." (Genesis 24:63)

THE RECENTLY PUBLISHED new translation of the Torah has aroused world-wide interest. During the past 50 years great advances have been made in the knowledge of Hebrew and other Semitic tongues. Many new insights have been obtained from a better appraisal of ancient and medieval Jewish sources, and from recent archeological discoveries. We are now in a better position to appreciate the setting against which our Bible was composed, and to comprehend its meaning more fully.

In the process of their work, each verse of the Torah was carefully examined by the translation committee. The learned men debated the meaning of each passage, and from the heat of their argument the new translation was hammered out on the forge of their joint efforts.

Our particular verse troubled the scholars. They were not certain as to the meaning of the Hebrew word *la'suah*. The translation which they finally accepted was, "Isaac went out to walk in the field toward evening" when he encountered Rebecca and her party. In a footnote, some of the translators suggested that the verb ought to be translated "Isaac went out to meditate in the field..." Maintaining their intellectual integrity, the translators went on to report that the exact meaning of the Hebrew word, whether it be to walk or to meditate, is uncertain.

WALKING IN THE FIELD

Man must learn to break away from routine. All too frequently, and sometimes tragically, physicians remind us that excessive stress and undue emotional strain are injurious to health. To recoup our emotional balance we must tear away from our normal activities, which, judged by objective standards, are often abnormal. We should recharge ourselves and bring our efforts into proper perspective. Walking in the field can be helpful in relieving the pressures of working in tense cities.

MEDITATION

There is a second level of recuperative experience suggested by our alternate translations. Walking in the field is good; intensifying that change through meditation is, perhaps, better. If one wants to regain inner stability, a pause, a vacation is not enough. The break may give us some physical rest and even some temporary relief for our flagging spirits. Soon, however, we discover the good effects have worn off, and we are back to our troubled selves. Meditation helps focus our attention on the lasting and the significant. Judaism appreciated meditation and encouraged it.

A THIRD WAY

There is, within the Jewish pattern, a third way by which we can bring our lives back into balance. This road is the path of prayer. The rabbis ascribed the establishment of the morning prayer to Abraham. Fancifully they said that Isaac, when he went in the field, was going to participate in the afternoon prayer. Prayer has meaning, as the Psalms say, "A prayer of the afflicted, when overwhelmed by his suffering, he pours out his plea before the Lord." Public prayer can help bring us back to our senses. Joining others in a group experience aids in lifting the burden which egocentric, self-centered thought places upon our shoulders. We no longer are like Atlas, bearing the burdens of the world alone. The company of other men lightens our tasks.

Many of you will retort very quickly, "This is not my experience. Public worship has little effect upon me. It leaves me cold." The truth is that we leave the synagogue cold because we have entered frozen.

The other day I read a small but significant work by a German Catholic thinker. He observed that no one with a serious task before him approaches it without preparation. "If we appreciate good music, we shall not arrive at the performance at the last minute, allowing for no transition between the noise and unrest of the street and the opening bars of the concert. We shall be there in good time and hold ourselves ready for the beautiful experience before us."

Let us ask ourselves honestly and candidly, "How many of us come into our service prepared for the experience which we are about to undergo? How many of us are like the early saints who spent hours in meditation before their minutes of prayer?"

If prayer is to have meaning for us, we must prepare for the ecstasy of our experience, and be able to concentrate upon it. What we Jews call *kavanna,* Christian thinkers label "collectedness."

Prayer can have little meaning if the worshipper has not focused his thought on the very activity in which he is engaged. Too often we are harried by life and disturbed by events which distract us. We are agitated by the hyper-activity which marks most of our schedules. We are perpetually in motion, either moved toward some desired goal or running away from some imaginary or real fear. It is hard for us to concentrate, but unless we master that mood our prayers will have little significance.

What Isaac did that afternoon can be understood in different ways. Whether Isaac was simply walking in the fields, or was a troubled soul trying to think things through, or whether his activity was actually a forerunner of public prayer, is not of ultimate importance. What is important is that at different times of our lives it is essential to our moral and spiritual well-being that we partake of one or the other varieties of this experience.

The Creative Pause

"And Isaac went out walking in the field toward evening..." (Genesis 24:63)

IN OUR TRADITION, with its veneration for the old, the more ancient an institution, the more authentic its character was regarded to be. The sages dated the practice of prayer to the age of the patriarchs. These founders of our faith, they said, were the first to worship. Abraham instituted the morning prayer, Isaac established the *Minha* prayer, and Jacob recited the evening service (Berakoth 26b). The rabbis interpreted "And Isaac went out walking in the field ..." to mean that he went out to meditate, and "meditation means prayer."

It is important for our modern generation to grasp the significance of the *Minha* service. Nahmanides, a 13th century scholar, interpreted the word *"minha"* as coming from the root "to rest." The purpose of our afternoon prayer, which takes no more than five minutes to recite, was to break into the day. *Minha* was the creative pause: it gave man the opportunity to find his spiritual bearings in the midst of a busy, and at times trying, working day.

If the morning service commences our day, and the evening prayers conclude our activity, *Minha* comes to correct our efforts.

What in our life stands to be corrected? Lionel Trilling, Columbia's Professor of Literature, in an article analyzing the mood of our modern age, observed that "the predilection for the powerful, the fierce, the personally militant, is very strong in our culture." This partiality for the powerful must be braked. Life cannot consist only of forward movement;

63

our existence must be marked by moments of rest and renewal. Our working day is filled with occasions that threaten
the annihilation of our soul, the destruction of our spirit,
and the demeaning of our better self. Much of our daily
work deadens our sensitivities. *Minha* comes in the midst of
the day and summons our attention; bids us meditate on life
and stabilize ourselves.

The *Minha* service is opened by the reading of the 145th
Psalm, which ends with the words "Hallelujah, bless the
Lord." In a mystical passage of the Talmud, we read that
David composed 103 chapters of Psalms, and did not say
"Hallelujah" until he saw the downfall of the wicked, as it
says, "Let sinners cease out of the earth, and let the wicked
be no more. Bless the Lord, O my soul. Hallelujah." The
numerical value of the letters in *Minha* is 103 (*mem*=40,
nun=50, *het*=8, *hay*=5). The sages understood this to mean
that when a person recites the *Minha* service he takes on a
David-like mood. He tries to correct his shortcomings and to
recapture his basic humanity. Only then can he joyfully proclaim the triumph of his spirit and sing, "Hallelujah!"

A Frightened Man

"And Isaac trembled very exceedingly." (Genesis 27:33)

ALL OF US ARE familiar with fear. Fear can be both teacher and tormentor. A child, for example, is taught at an early age not to touch an open flame or an excessively hot object. Unwarranted fear, on the other hand, can ultimately destroy even our mental balance.

Isaac had known fear. He had been bound by his stern father, Abraham, on the altar of sacrifice. No one who has ever had a loaded gun pointed at him or an unsheaved knife menacing him can ever forget this experience. Isaac lived through such a grim moment of bone-chilling dread. Much later in Isaac's life his son Jacob, aided and abetted by Rebekah, tricked him. He posed as his older twin Esau and the blind father gave him his brother's blessing. A while later, Esau appeared on the scene, bearing savory food. Suddenly it dawned upon Isaac that a ruse had been pulled on him. He "trembled very exceedingly."

The rabbis questioned which instance of fear caused greater anguish. They were inclined to believe that the second was the more disturbing as the Bible read, "And Isaac trembled very exceedingly."

A 19th century commentator tried to explain the difference between the two harrowing experiences. He observed that a Jew trembles when the knife is upon him. A shudder goes through us whenever we learn of an incident anywhere which threatens Jewish security. Anti-Semites are cast in the mold of the Pharaoh who said, "Let us then deal shrewdly with them." There is a straight line from Pharaoh with his plan to destroy all Jewish male babies, to Adolph Hitler with his heinous plan for the final extermination of our people. The commentator went on to suggest that there is a second type of threat which causes us to shudder even more than when we are endangered physically. This is the approach of an Esau. He comes to us bearing savory food. His hands no longer carry the knife drenched in blood. Now they are covered with silken gloves. This type of potential destroyer utilizes another approach. Like Balaam of old, who was retained to curse the Jewish people, he reports to his master, King Balak, with a new plan. He advises him how the Jewish people can become the King's people. What is his scheme? He will weaken our moral standards and destroy us from within.

This interpretation was offered during the Emancipation when we were permitted to become citizens and to enter into the political life of Europe. The Emancipation, to be sure, was a mixed blessing. There were some leaders who went to extremes and opposed our entry into a fuller civic status. They listened carefully to the words spoken at the French National Assembly by Claremont Tonnere: "To the Jews as a nation, we must deny everything; to the Jews as individuals, we must grant everything." The Jew was expected to divest himself of his Jewishness and to become part and parcel of the host nation. This was the threat of the destroyer who wore silk gloves and bore gifts of savory food.

Professor Solomon Schechter, who was concerned with our people succumbing to a slow extinction marked by a loss of spiritual identity, wrote, "It is this kind of assimilation ... that I dread even more than pogroms."

One hundred fifty years of experience have tempered the negative aspects of the Emancipation and taught us how to live in a free society.

There remains, however, a second type of threat which comes dressed in silken gloves. These words are being spoken on Thanksgiving weekend. Though we are grateful for all of the bounties of our society, we shudder as we consider the impact of modern materialism. We dread to think of how it has affected the character of so many who live in this affluent civilization. We are concerned with the ultimate effects of our disproportionate emphasis on material living standards as compared to spiritual standards.

Perhaps the savory society is a greater threat than the menacing sword. Ultimately our over-concern with abundance can do more damage to the Jewish spirit than the threat of the enemy's knife to the Jewish body.

The Wisdom of Caution

"And it came to pass when he had been there a long time." (Genesis 26:8)

FACED BY FAMINE, Isaac moved to Gerar, where a more adequate food supply was available. Concerned about the possible designs of the men of that community upon Rebekah, his attractive wife, the patriarch identified her as his sister. After a while the Bible reports, "And it came to pass when he had been there for a long time" that Isaac (to use modern parlance) "dropped his guard." Through his actions towards Rebekah, it became evident to observers that she was his wife. A commentator explains why Isaac was less cautious. He had been there a long time and reasoned, "Now I no longer have to worry." He was less circumspect in his conduct and did not watch himself.

A Jew cannot afford the luxury of lowering his guard. He cannot lull himself into a sense of false security by saying, "I have been here a long time, now I no longer have to worry." We Jews ought to be mindful of the very nature of our being. You remember that when Abraham had to bury his wife, Sarah, he sought a final resting place for her. He went to the people of Heth and identified himself, "I am a stranger and a sojourner with you." This is the existential character of our being. We are sojourners; we are deeply committed to the well-being of the land in which we live. We seek the peace of the community and we make every effort to enhance the welfare of all. Yet despite our efforts, in the eyes of some we remain the outsiders, the strangers.

Although anti-Semitism in the 1960's does not pose the threat that it did during the brutal and bitter days of Adolph

68

Hitler, I do not believe that we can afford the luxury of thinking that as we have enjoyed a relatively calm period for so long a time, we can drop our guard.

Aspects of the recent American elections point to an upsurge in anti-racial feeling. The dregs of the 1966 election campaign will be sour to our taste for a long, long time. Across the length and breadth of our country some candidates for public office traded on fear and hatred. The "white backlash" to the civil rights movement was exploited for political gain. Unfortunately, racism, both Negro and white, and the recollection of the summer's violence were an encouragement to bigotry. The exploitation of false fears muddied the entire inter-group relations picture.

While overt anti-Semitism continues to decline, radical right extremism poses a continuous threat to our democracy. In the past, most of the extremist thrust was towards one political party; recent campaigns in the South have witnessed extremist involvement on behalf of candidates of the other major political party.

What the future will bring in this area has been the subject of much discussion. During a recent conference of the American Jewish Committee it was reported that there has been a sharp reduction of anti-Semitic attitudes in our country. Recently, the Committee published *Jews in the Mind of America,* a full length study on this subject. On the occasion of the publication there was a full dress discussion as to whether mass anti-Semitic hostility can reoccur in the United States.

The optimists pointed out that our faith is respected as one of the three major religions of America along with Catholicism and Protestantism. Our citizens are less and less concerned with differences of ethnic character. They are not vitally interested, the analysis ran, in where a man has come from; they are more concerned as to where he is going. Those who look hopefully on the American scene claim that the tensions of mass immigration provided the element that disturbed the tranquility of earlier years. As ours is no longer a country of immigrants, this source of tension will disappear, they hold, and they see anti-Semitism as a declining phenomenon. "It will fade away, for the intense anti-Jewish feeling was only transitory rather than a permanent phase of American history."

On the liability side of the ledger, some competent scholars stressed that one should not ignore latent anti-Semitic factors. True, they argued, there has been a more general acceptance of Jews in American society. Mankind has learned the tragic lessons of World War II as to where hatred and malevolent attitudes can lead. Israel has created a favorable image for the Jew. Yet despite it all, "The attitudes of Gentiles towards Jews are likely to remain uneasily balanced between acceptance and rejection."

Turning from our domestic scene to the European continent, we find sufficient reason for concern about the recent success of the neo-Nazi party in West Germany. The growing strength of the National Democrat Party in the 1966 elections has caused great consternation. This ultra-right-wing party includes many ex-Nazis in its ranks. In the national elections in neighboring Austria, anti-Semitic sentiments were frequently expressed. Former Nazis continue to hold high posts in German and Austrian cultural, industrial, and political life.

History can teach us many lessons. Perhaps one of its most important teachings is that one can never afford the luxury of false security.

We must strengthen our resolve to live as Jews; we must work for the enhancement of our own morale. Alongside of these positive actions, let us never ignore the threats which remain to our very existence.

Prerequisite to Peace

"And Abraham took sheep and oxen and gave them to Abimelech, and the two of them made a pact." (Genesis 21:27)

"And they said . . . let us make a pact with you." (Genesis 26:28)

AT THE ELEVENTH HOUR of the eleventh day of the eleventh month in 1918, a terrible world conflagration came to an end. In reality, the fires of war were never extinguished. The Second World War and the Korean conflict were direct results of the first global hostility. Thinking men and women ask, "Is there a possibility of permanent peace? What must we do?"

In a set of incidents recorded in Genesis, a suggested course of action is intimated. Abraham tries to make peace with Abimelech. The Bible tells us, "And the two of them made a pact." Apparently, the agreement was not binding. A generation later, Abraham's son, Isaac, is again involved in a controversy with Abimelech. What happened? Why weren't the arrangements lasting?

A 19th century preacher observed that the Hebrew text actually read, "And they made, the two of them, a pact." Though they had signed the treaty, they remained two separate parties. As a result, because there was no fusion of interest and concern, there was no permanent peace. On the other hand, in the case of Isaac and Abimelech, the latter said, "Let us make a pact with you." They tried to join their personalities together. Lasting peace is attainable only when nations are willing to surrender part of their national sover-

71

eignty for the sake of a higher purpose. As long as countries enter into treaty arrangements and they remain "the two of them," division and potential destruction remain ever present.

The Persian poet, Yallaladeen, tells a beautiful parable of a lover who knocked at his beloved's door. The young lady's voice asked from within, "Who is there?" and the lover responded, "It is I." Then the voice inside said, "This house will not hold you and me" and the door remained closed. The lover went into the desert, fasted and prayed in solemn loneliness. After a year he returned and knocked again at the door. The beloved asked, "Who is there?" and he answered, "It is you." The door opened. The moral seems to be obvious. The lover had crossed the boundary of personal selfishness. He had learned to identify his well-being with that of his beloved.

When we learn to put ourselves in another person's place, feel his hurt, rejoice in his hour of gladness; when nations learn to share on the highest level of human experience—then there is a possibility for peace. History will say of that generation, "You are truly the blessed of the Lord" (Genesis 26:29).

The Grief and the Glory

"Jacob left Beer-Sheba ... He came upon a certain place and spent the night there, for the sun had set. Taking one of the stones of that place, he put it under his head and lay down in that place. He dreamed and, behold, a ladder was set up on the earth and the top of it reached to the sky, and angels of God were going up and down on it." (Genesis 28:10-12)

JACOB'S DREAM has been one of the most favored passages in world literature. Many an author has used it as a springboard for developing his particular philosophy of life. A.D. Gordon, for example, speaking of the Jew's aspiration for a national home, said, "And what are we seeking, is it not a resting place for the ladder?" The Jew hoped for a national home in which he could rebuild himself and permit his spirit to grow.

Jacob's dream was extended by the rabbis in their legends. They commented on the patriarch's proclamation, "How awesome is this place. This is none other than the house of God and this is the gate of Heaven!" The sages felt that God had caused the sun to set prematurely so as to speak to Jacob in the greatest of intimacy. "It is as though a loving friend came to visit the king from time to time and the king said, 'Put out the candles for I wish to speak to my friend alone.'"

Some writers have protested against both the grief and the glory which came from Jacob's dream of our people's destiny, binding heaven and earth together. One writer, Yitzchak Lamdan, had Jacob musing, "Let me walk the roads of life, a slave to the toil of day, free to night's rest." The poet felt that our people were entitled to a better life than the sort of existence given to a distinguished folk. Unless God could give our people the blessings of a normal, placid experience, dwelling upon a verdant land, Lamdan wanted neither the honey of Jacob's destiny nor the sting of being God's ambassador to the world.

This philosophy of life is at the core of the argument of those who ask that our people become "a normal people" like all of the other nations. They want to enjoy the imagined peace of the ordinary.

On the other hand, the writer Richard Beer-Hofmann saw in Jacob's dream the summons of greatness. He visualized an angel telling Jacob what his future would be like, "It is true that you may wander eternally, but rest never! And Home? A word without meaning for you." Despite the warning of the angel, Jacob accepts the challenge of his fate. He is ready to bear God's burden.

We Jews accept proudly the pain which we have borne as Jacob's children. We know, as one writer expressed it, that it is our patent of nobility, the origin of our people's greatness and the fount of our pride. When we wonder whether history could not have given us a less meaningful assignment and a less difficult fate, we ought to proclaim with the words of Hosea, "Who so is wise let him understand these things, who so is prudent let him know them. For the ways of the Lord are right and the just do walk in them." The glory of being God's chosen has more than compensated for the grief that we have sustained.

The Father Image

THE MIDRASH concerning the life of Jacob enriched the Biblical account of the patriarch's life and tried to fill in the details of his career. When the Bible spoke of Jacob fleeing from the wrath of his brother, Esau, the legend amplified the Biblical account. Jacob was seen as pausing, not only for nocturnal rest, but to engage in petitionary prayer. He was visualized as reciting a verse from the Psalms, "I will lift up mine eyes unto the mountains, from whence shall my help come."

The Hebrew word for mountains is *harim*. It is close in sound to the word *horim*, parents. Jacob, in a sense, was saying, "I will lift up mine eyes unto my parents." From their courageous experience I shall draw my hope.

Observers have noted a lack of concern of American college youth for political questions, their general lack of involvement with the basic issues of the day. They have also commented that the present generation of college youth lacks admired paternal figures. These young people do not and cannot look up to their fathers. Contemporary American culture does not hold the father in high esteem. If we examine our modern literature, which is a good gauge of the mood of our times, we find that seldom is there a depiction of the father of our literary heroes. Our theatre, television, and even our comic strips, lampoon the head of the family. He is a good natured soul who has to be humored along.

American fathers seem unable to fulfill their traditional psychological role as exemplars. College teachers frequently hear their students bemoaning the fact that their parents give them little authoritative guidance. "If only they would tell me what they think I should do!" Our young people are looking for direction, which they apparently are not getting from their fathers. Dr. Benjamin Spock observed that "many psychiatrists and school counselors find adolescents wishing their parents were stricter." Our youngsters would like to have demands placed upon them.

They will look up to their fathers when their fathers' lives represent affirmative and positive values in action. Young people need these models after whom they can pattern their lives. They require the example of older adults "who will act as guardians of their identity while it is still fledgling. When such models and guardians are absent, the young people feel and indeed are cheated" (*The American Scholar,* Fall, 1962).

These two observations—one from an ancient source and the other from a current magazine—teach a most powerful lesson. Jacob was able to look up to his fathers. They stood for great values and realized them in their lifetimes. Let us honestly ask ourselves, "Can our children, who need our advice and counsel so desperately, do the same?"

A Legacy of Dreams

"And Jacob went out from Beer-Sheba, and went toward Haran. And he lighted upon the place, and tarried there all night, because the sun was set; and he took one of the stones of the place, and put it under his head, and lay down in that place to sleep. And he dreamed and behold a ladder set up on the earth, and the top of it reached to heaven; and behold the angels of God ascending and descending on it." (Genesis 28:10-12)

THE HEBREW WORD for ladder is *sulam*. Its letters are the same as the word for "symbol" *(semel)*. The account of Jacob's dream is one of the most beautiful in all of the Bible. It has been interpreted and reinterpreted in every generation. This vision of the night can best be understood in a symbolic sense.

The three-fold repetition of the word "place" suggests a relationship between Jacob's dream and the future fate of his children. The vision was a "signature of Jewish destiny," foretelling three temples which would be called the "place." The first two sanctuaries would go up in the flame and fury of wrathful enemy destruction but the third would stand forever.

Our own generation has seen the fulfillment of Jacob's dream. The third temple of Jewish life is being built this very moment in the land of Israel. To be sure, it is not on the site of the old "place." This temple is rather the sum of all that has come into being in the Holy Land.

One wonders where our people got the power to hope for

77

a restoration of Jewish life and a rebuilding of a temple amidst the adversities and the bitterness of two thousand years of exile. There was one great source of strength—a Jacob-like ability to dream, to be hopeful though the mood of the time was desperate, to be courageous in an atmosphere darkened by the stark realism of persecution and misunderstanding.

The world of the dreamer-people was sustained by the re-reading of the words of our inspired prophets of old who spoke of rebirth and renewal. The prophets were great not solely by virtue of the majestic grandeur of their gripping words, but by the very fact that they had the strength to speak forth. Their addresses were in contradiction to what life about them seemed to say.

Father Jacob had every right to be despondent. He was a refugee, fleeing from the wrath of his brother, running in order to save his life. Yet he had the courage in the darkest of his hours, with only the stars of heaven to comfort him, to dream of the ultimate restoration and redemption of his children. Jacob's strength is our legacy. His power has sustained our people across the many generations even unto this day.

May our generation, too, be blessed with the fulfillment of the prophet Joel's words:

"And it shall come to pass afterward,
That I will pour out My spirit upon all flesh:
And your sons and your daughters shall prophesy,
Your old men shall dream dreams,
Your young men shall see visions."

A Three-Pronged Question

"And he instructed the one in front as follows,
when my brother Esau meets you and asks you,
'Whose are you, where are you going, and
whose are those before you?' you shall answer,
'Your servant Jacob's; they are a gift sent to my
lord Esau; and Jacob himself is right behind
us.'" (Genesis 32:18)

MANY PEOPLE send gifts before them on the occasion of a visit. Jacob's presents were being sent in hope of placating a brother long angry for having been tricked out of receiving the blessing of his father. Jacob had to flee to the haven of his mother's family in the north. Though twenty years had passed, Jacob remained fearful that his brother would be unforgiving. On the way home to his birthplace, Jacob sent gifts before him and instructed his men: "When my brother Esau meets you and asks you, 'Whose are you, where are you going and what is before you . . .?' " This three-fold question is among the most incisive that any man can ask.

THE SEARCH FOR IDENTITY

One of the greatest problems which has always faced man and which troubles most modern men keenly is the question "Whose are you?" "To whom do you really belong?" The Yiddish writer, I. L. Peretz, tells a wonderful story about the ramblings of a student. As the story opens, he is rushing back and forth all alone in the small Bet Hamidrash. Suddenly, the student stops himself and asks, "Almighty God, who am I?" He knows that he bears a name, but a person is more than the name he carries. He goes on to realize that to different people he means different things. The student becomes more confused and he says, "But I must have some idea as to who I am!" The student reaches the point where he would like to step out of himself, to examine, search out, and find his identity. This quest to find ourselves, to answer the question "Whose are you?" goes on continually in the minds of sensitive men.

THE HUNGER FOR MEANING

"Where are you going?" is the second phase of this three-fold query. A story is told of a great rabbi who was put in a Czarist jail on trumped-up charges. He was awaiting judgment when the warden came in. The chief keeper noticed the serenity of the rabbi and mused to himself, "This must be a thoughtful man." The warden, a bit of a Bible student, decided to question his charge. "If God knows everything, why did He ask Adam when he was hiding in the Garden of Eden, 'Where are you?' Didn't God know where the first man was?" The rabbi paused for a moment and then answered, "God knew where Adam was, but did Adam know where he was?" The rabbi turned to the Russian officer and continued, "At various times in his life, God comes to man and says, 'Where are you in your world? Realize that you have a fixed number of days. So many of them have already passed and where are you going?'"

The Hebrew words "Where are you?" can also be read as "lamentation." If man does not know where he is going, surely there is much to cry about.

REAL ACHIEVEMENTS

The third part of the question is, "Whose are these before you?" What is the nature of our real achievements? We play so many different roles at the same time. We are driven by so many factors. At times, we support positions which are, upon deeper analysis, diametrically opposed to one another. For so many of us, our life is but a patchwork. We need what

80

Martin Buber once described as a "united soul." We need desperately a unified principle which will bind us together.

We are all traveling on the road of life. It is good for every voyager, after he has covered some distance on his life's journey, to stop for a moment and to ask himself three most probing questions: "Whose are you? Where are you going? Whose are those before you?"

The Changed Joseph

*"When Joseph came up to his brothers, they
stripped him of his coat, the coat of many colors
that he was wearing; and they took him and cast
him into the pit."* (Genesis 37:23-24)

*"And Joseph's master took him and put him
into the prison, the place where the king's
prisoners were bound; and he was there in the
prison."* (Genesis 39:20)

I HAVE OFTEN WONDERED about the transformation
in the character of Joseph. From a spoiled young man who
tormented his loved ones, he ultimately became a righteous
man. His first appearance on the stage of history was when
he strutted out, bedecked in his coat of many colors. His
final achievements were the loving maintenance of his family
and the wise leadership of all Egypt. Though he rode the
crest of personal success, Joseph banished all thoughts of
vindictiveness against his brothers who had mistreated him.
He provided amply for them and treated them with the
greatest of respect.

Obviously, Joseph changed as he grew from youth to
maturity, and the change was for the good.

What transformed Joseph? Might I suggest that his bitter
experiences of being thrown into the pit by his brothers, his
release, his going down to Egypt, and his imprisonment for a
second time on trumped-up charges, caused the decisive
change in him. Being thrown into the pit twice is the key
factor in understanding Joseph.

In *Joseph and His Brothers,* Thomas Mann describes
Joseph going down to prison and the pit for the second time.

He is submitted to the greatest of indignities. Transported on a small freight boat on the Nile, his arms are bound together at the elbows across his back, and he has to be fed. During the long and protracted journey, Joseph recalls what had happened to him, his father's love, his going down to Egypt, his temporary respite, and now the pit again. When his guard permitted him to walk on the deck of the small ox boat that was carrying him, Joseph watched the peasants at work on the fertile shore.

He saw them going through the mournful task of burying seed into the dark soil. "It is a time of weeping—Joseph wept a little himself at the sight of the corn-burying little peasants, for he too was being buried again into the darkness, and into hope only too far away—in token that a great year had come round as well and brought repetition, renewal of life, the journey into the abyss." But Joseph sensed that as the seed would come back into renewed life after the Nile had overflowed its banks, so he too would emerge. Though he was going as the seed into the pit, he would rise again. Joseph's hope was restored; he felt that he would come forth out of the pit to a higher life.

Some men go down into the pit and are destroyed. Their personalities are maimed and they are crushed forever. Others go down into the pit and they emerge all the stronger.

A number of examples fill my mind as I reflect on Thomas Mann's insightful interpretation. For the last few years, the intellectual community has been stirred by the posthumously published writings of Teilhard de Chardin. During World War II, this French Jesuit scientist was practically imprisoned in China for six years. He had been appointed to an important post in Paris, but the outbreak of the war prevented his traveling to France. The experience of this pit-like existence gave him an opportunity to reflect on his research and to develop his thinking. Sir Julian Huxley comments that "his enforced isolation . . . painful and depressing though it often was, undoubtedly helped his inner spiritual development (as the isolation of imprisonment helped to mature the thought and character of Nehru and other Indians)."

In our own country, Martin Luther King, Jr., who had been imprisoned frequently during the civil rights struggle, was once jailed in Birmingham. Eight clergymen of the community urged him to desist from his work. He had no paper but the margin of the newspaper on which the clergymen's statement appeared. Without the benefit of any library, King began his response. The answer was continued on scraps of writing paper supplied by a friendly Negro trusty. It was concluded on a pad that King's attorneys were eventually permitted to leave him. King wrote one of the great documents of human freedom. He called it, *Letter From Birmingham Jail.*

In the world of fiction, many of us have read the best seller, *The Fixer,* by Bernard Malamud. The hero, Yakov Bok, became a greater man as a result of his imprisonment. The harder his jailers pressed him, the more they tormented him, the greater he emerged. Even solitary confinement and being chained to the wall did not break him. A simple man became a giant of the spirit as a result of being in a Czarist pit.

What happens to man in the pit may be understood as an experience of solitude. In an essay, a boy of 17 visualizes "Michelangelo's Moses, head in hands, the attitude of a child who prays with eyes closed; of a pianist—his back to the audience; they must be alone that they may offer what is most treasurable, themselves."

All of us go through periods of isolation. We partake of the loneliness of the pit of life. May we emerge like Joseph—as ennobled human beings.

Staying Awake

"And Pharaoh awoke. He fell asleep." (Genesis 41:4b-5a)

"Jacob awoke from his sleep and said, 'Surely the Lord is present in this place and I did not know it.'" (Genesis 28:16)

AS I GROW OLDER, I find it more difficult to enjoy a complete night's rest. Going to bed with the problems of the day, I find that they awaken me during the night.

In Genesis there are two accounts of men whose sleep was disturbed. One was a fugitive fleeing from his brother who was determined to harm him. He slept on a hard stone and the Bible reports that Jacob awoke from his sleep and said, "Surely the Lord is present in this place and I did not know it." A little later in the Bible, we have the story of an Egyptian ruler who slept in a far more comfortable bed than did the patriarch. Nevertheless, his sleep was also disturbed. The Bible reports, "And Pharaoh awoke. He fell asleep (again)."

What a remarkable difference we see in the two experiences. Jacob is aroused and declares his faith in God. Pharaoh awakens, turns over to the other side and goes back to sleep again. This is the nature of human experience. Two people live through a similar event, one is stirred into action and the other goes back to sleep again.

A Viennese journalist, Theodor Herzl, was among the spectators, surely including other Jews, who witnessed the humiliation of Captain Alfred Dreyfus in Paris in 1895. Herzl was so moved by his experience that he could not rest until he developed a plan to restore Jewish dignity. Other Jews merely went back to their pedestrian activities.

You surely remember Rip Van Winkle. He went to sleep, a subject of King George III. He awoke 20 years later a citizen of the newly established United States. He slept through a revolution. It is hard to imagine that Rip Van Winkle's sleep was not disturbed by all of the fighting which took place up and down the Hudson River Valley. But Rip Van Winkle did not remain awake. Like Pharaoh, Rip Van Winkle did not stir himself to find out what was happening. He went back to sleep again.

The late brilliant Aldous Huxley, though nearly blind, saw more in human life than most better-sighted men. In his last essay, he made this observation, "Our business is to wake up ... We must not attempt to live outside the world which is given us but ... somehow learn to transform it and to transfigure it." Man's duty is to see the potentialities which are before him. A better life does not come automatically unless we are stirred inwardly to its possibilities.

Unfortunately, we miss our opportunities. We incorrectly gauge the situation in which we find ourselves. At times, we reveal another shortcoming. We do not properly estimate the abilities of the men and women whom we encounter.

A remarkable incident is told by one of the great rabbinic leaders of the American-Jewish community. Early in his career, he served as adviser to Jewish students at a renowned Eastern university. The dean of the university invited him in to review his responsibilities. The dean was disturbed that the Jewish students, immigrants or the sons of immigrants, were burning too much of the midnight oil. They were bookworms, "grinds." They did not have enough of the old "college spirit." Finally, the administrator revealed his bias and said, "Perhaps they would be better off if they were tailors or carpenters like their fathers." The dean underestimated these wonderful human beings who have since brought great glory to their university and have helped to enhance American life.

86

So many of us, as we see the latest group of immigrants to our city, those who come from Puerto Rico, or from Mexico, those who move from the south, both Negro and white, underestimate their ultimate potential. Let us see the traces of greatness in every human being and not miss the opportunity of building a better America.

As the great New England philosopher, Henry Thoreau, once observed, "Only that day dawns to which we are awake."

Brother or Other

ALL OF US are familiar with the dream of Pharaoh. "He was standing by the Nile," when out of the river, "came up seven cows, handsome and sturdy, and they grazed in the reed grass. And behold, seven other cows came up from the Nile after them, ugly and gaunt, and they stood beside the cows on the bank of the Nile; and the ugly, gaunt cows ate up the seven handsome, sturdy cows" (Genesis 41).

There is more to this account than a Sunday school story. The Hebrew word for reed grass is *ahu.* This word is close in sound and has the same first letters as *ah,* meaning brother. One commentator interpreted the word *ahu* as follows: When good years come to the world and there is enough for everybody, men are *ahim,* brothers, feeling akin to one another. When the years are bad and the pickings are lean, men become *aherim,* others. That is why the Bible speaks of "seven other cows." The seven handsome, sturdy cows saw their fellow creatures; yet they turned their faces from them.

This intepretation seems to strike a familiar note. Since the birth of time there have been the 'haves' and the 'have nots,' the ingroup and those who remain out of bounds. When those who are in a good position concern themselves with the less fortunate and regard them as brothers, society benefits from the considerate behavior of the affluent. On the other hand, when men turn their faces from their fellow human beings and reckon them as others, what happens? As in the dream story, the seven ugly, gaunt cows consume the fit cows who could have been helpful and chose not to be.

How different the story of turbulent Latin America and pulsating Africa would have been if the more developed countries would have truly regarded the under-developed lands as brothers, and faced their problems squarely. Much of the convulsion of our day and the strife of our decade would surely have been avoided.

Carlyle related a penetrating story. It tells of a destitute Irish woman with three helpless children. She applied for help to many quarters and was refused. She persisted and struggled. She contracted fever, her strength ebbed and finally gave out. The author speaks of her situation and pictures her pleading in anguished desperation. "I am sinking and in need of immediate help. Come to my rescue. I am your sister . . . One God has made us. You must help me." "No!" the answer shot back. "You are no sister of ours." The woman demonstrated her kinship by dying and infecting many others who succumbed. "Hide not thyself from thine own flesh" (Isaiah 58) has been translated as "Never turn from any fellow creature."

Let us learn to look upon men as our brothers. In that splendid vision we shall have our blessing, and mankind shall enjoy its peace.

Tone, Tome and Tears

"You can see for yourself... it is indeed I who am speaking to you." (Genesis 45:12)

A DRAMATIC CLIMAX is reached in the Joseph story. The long-lost brother is no longer able to control his emotions. He identifies himself to his brothers. In capsule form, he reviews what happened to him, warns them of the continuing famine, and finally invites them to come and live with him in Egypt. He adds, "You can see for yourself... that it is indeed I who am speaking to you."

The commentators speculated on the identification marks used by Joseph to prove that he was really their kinsman. One sage explained that Joseph spoke to his brothers in Hebrew; literally, in the holy tongue. Other observers challenged this interpretation. "What does that demonstrate?" they asked. Many capable public officials, schooled in the art of diplomacy, can speak several languages.

It was not the language used by Joseph which was important, but the manner in which he spoke. It is not the tongue which we use which is essential, but the tone in which we say the words. We show the world who we are by the tone in which we speak.

Another student, in a flight of fancy, suggested that Joseph showed them his chest of books. It was filled with holy works rather than the books of the Egyptian magicians.

This particular thought has some interesting connotations. Joseph wanted to identify himself, so he showed them his tomes. When we want to identify ourselves, what physical possessions do we show to other people? What do we want observers to see of our belongings? What image do we

90

project? How do we try to impress others with the things we have? The demonstration of our physical possessions is a great indicator of what we think important or unimportant. Joseph showed his tomes. One of the wealthiest men in Egypt, he used the symbols of his cultural attainment as his assurance to his brothers.

Joseph revealed himself in yet another way. He asked that all who were present, except for his brothers, leave the room, to spare his brothers the embarrassment of the re-telling of the tale of how they sold him into slavery. He cried out in a loud voice, and he recounted his experiences amidst his tears.

A man identifies himself by his behavior with his family and by his regard for another's sensitivities. The tears which we shed reveal our feelings for our loved ones.

What people see of us is not only important for us but is important to them also. Perhaps more important than what the world sees of us, and most people are usually guarded in their public conduct, is what our families, and particularly our children, observe. Everything we do is a sort of identification mark, not only who we are in terms of our name and address, but what type of people we are. What are our values? What is important to us? What motivates us? These identification bracelets, which we always wear, are most evident to our children, for we are their prime teachers, their models. They mimic our speech, they reflect our values, and they are affected by our behavior. What do we show to our child that "You can see for yourself"?

> "If a child lives with criticism,
>   He learns to condemn.
> If a child lives with hostility,
>   He learns to fight.
> If a child lives with jealousy,
>   He learns to feel guilty.
> If a child lives with fear,
>   He learns to be apprehensive."

91

On the other hand,

> "If a child lives with tolerance,
>   He learns to be understanding.
> If a child lives with acceptance,
>   He learns to love.
> If a child lives with fairness,
>   He learns justice.
> If a child lives with security,
>   He learns to have faith in himself
> and the world about him."

The Power of Shame

"Joseph could no longer control himself before all his attendants . . ." (Genesis 45:1)

THE STORY OF JOSEPH has been recognized as one of the most exciting in all of world literature. Many questions arise from its numerous incidents. Why, for example, did not Joseph identify himself immediately to his brothers upon their arrival in Egypt? Why did he continue to torment them, to play with them as a cat with a mouse?

The Bible reports that Joseph could no longer control himself before all his attendants and cried out, "Have everyone withdraw from me." Then came the moment of identification. "I am Joseph." Without hesitation he continued, "Is my father still alive?" While many interpretations of Joseph's actions have been offered, one theory appeals greatly to me. Joseph had not really intended to identify himself to his brothers until his aged father had come down and pleaded for Benjamin. He was committed to a course of continued emotional harassment. He wanted the old Jacob to plead before him. This would be the fulfillment of the old dream that the sun and all of the stars would bow down before Joseph's star.

What brought Joseph back to his senses? One commentator suggested that instead of reading our text, "Joseph could no longer control himself before all his attendants," we should read rather, "Joseph could no longer control himself because of all his attendants." Suddenly it dawned upon Joseph that he was in a potentially embarrassing position. Joseph wondered "Does it really pay for me to continue to play this

93

hard-hearted role? When I finally identify myself, what will these members of the palace staff think of me as a human being? How cruel, how sadistic, can one person be?" Joseph, according to this theory, was brought back to common sense because of the presence of the bystanders.

Though Joseph was a great man, he had some of the short-comings inherent in all of us. In every man there remain traces of animal origins. We are heirs of the jungle and primitive instincts survive within us. At times, the worst of our nature gets the best of us. Fortunately, in most cases we are able to master our baser impulses. The animal and the primitive in Joseph was tamed because he was ashamed. This theory is perhaps a key to an understanding of much of human behavior. Joseph was compelled to change his strategy and become a human being again because he was ashamed. We are ashamed of what other men will think of us and because of that shame we become more human. This is the civilizing power of society. The awareness of living together with other men causes the primitive to become civilized.

This point, I believe, can be very carefully documented. Much has been written about our splendid Jewish charities. One national magazine featured an article, "The Tithe That Binds," explaining the dynamics of Jewish philanthropy. One phrase describing the motivations of philanthropy was "Piety or Pressure." Many fund-raising drives publish a "Book of Life," a public revelation of what people give. A business man admitted, "We all know that these books are nothing but a form of pressure. But they work and that's what counts, if the cause is good." One wonders how many donors were tamed because they were ashamed.

One should not discount the significant role which shame plays in motivating recalcitrant individuals into doing what is right. Maimonides, our great medieval teacher, spoke of eight degrees of charity. The lowest degree is of the person "who gives grudgingly, reluctantly, and with regret." That donor is a long way off from the highest degree where a man gives charity anonymously and helps another man to earn

94

a living by mastering a craft. Yet we must acknowledge and recognize that even the grudging giver is at least doing a good deed. There are some who may have initially given because of shame, but through the process of doing the good deed, they are trained in kindness.

Rabbi Yohanan's parting words to his son were, "May it be God's will that the fear of heaven will be upon you like the fear of flesh and blood." The fear of other men, the shame of what people will think of us, is a powerful force in life. Fortunately, starting from motives which are less than noble, men have learned ultimately to follow the right and charitable course.

A Nation Under God

"Pharaoh said to Jacob, 'How many are the years of your life?' And Jacob said to Pharaoh, 'The years of my existence are one hundred and thirty. Few and hard have been the years of my life, nor do they come up to the lifetime of my fathers in their existence.'" (Genesis 47:8-9)

AN 18th CENTURY RABBI asked a fascinating question concerning the rather extensive answer which Jacob gave to Pharaoh's query. "What motivated the patriarch to answer as he did? Could he not have replied simply by stating 'I am 130 years old?'" A further matter of interest concerned Pharaoh's eagerness to know Jacob's age. Having posed the questions, the commentator went on to make a very cogent interpretation. He drew attention to an old legend which told that with the coming of Jacob to Egypt, the land which had been barren and plagued by famine began to blossom again. Pharaoh felt that the well-being of his country was somehow connected with Jacob's presence. The ruler looked upon the aged Jacob and thought to himself, "This old man will not live very long." The monarch's question revealed his inner fear that with the imminent death of Jacob, Egypt's soil would again be barren.

Jacob was a good student of human nature. He sensed the real motive behind the ruler's question, "How many are the years of your life?" The patriarch answered the question fully, touching at its hidden implications. "Nor do they come up to the lifetime of my fathers in their existence," means, in a sense, "Don't worry, Pharaoh, I have more years to live and your land will continue to flourish."

These two, Pharaoh and Jacob, men of varying background, personality and experience, provide a striking contrast. Pharaoh was urbane, the head of a great kingdom, brought up in the proverbial lap of regal luxury. Jacob, on the other hand, came from a comparatively primitive, pastoral background. Jacob was a believer in one God, and Pharaoh was an idolator even though there were glimmerings of a monotheistic faith in Egypt.

The essential difference between the two men lay in their conception of the relative place of God and man in the order of things. Both men had dreamed. Pharaoh dreamed about the Nile: "Behold, he was standing above the Nile." Jacob had dreamed of a ladder ascending to heaven, and "Behold, God was standing above him." Pharaoh worshipped the Nile as one of his gods, yet he was presumptuous enough to say, according to the prophet Ezekiel (29:3), "My river is mine own and I have made it for myself." Pharaoh felt that he stood above his God. He thought of himself as being the strength and productivity of Egypt. The king himself was a god, the son of Amon-Re, who was the chief deity of the land, and the divine blessings of the country were believed to be mediated through his person.

Jacob differed from Pharaoh. He placed himself under God. An ancient sage noted this difference between these two and said, "The wicked stand over their gods, but as for the righteous, their God stands over them."

In the course of history there were many despots, ranging from Pharaoh in ancient Egypt to Hitler in modern Germany and the Russian dictators in the Soviet Union, who tried to put God and religion beneath them.

The wise ruler places his state and himself under God and His moral law. Properly, we Americans have added to our Pledge of Allegiance the affirmation that ours is "One nation, under God, indivisible, with liberty and justice for all."

May the day soon come when the prophecy of Ezekiel, which we read in the synagogue on the same Sabbath when we hear the story of the encounter between Pharaoh and

Jacob, be fulfilled: "My dwelling-place also shall be over them: and I will be their God, and they shall be My people" (Ezekiel 37:27). When the nations and their rulers learn that God is above them, when the world will be perfected under God's reign, then mankind will enjoy peace and tranquility.

Joseph the Zaddik

MANY OF THE GREAT personalities of our people are known by a specific title. All of us are familiar with the names Abraham our father, Moses our teacher, and David the king. Joseph is referred to as Joseph the righteous.

Perhaps the reason for this particular name "the righteous" can be found in the life story of Jacob's favorite son. He had been hated by his brothers, thrown into the pit, sold into slavery, submitted to the indignities of false accusation, and had been imprisoned on trumped-up charges. Yet, Joseph earned the title of *zaddik*, a righteous man. His character and personality were refined in the fiery crucible of most trying experiences. He had overcome his difficulties and had been purified by them. He emerged from all of his testing as a much finer human being.

An expression coined by Shakespeare has passed into common usage: "Cowards die many times before their deaths, the valiant taste of death but once." We Jews have a different notion concerning the hero. We have looked upon the righteous man as the ideal heroic type whose character was tempered by his life career. The sages interpreted the verse, "For thy sake are we killed all the day, we are accounted as sheep for slaughter," as referring to the *zaddik*. "Is it possible," the rabbis queried, "for a man to be killed every day?" A righteous man, they believed, passes through trying experiences which are tantamount to daily destruction, which could annihilate one's personality and so deaden the character of weaker souled individuals. Yet, the righteous man is not submerged by his experiences. He is buoyed up by an inner strength which permits him to overcome the tests of time.

The Jewish attitude concerning the *zaddik* is not to be

99

confused with the Christian conception of resignation. The righteous man is ready to die to sanctify God's name. Rabbi Gershon Hadas in his thoughtful translation "The Psalms in Current Speech," sensed this when he translated the verse, "For thy sake are we killed all the day," as "Daily we face death."

The Jewish hero faces a thousand deaths, but proudly he proclaims, "I shall not die but live to tell the wonders of the Lord." The righteous man is sorely tested by adversity, but it does not overwhelm him. He senses that which Victor Hugo once felt when he wrote, "Adversity makes the man, prosperity makes the monster."

Joseph was a *zaddik*. He passed through the vale of misfortune to the highlands of God's full blessing. He emerged from all his trials as a superior human being. The spoiled lad of seventeen, who had strutted across the stage of history bedecked in his coat of many colors, developed into a spiritual hero, a truly righteous man. Though he rode the crest of personal success, he banished all thoughts of vindictiveness against his brothers who had mistreated him. He sought only their well-being and the welfare of his adopted nation.

Man's spirit does triumph over destructive experiences, but only when he passes through them. Joseph successfully passed through the great trials of life. May we emerge from all encounters with adversity and hardships as ennobled human beings.

Caretaker or Creator?

MAN IS A UNIQUE combination of hope and aspiration, coupled with anxiety and worry. One of his great concerns is the disturbing thought of being unrecognized in life and forgotten after death. Man's striving for recognition and remembrance is often motivated by this ever present, though not always articulated, fear.

Jacob, like all men, shared this concern. Towards the end of his life, he recalls to one of his sons the reassuring promise which God had made to him as a young man: "I will make you fertile and numerous, making of you a community of peoples; and I will give this land to your offspring... for an everlasting possession." (Genesis 48:4)

As understood by tradition, the key words in God's pledge were community and possession. The sages developed a very interesting principle from this verse, teaching, "He who has an inalienable possession is designated as a community, but he who has no everlasting possession is not designated as a community." In Jewish law an *ahuzah* meant a permanent possession. The root meaning of *ahuzah* reflected taking hold, having a firm grip. Whatever is given into our hands for custodial care is subject to the demands of time. We must give it back. That which we create, develop, add to, re-fashion, represent our own achievements. Limited by mortality, we cannot hold these possessions forever, but they are undeniably ours. We make our life permanent by creating that which is permanent.

In the life of a congregation (in Hebrew, the words 'congregation' and 'community' are the same), there are those who regard themselves as trustees of the past, guardians of the legacy, preservers of the memory, custodians of that which has

101

been transmitted to them and which they will turn over, unchanged and unimproved, to others. By their actions, they demonstrate that they consider themselves to be mere transmission belts. To be designated a congregation or community in the full sense of the word we must not only be guardians of the gate, but expanders of the horizon; not only protectors of the past, but progenitors of the future; not only custodians of the heritage, but creators of a brilliant tomorrow.

We will be remembered when we have created, when we have fashioned an everlasting possession.

Your Grandfather's Sword

*"And then Israel said to Joseph, I am going to
die, but God will be with you and bring you
back to the land of your Fathers ... and now
I give you one portion more than to your
brothers which I wrested from the Amorites
with my sword and bow."* (Genesis 48:21)

WHENEVER I THINK of the patriarchs, Abraham, Isaac
and Jacob, my grandfather comes to mind. He was a rabbi of
the old school, devoted to his studies; a person who would
never harm a living thing. Who could ever imagine that my
saintly grandfather would be found with a weapon in his
hand? Likewise, when the sages came to the passage in Genesis which describes Jacob as a combatant with sword and
bow, they had a similar reaction. Could you imagine, they
reasoned, that grandfather Jacob, "the mild man who stayed
in his tent," was an aggressive warrior? And did not the
Psalmist say, "For I trust not in my bow, neither can my
sword save me!"

The scholars took great liberty in consciously changing
the text and reading another meaning into it. They interpreted "my sword" to mean "my prayer," and "my bow" as
"my supplication." (The same Hebrew letters for "with my
bow" can be read "with my supplication.")

The rabbis were engaged in more than a play of words.
They changed the text and transformed the literal meaning
of the Bible to conform to their philosophy of life.

In our own age, we have seen the reverse process in operation. For many centuries our students have been nurtured
on a splendid tale. It tells that during the siege of Jerusalem,
Rabbi Johanan ben Zakkai saw the futility of continued

103

resistance, and determined that he would be smuggled out of Jerusalem by means of a ruse. He appeared before the Roman general and informed him that within a few days he would become emperor of Rome. When Johanan's prophecy was borne out, the grateful general asked him to name his reward. Johanan responded, "I ask nothing of you save Jabneh where I might go, teach my pupils and establish a prayer house..." This account, whose historicity can never be completely checked, as it occurs in several varying versions, has been challenged by a modern Israeli historian, Gedaliahu Alon. For years Johanan's choice had been hailed. He had, through a seemingly harmless request, given Judaism a renewed lease on life. Our humbled faith and defeated people managed to outlive Imperial Rome. Professor Alon, in a learned article, argues that the origins of Jabneh as the successor of Jerusalem were quite prosaic. Jabneh had not been chosen by Rabbi Johanan but was rather a quite mundane Roman prisoner camp for Jewish leaders.

Whether or not Professor Alon's point is a valid one is not important. What is significant, to my way of thinking, is that the older account was trying to place emphasis upon the spiritual element of Jewish experience. The rabbis had redirected the spirit of the Jewish people and affirmed that the best possibility for Jewish survival was through study, prayer, observance and ethical living.

In our own century, the great philosopher, William James, spoke for transforming the war-like energies of man and placing them into peaceful channels. James argued for the "Moral Equivalent of War." Instead of attacking people, men ought to devote their strength and energies to building the better society.

As we think of the future of our people, as we search for the key to our continued existence, the insight of Ahad Ha-Am comes to mind, "The secret of our people's persistence is...that at a very early period, the prophets taught it to respect only the power of the spirit and not to worship material power." There are many techniques of survival. In a world which places supreme reliance upon force, the Jew must ever remember the role of prayer and supplication.

104

A Man's Last Words

"And when the time approached for Israel to die, he summoned his son Joseph ..." (Genesis 47:29)

FREQUENTLY, when a loved one or friend passes away suddenly, we hear this remark: "Oh, if only he could have spoken some last words to us before he died." We are frustrated by our failure to receive a final message.

There is a legend which tells that until the death of Jacob, death had always come upon men suddenly. They were taken away before they were warned by illness of their approaching end. Jacob, however, spoke to God, saying, "O Lord, a man dies suddenly. He is not laid low first by sickness. He cannot acquaint his children with his wishes regarding all he leaves behind. If your world were different, if a man first fell sick and realized that his end were near, he would have time to set his house in order." God responded, "Your request is intelligent and you shall be the first to profit by a new arrangement." So it happened. Jacob fell sick shortly before his death. He had an opportunity to speak frankly and forthrightly to his children.

Modern men and women prepare a long time before their passing for their end. Our atmosphere is sated with a constant stress on insurance coverage and estate planning. Magazines and newspapers frequently carry articles on the general theme of "Have You Prepared Your Will?" All this is good. One ought not leave behind confusion and chaos to confound loved ones in their trying days. A fundamental question, however, that I would like to ask is "What sort of spiritual legacy do we leave behind?" The heritage that Jacob promised in his final words was more than an assurance that the real estate of Canaan, which belonged to Abraham and Isaac, would some day be the possession of his children. The testament which Jacob left in his final blessing was essentially a spiritual one. He hoped that his family would be adherents of "God before whom my ancestors walked"; that his children would be strong enough, like their forebears, to walk before God, continuing his pioneering in the realm of the spirit.

The pattern of leaving a spiritual as well as a material bequest is reflected in the rich Jewish literature of ethical wills. Jewish history includes magnificent examples of moral instruction, from the days of Jacob and Joseph through the lives of Moses and Joshua and down to our own generation.

Recently, an Egyptian Jewish cotton millionaire, whose family had been awarded more than nine million dollars by a claims group in compensation for property seized by Nasser, passed away. In his will, this gentleman laid down a code of conduct for his survivors. He stated, "I desire to thank my dear wife, for all her kindness, devotion and help, and I confidently commit to her care our dear children. I beseech my children to be upright and of pure character in all their undertakings, to nurture no ill will towards anyone, and to remain true to the religion of their fathers, to love each other and throughout life to remain united . . . I rely on my wife and children to give freely to charity."

An American Jew of our generation has left a will which reads, in part, as follows: "I beg you, my dear children, always to be at peace with one another, bound together as one. No rifts, no quarrels, God forbid. Help one another with counsel and also with funds, if, God forbid, any of you are in need. You know that this has always been my wish and my consolation. Guard zealously good will and peace among you at all times.

"Cling to the Jewish atmosphere in your homes. Do not let your children become estranged from Jewish traditions, from the Jewish people, and from the God of Israel.

"When my time will come, let there be no manner of eulogy . . ."

Let us not be over-concerned about whether or not we will have an opportunity to deliver a final message to our children. Every day of our lives we communicate with them. Our youngsters observe us in action. Not only our words but our deeds speak to them. May the message we transmit be clear and purposeful; may we inspire them by our deeds, so that they, too, may keep God's way to do righteousness.

To Tell the Truth

"When Joseph's brothers saw that their father was dead, they said, 'What if Joseph seeks to pay us back for all the wrong we did him!' So they sent this message to Joseph, 'Before his death your father left this instruction: So shall you say to Joseph, Forgive, I urge you, the offense and guilt of your brothers who treated you so harshly. Therefore, please forgive the offense of the servants of the God of your father.'" (Genesis 50:15-17).

AFTER THEIR father's passing, Joseph's brothers were deeply distressed. They had been reconciled with the "lost one," yet they could not bring themselves to believe that all had been forgiven. Though the old Jacob had left no instructions for Joseph, the brothers fabricated a statement.

There are some serious questions about their behavior. We are the possessors of a tradition which stresses the truth. "The seal of the Holy One, Blessed is He, is truth." While devoted to the principle of telling the truth, the sages explained the brothers' action.

In a classic Rabbinic passage they taught that in some instances the truth should be modified in the interest of peace. The brothers ascribed this request to their late father for the sake of preserving peace between themselves and Joseph. The Talmud goes on to relate that not only are men permitted to tell a "white lie" when circumstances of peace demand it, but God Himself modified statements for the sake of domestic harmony. When the aged Sarah heard that she was to be blessed with a child, she laughed to herself saying, "Now that I am withered, am I to have enjoyment—

108

with my husband so old?" If God had quoted Sarah verbatim, this repetition would have hurt Abraham. When God spoke to him, He modified Sarah's expression which Abraham might have resented. The Lord said to him, "Why did Sarah laugh saying, 'Shall I, in truth, bear a child—old as I am?' "

This passage is, indeed, a remarkable one. Truth is the seal of God, but peace is a higher ideal. We cherish peace, yet we regard peace between man and his fellow man as well as inner tranquility as the expression of a higher ideal. The rabbis did not accept the rigid, absolute position towards truth expressed in Fichte's statement, "I would not break my word, even to save mankind." The Jew who daily prayed, "Man should always revere God, in thought as in deed, acknowledge truth, and speak the truth even in his heart," knew that at times one is absolved from telling the truth.

Judaism is sensitive to human feeling. Our approach to living is not as intractable as the philosophy of life crystallized in the statement, "Let justice be done though the world perish."

In recent months I have been trying to clarify my thinking on the question, "Shall the patient know the truth?" In meetings of the Committee on Medicine and Religion of the American Medical Association I have discussed the vexing issue with my Protestant and Catholic colleagues. Their answer is usually an absolute one—"The truth is the truth." I believe that in Judaism there may be a more delicate understanding of man's emotional needs.

Obviously, the truth is to be preserved when not telling the truth would lead to harm. There are times one *must* tell the truth, as in the case of giving evidence. It is a positive commandment to speak forth, not to hold back the facts when one's evidence affects the conduct of justice. Is this involved in the case of a patient who is afflicted with a terminal physical condition? I wonder if the truth has to be told to him!

There is a magnificent legend which tells that when God was about to create man, the angels formed themselves into two parties: Love said, "Let man be created because he will

109

be an instrument of love." Truth said, "Let him not be created because he is compounded of falsehood." Righteousness said, "Let him be created for he will do just deeds." Peace said, "Let him not be created because he is full of strife." What did God do? He took Truth and cast it down to the ground.

Louis Jacobs, in his splendid volume *Jewish Values*, observed, "If absolute truth were always to prevail, man could not endure; but the world cannot endure without truth. Consequently, man must try to live by the truth, but there are times when truth imperils man's existence and then truth must be cast to the earth."

There are valid arguments for telling a patient the complete facts about a fatal illness. Telling the truth may help a patient prepare his soul, put his affairs in order and make peace with his fellow men.

On the other hand, what we may consider to be the truth may not be so. We may be telling a lie, for who can say with exactness what is ahead for any person? Judaism believed that it was improper to subject the patient to torture through words and to cause him harm by what is said. Delicacy is important, even in the transmission of bad news. Sad tidings should be related in such a way as to lessen the shock. Great is peace. At times it is more important than truth.

There is no absolute answer to our question, "Shall a patient know the truth?" Each case must be dealt with in its own context, depending upon the circumstance. The most important element in helping to resolve our dilemma—to tell or not to tell—is the determination of what will be the greater good—telling the truth or maintaining the peace.

Babes in Toyland

"Not by might, nor by power, but by My spirit,
saith the Lord of hosts." (Zechariah 4:7)

IN THE MIDST of the holiday shopping season a most unusual news item caught my eye. It reported that there had been a big increase in the number of warlike toys that were available as children's gifts. Some parents, reacting negatively to the toy rockets, junior missiles and guns, began a campaign against these items that "represent extremes of death, war and destruction." A consumer trend is always exciting news and the *New York Times* ran a background story on this parental revolt. Noted for its thoroughness, the newspaper checked with stores, trade associations and children's experts. The business community reported that sales had never been better. The chairman of the psychology department of an important university refused to comment at length, hedging with the argument that there had never been a thorough study to determine the impact of children's war toys. One could not say, for lack of scientific evidence, whether or not Johnny's playing with war toys at a young age led to violence in later life.

These responses I expected. I was taken aback, however, by the answer of a psychiatrist—"Playing is preparation for adult life. When boys play with toy guns they are preparing to use real guns when they go into military service. There is nothing wrong with developing aggressiveness. After all, this is not a gentle Tahitian world. It's a rough, tough, competitive society." The psychiatrist then revealed that his holiday gift to his 13 year old son was going to be a .22 caliber rifle.

Reading our verse, "Not by might nor by power, but by

111

My spirit ..." against the background of this last statement challenges us to understand who we are and what we are. People should not shy away from the realization that there is violence, roughness, toughness, brutal competition, aggressiveness in this world. These are, unfortunately, the stark facts of life. It is far different, however, to say that this is a situation which we must accept.

One runs the entire gamut of values when one goes from the prophet's statement with his inherent humaneness, to the extreme position of Benito Mussolini, the leader of Italian Fascism—"War puts the stamp of nobility upon people who have the courage to face it." Might and physical power, if they are not curbed by spirit and religious value, can destroy the world. Peace begins in the hearts of men. A passion for peace can well begin with proper toys in the stubby fingers of little children.

Recently, some of our local papers carried this unsigned article about toys and children.

VIOLENCE is abroad in our land...
Murder is with us in the headlines and TV...
Homes are bombed in the North...
Children in church are killed in the South...
We rely on the weapons of annihilation to secure our "way
of life"—
Violence is so commonplace in our lives that we hardly
notice it...
Until finally, our young and vital President is killed by an
assassin's bullet
Setting off a chain of even more violence.
And we are ashamed.
Let us begin to question the violence of our lives—
Let us bring love and understanding to our families—
Let us begin with our children—
Ought we supply them with the toys that make violence so
commonplace, so accepted...
The gun, the tank, the rocket, rather than tools, paints, or
the books of other lands?

112

I hope that the older members of our community will continue to buy toys for their children, grandchildren and loved ones. It would be good if they were toys that helped develop in the child those qualities which have always been the hallmarks of the Jew—wisdom, compassion, kindness, gentleness. "Train a child in the way he should go, and when he is older he will not depart from it."

Exodus

The Ideal and the Real

THE CENTRAL FIGURE of the Pentateuch is Moses. His early years were spent in palatial surroundings. By virtue of his adoption by Pharaoh's daughter, he was brought up in a princely manner.

One day, Moses ventured forth, drawn by inexplicable curiosity. He went to seek his brothers. A completely new world opened to him. In place of gracious living he found a grievous slave society. Harshness and cruelty replaced gentility and courtly manners.

From the background in which he had been reared, Moses was suddenly projected into the grim realities of life. In essence, all of us are brought up in an ideal world. We are sheltered and protected by our parents. Only as we mature do we awaken to the realization that there is a "world as we would want it to be" and a "world as it is."

The Bible speaks of Moses growing up. As evidence of his spiritual growth, we find him suddenly comprehending the meaning of the task-master smiting a Hebrew slave. The impact of this experience made Moses suddenly aware of the vast chasm that divides the ideal from the real. Moses' swift action was evidence of the fact that he knew that he must bridge the gap between the way things are and the way they ought to be.

All too frequently the difference between preachment and practice, the ideal and the real, is apparent to us. Yet we fail to act. Such was not the case with Moses. He saw iniquity; his moral fibre was firm and he acted with prophetic zeal.

There are many instances of this frustrating gap between the ideal society and the real world. In the vexing area of American race relations we need but recall the words of James Baldwin, author of *Nobody Knows My Name*: "People

117

don't live by the standards they say they live by, and the gap between their profession and the actuality is what creates this despair, and this uncertainty, which is very, very dangerous."

In our political life, we have this description of Washington, our nation's capitol, in the novel *Advise and Consent*. "There was a sort of necessary workaday hypocrisy, as inescapable here as it was back home on a thousand Main Streets, that imposed its own adjustments on a society caught in the overriding need to keep things going ... this enforced a combination of front-door idealism and backdoor acceptance of human realities."

Our professions, with their highly vaunted code of ethics, have their problems, too! The great novelist, James Cozzens, described these in his novel, *The Just and the Unjust*. Using the promising career of a young district attorney as the backdrop for a drama in life, Cozzens describes the dilemma faced by a young lawyer when he is asked to accept a retainer to uphold a will which is cruel and unfair to the sisters of a woman who left a sizable sum of money. What are the young barrister's responsibilities? Shall he follow the dictates of his conscience, adhere firmly to the standards of his ideal, or shall he pursue the goal of a successful practitioner of the legal arts?

Complicating our moral dilemma in making decisions between the ideal and the real is yet another factor. Frequently, life does not permit us to choose between clearly and sharply defined cases of right and wrong—between virtue and vice. At times we must decide between two nearly right courses of action. We protest, "Oh, if there were only a single right alternative which we could take."

Religion and ethics present us with a vision of the perfect society we ought to seek. It has been wisely said, "The vision of the future is our guide; the realities of the present are our limitations."

We must hope for the ideal world, and blend what Martin Buber called "a drop of Messianic fulfillment" in every hour.

118

The greatness of Moses was in his knowledge of how to annihilate the distance between the ideal and the real. Not all of us can reach this level. We can, at least, try to approximate him. We can, like our teacher of old, hope "Were that all of God's people were prophets."

Positive Persuasion

OUR FAITH has a strong democratic impulse. Professor Milton Konvitz of Cornell observed that as Judaism posits the ideals of social and economic equality, so, too, it posits political freedom and equality. Israel was conceived as a holy nation. Each Jew was to be a member of a kingdom of priests. If God alone is Master of the world and ruler of Israel, what need is there of a mortal king? When our ancestors asked Samuel to appoint a ruler over them so that they could be like all other peoples, the judge tried to discourage them. He warned them as to what was in store. The king would seize their fields, tax them mercilessly and compel them to do enforced labor. Samuel summed up his attitude by warning solemnly, "You shall be his servants."

An echo of this passionate love of liberty can be seen in the rabbi's intepretation of Moses' first prophetic experience. Moses was tending his father-in-law's flock in the wilderness near Horeb when he saw a marvelous sight. A bush was aflame, yet the bush was not consumed. God's voice was heard calling, "Moses! Moses!" Moses responded, "Here I am." God said, "Do not come closer. Remove your sandals from your feet, for the place upon which you stand is holy ground" (Exodus 3:5).

The expression "Do not come *halom* (closer)" reminded the rabbis of a similar phrase in the story of King David. At a critical point in his reign, the shepherd king exclaimed, "Who am I, O Lord our God" . . . that Thou hast brought me *halom* (thus far)." The rabbis, who had the greatest respect for Moses and affectionately called him "Moses our teacher," read an interesting idea into God's words "Do not come closer." Moses wanted to become a king and this re-

120

quest was not granted to him. God was warning Moses not to draw closer to his fond expectation.

The legend is hard to understand. Was anyone worthier than Moses? Was he not the mightiest of the prophets? A commentator suggested that the passage came to teach that one does not establish decisive leadership over a people by virtue of position. What influences the life of the people is the benign power of positive persuasiveness.

In commenting on the history of leadership, Dr. Louis Finkelstein said that one could divide its development into three stages. The earliest level finds the leader dependent upon the power of his *might*. Whoever was strongest was in the dominant position. He ruled over men as the cock rules the roost, by strength, dependent upon his own power and the might of his hand. During the second stage, the leader ruled by virtue of his *status*. His office opened the door to all privileges and prerogatives. His position was transmitted to his heirs. Though he might be the weakest person physically in the realm, the power of his office gave him control over the life of men. The most creative and fruitful level of leadership, however, finds the leader recognized by his *spiritual* teaching. He is a statesman of the spirit, who does not rely upon physical force or office, but rather on the power of his doctrine.

As we think of leadership in our own troubled age, we know that brute force is practiced only in police states. Men, however, attempt to establish themselves and rule over the lives of others through the power of their position or of their possessions. They maintain hegemony over others by arbitrary orders, by command. At times the command is masked in velvet tones; in other instances, it is heard as a bully's bark. How lasting is the influence of the domineering, demanding parent who perpetually orders his children about? How lasting is the influence of any person who lives by the rule of demanding obeisance?

Men attempt to buttress their leadership by buying it through gifts. The practice of gift giving has become an integral part of American life. Many gifts are given for

121

altruistic reasons, with no strings attached. They reflect our affection and admiration for the recipient. Other gifts are given in return for past favors and in expectation of future rewards. John Steinbeck, in a moving letter to Adlai Stevenson, described the revolting experience of seeing some American children who, after receiving present heaped upon present, ask, "Is that all?"

Do we really buy people's affections by gifts alone? Let us reflect for a moment on our foreign aid program. It must be granted that this multi-billion dollar effort has played an important role in European economic recovery, and has aided immeasurably in the development of the emerging nations of the world. Have our gifts to a land like Egypt, however, won us a true friend and a constant ally or have we earned the title of "The Ugly American"? We achieve the most lasting influence over people and nations by the example of our personal dedication. We win respect for ourselves by our commendable actions. We cannot command people's actions nor buy their loyalty. It is our own practices which will inspire and persuade them to emulate us.

Even the great Moses was human and wanted to be a king; God taught him a lesson that his most decisive contribution would be through the positive influence of his spirit.

Character of Moses

"Sometimes after that, when Moses had grown up, he went out to see his kinsfolk and witnessed their burdens." (Exodus 2:11)

MOSES HAD LIVED for many years in the royal palace as the adopted son of Pharaoh's daughter. An unexplainable impulse moved him to seek his own and to come into direct confrontation with his people. He "witnessed their burdens" may be translated figuratively as he "saw their patient suffering *(sivlotam).*"

Judaism developed a most significant concept called *savlanut,* teaching men to be patient under stress and to be hopeful under the most trying circumstances.

The *Paths of the Righteous* explains that from patience comes peace. Patience was regarded as a manifestation of modesty. The element of the patient, suffering people, which attracted Moses' concern, has appeared in the life story of other liberators. Mohandas K. Gandhi was conducting a successful law practice in South Africa when the plight of his Indian people came to his attention. Emile Zola was attracted to the cause of Alfred Dreyfus by the forbearance of the falsely accused French captain. After Zola's passing, Anatole France eulogized his colleague and extolled his efforts in publishing *"J'Accuse"*, the explosive document which caused the reopening of the case. France spoke of Zola as "a moment in the conscience of mankind." These men were attracted by the patient suffering of the afflicted.

It is one thing, however, to be drawn to a cause; it is another to do something about it. Moses saw that there was no labor more arduous than the handling of mortar. What did he do? He would help shoulder the heavy load and assist everyone that he could. A leader must do more than commiserate with his people. He must partake directly in their physical burdens. The legend went on to say that Moses did other things. He saw that the slaves were like cattle—that they had no relief from their labors. He went to the Pharaoh and said, "If one has a slave and he does not give him rest at least one day a week, the slave is worn out and will die. If you do not give your slaves a day's respite, they will surely perish." Moses then suggested that the Sabbath Day be the occasion for the rest. Pharaoh thought it was a good idea, for the Sabbath Day was regarded as an unlucky day. "How much would I really lose?" the monarch thought to himself.

What did Moses do on that day for the Hebrews? Having procured for them a day of physical rest was not enough; he began to teach them and to read with them. That is why, a tradition explains, in our Sabbath *Amidah,* we joyfully sing "Moses rejoiced in his gift of the portion." The Sabbath Day was Moses' day. When God commanded at Sinai that the Sabbath Day be a day of rest forever, this was a token of recognition for the efforts of Moses. He not only participated in the affliction of his people, but tried to raise them from the level of physically refreshed slaves to spiritually cultured men and women.

Moses did still more for the slaves. He gave them a vision of a better tomorrow. An old source tells us that Moses used these words, "My dear brothers, bear your lot with fortitude. Do not lose courage and let not your spirit grow weary with the weariness of your body. Better times will come when tribulation shall be changed into joy. Clouds are followed by sunshine, storms by calm and changes in the world tend towards their opposites: nothing is more inconsistent than the fortunes of man."

He taught them that which is later recorded in the Book of Job, "Thou shalt be secure because there is hope."

In our own lifetime, we have witnessed the attempt of a modern Pharaoh not only to enslave but to destroy our people. During the Hitler tragedy there were great leaders,

Leo Baeck and others, who in addition to their efforts to save lives, sought to maintain the psychic balance of German Jewry. Jewish adult education in Nazi Germany was a most powerful antidote to the poisons of Nazi propaganda. Every attempt to wear down the morale of the Jew was resisted; the rabbinic leaders and teachers of Germany helped to maintain the moral fibre of the Jewish community. They gave to the Jew, and especially to the young Jew, unshakeable support. The German educators applied the techniques taught by Moses and under the most massive attacks aimed at the humiliation and degradation of German Jewry, our people did not lose their self respect and sense of dignity.

The task of the leader is to participate personally in his people's lot, to teach them and to bring them, even under the direst of circumstances, a measure of hope.

Why Don't People Listen?

*"And Moses spoke so unto the children of Is-
rael; but they hearkened not unto Moses for
impatience of spirit, and for cruel bondage."*
(Exodus 6:9)

HAVE YOU NOT HAD this experience? Someone comes to
you with an important message and you fail to hear it. What
caused your inattention? In most instances, you were over-
concerned with something; another thought preoccupied
your mind.

Many centuries ago, Moses came to the Jewish people.
They had been enslaved for hundreds of years. The leader
arrived with a great message that the God of their fathers
would set them free. The people did not listen to the would-
be emancipator, and the Bible gives as the cause of their
deafness "impatience of spirit and cruel bondage."

The Hebrew words "impatience of spirit" actually mean
"shortness of breath" or "shortness of spirit." This literal
meaning is extremely suggestive. Why is it that modern man,
who is so full of anguish concerning himself and his lot in
the world, fails to hear the voice of religion? Though we are
desperately seeking meaning in life, we are spiritually short-
sighted, religiously deaf.

Moses' generation was regarded by the ancients as an age
that was lacking in faith. Their short-coming is also ours.

Yet a second factor blocked the attention of the children
of Israel: the "cruel bondage." The Egyptian taskmasters
prevented the Hebrew slaves from listening by continually
driving them. Cruel bondage can surely be interpreted as
over-concern with work. Paradoxically we moderns are free

men, yet we are our own task-masters. We enslave ourselves to our material needs. How difficult it is for us, because of our fatigue, to listen to the liberating voice of faith.

In our generation, when the actual work load has become lighter and the work-week shorter, the modern businessman works the longest work-week of all American occupations. "Managers and proprietors today generally work a 53 hour week . . . the 70 hour week is nothing strange for top management circles." This is true also of many professionals.

Our ancestors were in bondage to Pharaoh. We are our own slaves.

We moderns pay a tremendous toll caused by our hunger for material things. The price is paid in the currency of insecurity and anxiety. The more we emphasize our material needs, the less we remember the real satisfactions which come from faith. The great material goals we set for ourselves can be attained only in terms of the tremendous personal sacrifice of our physical well-being and our spiritual health. Our modern slavery has produced what one observer called a society "full of restless people, living frantically in a pursuit of success and approval." Our insatiable hunger leaves us little time for spiritual contentment and true serenity.

Our freedom will be won when we break our own shackles and learn to listen.

Who Goes First?

*"It is the same Aaron and Moses to whom the
Lord said, Bring forth the Israelites from the
land of Egypt...It was they who spoke to
Pharaoh king of Egypt to free the Israelites
from the Egyptians; these are the same Moses
and Aaron."* (Exodus 6:25-27)

WE ARE ALL at the mercy of protocol and the demands of
etiquette. How our dinner guests are to be seated is spelled
out carefully by an Emily Post. At times, the questions, Who
goes first? Who sits up front? find normally sensible people
jockeying for position. Claims are advanced that by status of
service, real or imagined, they are entitled to the most promi-
nent location. "Who goes first?" is asked every time we print
a listing of names.

The proper listing of names was also of concern to Bible
students. They noticed that, in most cases, Moses, though
younger in years, was listed before his older brother, Aaron.
Moses as liberator and lawgiver was given priority over his
senior. In our text, though, Aaron is listed first. This change
in order was used to teach an important principle: Aaron
and Moses are equal to one another.

Judaism seeks to emphasize the basic equality of all men.
In our High Holiday *Mahzor*, God is called *Ha-Shaveh*, the
Just One, who restores equilibrium and balance in human
relations. God who lifted man above the beast, who elevated
man to pre-eminence in the natural order, levels the arrogant
who mistakenly think that they are more important than
other men. Moses and Aaron are equal; they balance one
another. The principle underlying the change in the order
of their names must be extended to the life of all men,
demonstrating the worthwhileness of every man.

128

Another interpretation of "they are equal to one another" may be found by comparing the respective roles of the brothers. Moses was the mightiest of the prophets, Aaron was the first of the priests. Professor A. J. Heschel, in his book *The Prophets*, compares the work of the prophet with that of the priest. The task of the prophet is the turning of God toward man. The turning of man toward His maker is the work of the priest. The priest, functioning through ritual and prayer, attempts to bring man closer to God. He acts for the people and attempts to carry out God's will. (The word, *korban*, sacrifice, comes from the root "to draw near.") The prophet speaks for God and His concern for man, declaring what God desires of man. The prophet speaks by the strength of Divine inspiration; the priest functions by merit of his official status.

Both priest and prophet have had their modern advocates. Those who attempted to teach Judaism as prophetic lessons alone deprived their students of an essential aspect of our faith. The ritualists who ignored the ethical dimensions expressed by the prophets have been compelled to acknowledge the narrowness of their position.

In Reform Judaism, which long identified itself with the prophetic impulse, there is growing awareness that ritual is indispensable for vital religion. Powerful ideas give significance to a people but these ideals must be preserved and transmitted through an institutional framework. Otherwise, the values evaporate and are dissipated.

Prophet and priest complement each other. Their respective disciplines, the prophet's emphasis on ethics and the priest's use of ritual, are not mutually exclusive. A man who is trained through ritual to serve God selflessly learns to serve his fellow man selflessly.

It is foolhardy to attempt to choose which approach to meaningful religious experience is more desirable. Rather than state which goes first, I would echo the phrase "they are equal to one another." We need both the words of the prophets and the works of the priests.

Do You See Your Brother?

"And Moses stretched forth his hand toward heaven; and there was a thick darkness in all the land of Egypt . . . They saw not one another . . ." (Exodus 10:22, 23)

THE EXPERIENCE of darkness is familiar to all. At times darkness appears as a promise of nocturnal rest. On other occasions, the coming of night heralds fear and terror. Darkness has been used alternatively as the symbol of gloom and of peace.

The sages commented at length on the meaning of the word "thick darkness." One simple yet profound intepretation explained the Egyptian experience of darkness in this manner: the words "they saw not one another" literally meant "man did not see his brother." The affliction was more than a physical phenomenon. It was not in the eyes of men, but more significantly, in their hearts.

There is no darkness in the world which is more devastating than the experience of one brother not seeing, nor wanting to see, his own. When a person worries only about himself and thinks that the sun rises and sets only for him, that is thick darkness.

In analyzing our contemporary scene, there is a feeling among many that the American and world communities are entering into a period of thick darkness. Men continue to refuse to see their brothers and to comprehend their needs.

Though the American community elected a Catholic President in 1960, the underlying bitterness between Catholic and Protestant still remains as an ever-present disturbance in American life. Thick, dark clouds have re-appeared in the

130

Jewish heavens. In our own city, we have experienced synagogue defacings and swastika markings. Though the Negro community has achieved many symbols of equality, there is a marked heightening of tension between Negro and white in our country. Some thoughtful Jewish leaders are quite concerned about the rise of a Mohammedan conversion effort among American Negroes. They see in that volatile and sensitive community influences of all sorts of propaganda, including the Arab League, spreading bitterness against American Jews.

We may rightly ask why it is that sixteen years after the Nazi beast was beaten back into his lair, after a splendid period of sunny days when men saw and understood their brothers, genuine progress in inter-group relations has been arrested.

There are many explanations. Historic changes are always due to a host of factors. Yet, the one important element in the changing scene is the fact that a generation has arisen that "remembers not Joseph." Despite all of the publicity of the Eichmann Trial, there are millions of young people in the world for whom Hitler, death camps, brutal slaughter, genocide, are only a footnote in a social studies textbook. At times, even that footnote is distorted. Until schools in America and all parts of the world teach the facts about the last world war, thick darkness will remain.

It is our hope that the darkness will not represent a permanent blackout. Men must learn to band together, not merely to repel the common foe in war time, but to sense that they are brothers in peace. Let us see one another and in that splendid vision we will have our peace.

Why Did We Come?

*"They shall take some of the blood and put it
on two door posts and the lintel of the house
in which they are to eat it."* (Exodus 12:7)

WE KNOW THE STORY of the last plague of Egypt well.
If we think of it only as a tale which we heard as children,
we may miss its basic message. The Angel of Death passed
over the houses of the Hebrews; thus we have one of the
origins of the name of our festival, Passover.

The early rabbis were uncertain as to the exact location
and purpose of the sign on the doors. One sage said that the
sign was essentially for God's sake. "When I see the blood I
will pass over."

Another scholar said the identifying mark was to be on the
inside: "And the blood on the houses in which you dwell
shall be a sign for you."

A third teacher said the mark should be on the outside to
impress the Egyptians.

This commentary calls to mind an interesting analysis by
the noted American sociologist, David Riesman. He suggests
that there are three types of people: those who are traditionally-directed; those who are inner-directed; and those who
are other-directed.

The traditionally-directed person is motivated by his religious heritage. The inner-directed person draws his control
from himself. He has a control that keeps him on an even
keel, a sort of psychic gyroscope.

The other-directed person get his motivation from the
community in which he lives. He has his antennae out to
learn what people are doing and what is expected of him.

132

Why do we come in such vast numbers to recite the *Yizkor* memorial prayer? I think that we can safely offer three reasons.

There are those who come out of a sense of religious duty. Their faith is that God hears their prayers. Others gather on this day because it does something for man internally. We are helped by the catharsis of our tears. Still others come essentially because they are moved by the fact that this is the correct thing to do.

In a sense all three reasons have validity. Our prayers do have meaning. There is something normal and healthy for the expression of our grief through this channel of prayer to God. Our service affects our inner life and allows us to function again as individuals. The third element is also important. Though we are committed to the integrity of our lives as individuals, our existence depends upon a continued relationship with others.

Men do things for many and mixed reasons, some of them known to us and others only to God.

People Without Faces

"This month shall mark for you the beginning
of months. It shall be the first of the months of
year for you." (Exodus 12:2)

THE MONTH OF NISAN marked the freedom of Israel
from Egyptian slavery. In the old biblical calendar, this
spring month was counted as the first of the months of the
year. The rabbis remarked that the observance of this month
of Nisan was the first uniquely Jewish commandment given
to our people. Prior to this specifically Jewish commandment, there were other commandments to be kept by all of
mankind: there was the instruction to Adam to be fruitful
and multiply; there were the seven laws of morality incumbent upon all of the descendants of Noah. Here, however, for the first time, we have God's legislation for His
people alone.

Is it too much to assume that the human mitzvot were
given first, before the specifically Jewish commandments, to
indicate to our people that we are part of humanity before
we are Jews? The Bible emphasizes that we were not the
original human beings. We were, and remain, part of a
greater humanity. Specific religious responsibilities are ours
alone, but never are we to forget Judaism's basic respect for
all who live.

This idea of the inherent dignity of man is stressed in the
writings of Professor Abraham Joshua Heschel. He observes
that we do not speak of "What is man?" but rather of "Who
is man?" When we question, "What is man?" we label man
as a thing and ask regarding his worth. We are only con-

134

cerned with his utility to us. When we ask, "Who is man?" however, we seek for his identity as a person.

I should like to quote from a play by a brilliant French writer, Jean Anouilh. He describes how a group of modern Frenchmen came to a masquerade ball. Each individual assumed the personality of a famous historical character of the French Revolution. In one very moving scene, Lucile pleads with the tyrant, Robespierre, for the life of her loved one.

"Lucile: You can't have Camille killed, Robespierre.

Robespierre: I would sacrifice myself if necessary. Greatness is very costly.

Lucile: What is greatness?

Robespierre: The ruthless fulfillment of one's duty.

Lucile: And what is your duty?

Robespierre: To follow a straight road whatever the cost, right to that clearing in the forest where the Revolution will at last be complete.

Lucile: What if that clearing receded as it does in fairy tales?

Robespierre: Then we should have to continue the struggle.

Lucile: Forever?

Robespierre: Forever.

Lucile: Without concern for people?

Robespierre: Without concern for people.

Lucile: But it's for people that you want this Revolution.

Robespierre: For other people, without faces.

Lucile: Robespierre, I'm only a woman. But women know things that you don't know. Life is made in the depths of their wombs. They have known since always, that in the daytime, there are no men. You've, all of you, stayed little boys, with your ideas, your assurance which nothing can shake, your fits of violence . . .

Robespierre: Excuse me, Lucile, but I have important business . . .

Lucile: Of course! Right from the age of fifteen, you've all had too many things to do always! Becoming generals, discovering the North Pole, getting rich, building the reign of Justice, taking your revenge. Your plans haven't changed since your voices broke. And not one of you set yourself the task of just becoming a man!"

How pregnant with meaning are some of these phrases! The playwright is deeply concerned with preserving the dignity of humanity. So many of us act tyrannically in our constant disregard for people. We espouse high ideals, but we forget that in the long run, the acid test of our efforts is measured in the lives of men and women. The task of just becoming a man is our real destiny here on earth.

Let us learn to deal with people. Let us understand that as Jews there are many mitzvot which we ought to keep, but that the first mitzvot were given to all of mankind, stressing man's basic dignity.

The Courage of Our Confusions

SPRING IS THE QUESTIONING season. Together with the rest of America, each one of us has to answer many questions, posed by the Federal government concerning our income and expenses. As Jews, we sit around the *seder* table, and ask four questions as to the meaning of our ritual. A delightful story is told of Professor Isadore Isaac Rabi, the brilliant Columbia University professor who won a Nobel Prize in Physics in 1944. When asked by an interviewer, "To what do you attribute your success?" he answered, "I owe it all to my mother." (Incidentally, Rabi was born in Austria and was brought to the U.S. as an infant.) The questioner went on to ask for an explanation. The professor said that whenever he came home from school his mother would inquire of him, "What good question did you ask today?"

Questions are important but at times they are annoying. A story is told of a little boy who kept firing inquiries at his father. "Why is the grass green?" His father responded, "I don't know." Shifting from earthbound queries to more celestial ones, the youngster asked, "What makes the stars hang up in the sky?" The harried father rebuffed him with, "I don't know." This went on for a while and the little boy was getting nowhere. He made one last great attempt and began to ask a question. In the middle of a sentence he stopped himself and shouted, "Oh, never mind." At this point, his father retorted, "Go ahead son, ask your question. How else are you going to learn?"

A great English philosopher once declared that every statement ever made was made in answer to a question. Yet people resent questions, or are afraid to ask questions at times. There are so many men and women who think that they are polymaths, knowing everything there is to know about every conceivable subject under the sun. A well posed question may disturb their self-image. It is important to be able to say that one knows the answer, if one really does. On the other hand, this advice is well taken, "If a man asks you something and you are not completely conversant in the subject, answer him, 'I don't know.'"

We may be afraid to ask questions, lest they reveal that we are not quite certain about life itself. We are confused and afraid to expose our confusion. Our age is one which respects a person who seems to know where he is going. We do not admire the indecisive. We hail the activist and the determined.

John Ciardi once wrote in the *Saturday Review* that it is important to have the courage of our conviction and that it is equally important to have the courage of our confusion. He said, "Man needs the courage of his confusions. Show me a man who is not confused and I will show you a man who has not asked enough questions. The world is worth being confused about."

Judaism believes that man reaches the heights of religious experience when he is courageous enough to ask questions even of God Himself. This questioning does not label him as an unbeliever. The great Pascal, the 17th century French philosopher, had questions to ask of God. He was deeply troubled until he heard God say, "Thou wouldst not be seeking Me, hadst thou not already found Me. Be not therefore disquieted." Honest doubt leads to a stronger faith.

Alfred Lord Tennyson, in his "In Memoriam" writes:

> *"Perplext in faith, but pure in deeds,*
> *At last he beat his music out.*
> *There lives more faith in honest doubt,*
> *Believe me, than in half the creeds."*

The old grandmother's view that one doesn't ask questions, is not the epitome of Jewish religious experience. Passover is the time when we ask questions. The Bible predicts...
"And when, in time to come, your son asks you, saying, 'What

does this mean?' you shall say to him, 'It was with an almighty hand that the Lord brought us out from Egypt, the house of bondage' " (Exodus 13:14).

The Bible stresses that everyone, including the child, and perhaps most particularly the child, has the right to ask. We are of the seed of Abraham, who asked of God Himself, "Shall not the judge of the earth do justly?"

As there is the right to ask, there is the commensurate responsibility to answer.

All of us are entitled to the courage of confusion but we ought also to seek our way out of our spiritual dilemmas and intellectual difficulties. We must acquaint ourselves with more and more of our tradition and its religious philosophy, so that we can answer the questions which are posed to us by our children as well as by life itself. "A man's wisdom maketh his face to shine," the wise King Solomon said (Ecclesiastes 8:1). Man's spirit grows when he is asked a question and he is able to answer.

What's New?

"This month shall mark for you the beginning of the months. It shall be the first of the months of the year for you." (Exodus 12:2)

THE HEBREW WORD for the month, *hodesh,* is related to the word for new, *hadash.* People like new things. One of the outstanding characteristics of American society is its quest for the new. Our daily speech is marked by expressions like "What's new?" Every fall the rush is on to get the latest model car. Although we know full well that there may be little difference between this year's auto and last year's we want to have the most recent vintage.

It is reported that in Palestine, 30 years ago, street peddlers used to attract customers by shouting *"Davar hadash ba-aretz!"* which means, roughly, "Something new in the land." Everything new seems to carry the connotation of being better than the old.

We ought to recognize that the hunger for newness is a legitimate human desire. A 13th century scholar, Menachem Meiri, observed that "the nature of man is aroused by every new thing. The novel stirs him more than the familiar and customary." In an age which rigidly guarded against religious innovation, Meiri permitted new prayers to be introduced into the most sacred portions of the High Holy Day liturgy.

While appreciating that the new is significant, we should, at the same time, be apprehensive as to its potential dangers. A writer once commented on the hunger for the new and the striving after novelty, "Novelty is one of those toxic stimulants which, in the long run, become more necessary even than food. Once they have enslaved us, we have to go on increasing the dose to a point at which it becomes destruc-

140

tive to life. It is strange, indeed, to become so dependent on precisely what is most perishable in things — their quality of newness" (Paul Valery). The latest creation from the designer's drafting table, the couturier's sketch pad, or even the philosopher's mind is not, by its sheer novelty, necessarily good.

May I suggest two tests which may be used to determine the advisability of the new and the novel. A reasonable test for any new thing is whether or not the innovation is worthy of being sanctified. Does it ennoble our lives and enrich our existence? Every month, when we welcome the new moon, we sanctify it, for the new moon means new opportunity and new hope. The late Chief Rabbi of Israel, Abraham Isaac Kook, offered a splendid formula: *hayashan yithadesh, hadadash yitkadesh*, "the old must be renewed, the new must be made holy."

Another test of the new is suggested by the fine custom which we have when we see someone in a new garment. When we wish him well on his new clothes, we say, *tithadesh*, "may you renew yourself." Newness is not only that which comes from without; it must also come from within. Too often we look for the thrill which comes to us from life, rather than the excitement which we can bring to life from within ourselves.

Let us search for the new, for it is a natural longing of the human heart; let us attempt to renew ourselves by bringing that which is positive, edifying and uplifting, into our lives.

Signs and Reminders

"And this shall serve you as a sign on your
hand and as a reminder on your forehead—in
order that the teachings of the Lord may be in
your mouth—that with a mighty hand the
Lord freed you from Egypt." (Exodus 13:9)

RECENTLY FIVE Nobel Prize-winners participated in a
symposium on "What Can We Do to Keep Peace on Earth?"
One of them, Father Dominique Pire, who won the award
in 1958, was asked, "On what do you most pin your hopes
for world peace?" Father Pire answered that he believes in
the basic goodness of man.

He emphasized his answer in a most striking illustration.
Some years before, he had visited a camp of Algerian refugees
in Morocco. A poor Moslem received him with the traditional
Oriental hospitality. There was little food in the tent, and
he had nothing to offer except an egg. The priest was so
touched that he had the egg preserved. It rests on his desk
and recalls the goodness of man.

Side by side with this object, Father Pire has a tile that he
brought back from Hiroshima. It was subjected to an atomic
blast accompanied by 3,000 degrees of heat. Father Pire often
finds himself pondering which object weighs more in the
scale of man, the egg or the tile. "If it is the tile," he fears,
"the world is lost; if the egg, the world is saved." The heart
of the question remains: "Is there more cruelty in man than
good; or more good than cruelty?" The desk objects are
symbols intended to remind a most thoughtful man of the
great choice which every man and the entire world must
make.

142

All of us have signs and reminders before us. They recall maxims for living, remind us of significant responsibilities. The Jew was to have the annual reminder of his redemption from slavery through the Passover seder. Beyond that, each day we were to be reminded of our liberation. *Tefillin* were to be placed on the hand and the head. "This shall serve you as a sign . . . as a reminder . . . in order that the teachings of God may be in your mouth." The symbol is important, but teachings for which it serves as a reminder are more important. The teachings of God have to be expressed, clearly articulated.

Surely you remember this poem which stirred us years back:

"Mourn not the dead that in the cool earth lie—
Dust unto dust—
The calm sweet earth that mothers all who die
As all men must;
Mourn not your captive comrades who must dwell—
Too strong to strive—
Each in his steel-bound coffin of a cell,
Buried alive;
But rather mourn the apathetic throng—
The cowed and the meek—
Who see the world's great anguish and its wrong
And dare not speak!"

We must speak forth on that which we consider to be significant. We must dare to speak for that which we regard to be precious. For too long religionists have been satisfied with signs and reminders and have forgotten to speak forth.

What's in a Name?

*"And he called for Moses and Aaron by night,
and said: 'Rise up, get you forth from among
my people, both ye and the children of Israel;
and go, serve the Lord as ye have said."*
(Exodus 12:31)

RECENTLY a SOVIET writer found himself in an unique
predicament. Seated next to a lady at a public function, a
salad was placed before him. As he did not care to eat it, he
wanted to offer the course to the lady next to him. The
woman, however, was facing the other way, and he was at a
loss as to how he was to attract her attention. Not knowing
her name, he could not say, "Nina, would you care for some
salad?" He dismissed the thought of tapping her and saying,
"Hey." He could not use the old revolutionary *"Tovarich,"*
as this seems to be *passé.* Unless he knew her name or how
to address her properly, our friend found that he was unable
to offer the dish to his dinner companion. The author mulled
over his dilemma and after a while decided to write an
article. He proposed that the Russians re-introduce the
use of "sir" and "madam" which were discarded after the
revolution.

Knowing a person's name and how to address that individual correctly is of utmost importance. In the Biblical
account of the Exodus there is a vivid description of the
intense final hours prior to the redemption. Having been
inflicted with the most grievous of plagues, the death of his
first born, Pharaoh in despair called for Moses and Aaron.
The monarch said to them, "Rise up and go you forth from
among my people both you and the children of Israel
with you."

144

One commentator observed that this was the first time that Pharaoh called our ancestors *B'nai Yisrael*. In the prior encounters between the ruler and Moses, he had used the word *am*, in the sense of masses. The very fact that our people were called by their proper name—*B'nai Yisrael*, or Children of Israel—was an important stage on their road to freedom.

We in America are witnessing and participating in a nation-wide Negro revolution. When Dr. Martin Luther King, Jr., one of the great voices in this struggle for human dignity, was incarcerated in the Birmingham city jail, he wrote a letter to a group of eight clergymen who had labeled his activities "unwise and untimely." The epistle is one of the great documents of human liberty, composed without any books available to him. It reveals not only the intensity of King's feelings but the profundity of his knowledge.

He wrote in passing, "When your first name becomes "nigger" and your middle name becomes "boy" (however old you are), and your last name becomes "John," and when your wife and mother are never given the respected title "Mrs.", then you will understand why we find it difficult to wait." King spoke of the problem which the Negro has in fighting what he calls "a degenerating sense of 'nobodiness'." You are a nobody if people refuse to address you by your correct name.

James Baldwin published a series of articles with the title, *Nobody Knows My Name*. See how this stamp of "nobodiness" troubles the Negro! Baldwin testifies to his personal experience. He relates the price of self-discovery and the pain of becoming a man. Baldwin stresses that nobody can become somebody without freeing himself. Personal growth, self-liberation, means discovering more and more what we are by forcing oneself out of hiding.

In our own people's experience, after the British evacuated Palestine and the State of Israel was proclaimed, the former masters of the Holy Land didn't see fit to recognize the new government. Yet they had to communicate with the new state. The British kept sending messages to what they labeled "the Jewish authorities" in Tel Aviv. When they finally came around to recognizing the State and calling it Israel, they acknowledged that this little republic was now a free nation which had to be reckoned with.

A person is on the road to freedom when he is properly addressed by others and when he himself recognizes his own name.

Thoughts for a New Month

TWELVE TIMES A YEAR the Jewish people recognize and consecrate Rosh Hodesh, the new month. Each recurrent appearance of the new moon, as predictable and unstartling as it may be, is a cause for the celebration and sanctification of God's name.

The inevitable passage of any month, the ebb and flow of day and night, arouses the question, "What is time?" We see the days and the years move by and we wonder, "What is it all about?"

Different cultures viewed the passage of time against the background of their distinctive outlook on life. The primitive personality had little concept of time. Life was without hope; there was nothing to look forward to or to strive for beyond the immediate date. Tribesmen in darkest Africa and Eskimos in the bleak reaches of the Arctic have little notion of a calendar.

To the Hindu, living in an atmosphere heavy with mystery, time was an illusion. The movement of the hours was like a ripple in a deep pool rather than the flow of a stream.

For the Greek, time was an enemy. It brought furrows to his brow and gray hair to his head.

Most Americans experience time in another sense. Time symbolizes the possibility of material achievement. Viewing time as a commodity, we glibly say, "Time is money." We gear our life to conserve the hours so that we may translate the minutes into material success.

The Jew views time in a completely different fashion. It is not an illusion nor an enemy of man. Time is the only instrument granted unto us with which we can freely serve God. For the Jew time has meaning; its passage reveals to us the will of God. Man's chief task is to sanctify time, to look upon it as an opportunity for hallowing our lives by calling upon the name of the Lord.

147

Darkness and Light

JUDAISM STRESSES THE FACT that God is the "fashioner of light and creator of darkness." Yet the Bible, in many instances, identified darkness with gloom and associated it with anguish and distress.

Our people, through the centuries, knew the meaning of darkness. Through sufferings of body and spirit, they felt the absence of light. To our people there could be applied the verse of Job, "He knows that the day of darkness is established for him." The nations of the world had sustained a centuries-long "day of darkness," prepared for the Jew.

When the nations of the world barred the Jew from universities and schools of learning, when they tried to stamp the imprint of cultural darkness upon him, the Jew kindled his own lamps of culture. He knew the meaning of the Psalmist's words, "The commandment is a lamp and the Torah is a light." Our people devoted themselves wholeheartedly to the fashioning of beacons of learning. They never stinted in the maintenance of their schools. Even the night itself, symbol of the darkness, was transfigured into an instrument of hope. The rabbis taught, "The night was created only for study." God rewarded the Jewish people's devotion to the lamp of learning and fulfilled the promise, "I shall light a candle of understanding in your heart which shall not be put out."

A second type of darkness was established for the Jew—the bitterness of political oppression and the humiliation of social ostracism. Our people were outcasts of society, barred from the life politic of the state, permitted to live only upon the fringes of the community.

As the Jew stepped forth into the work-a-day world at the

end of the Sabbath, he proudly proclaimed, "I will trust in my salvation and will not be afraid." The candles which he lit as the new week beckoned, the lights we cause to glow at Hanukkah time, served the Jew well. They reminded him that ultimately he would have to strike forth, in God's own good time, to re-acquire his political freedom. The candles were small, but their message was powerful. "How far the little candle throws its beam," Portia said. How strong was the impact of these lights of hope, these mighty torches of courage. They heartened the Jew with their beams of faith; they strengthened him with their rays of confidence.

May the lights of learning and the lamps of freedom burn brightly for our generation.

The Hands of God

"You will bring them and plant them in Your
own mountain, the place You made Your
abode, O, Lord, the sanctuary, O Lord, which
Your hands established." (Exodus 15:17)

AFTER THE MIRACULOUS crossing at the Red Sea, the
Bible reports that "when Israel saw the wondrous power
which the Lord wielded . . . they had faith in the Lord."
Many people refuse to believe in God. They reject a theistic
faith, because they feel that such a belief leaves man powerless. They argue that the idea of an all-powerful God leaves
man weak and impotent.

Against such a background, it would be worthwhile to
consider the remarkable statement of Bar-Kappara, a talmudic sage. He stated quite boldly, "The work of the
righteous is greater than the work of heaven and earth."

To prove his point, the scholar contrasted two Biblical
texts. Reflecting on Creation, God says, "My hand laid the
foundation of the earth, My right hand spread the heavens
above."

Describing the work of the pious, it is written, "The place
You made Your abode, O Lord, the sanctuary, O Lord,
which Your hands established." To Bar-Kappara's way of
thinking, more effort was involved in constructing the
Temple in Jerusalem by its righteous builders than in creating the world. With regard to the creation of heaven and
earth, the singular, "hand," is used, while concerning the
Temple, "hands" are mentioned. (Bar-Kappara interpreted
"Your hands" homiletically, to mean not God's hands but

man's hands. When man does good deeds he becomes God's hands.)

This interpretation seems to stress, in the strongest of terms, that the man of faith is not powerless to act. Man has been assigned a role of great significance, not the part of a servile weakling. He is called upon to become God's partner in completing creation.

There once was a Roman governor of the Holy Land named Tineius Rufus. At first, he was friendly with Rabbi Akiba. In the end, however, he was the very judge who ordered the martyr's execution. During the days of their better relationship, the Roman asked Rabbi Akiba, "Which are more to be admired: the works of God or the deeds of men?" The sage replied, "The works of men." To illustrate his point, Rabbi Akiba asked that a handful of grain and some freshly baked cakes be brought before him. "These," the sage said, "are the works of God and the works of men. Which are to be more admired?" To accentuate the point he had made, Rabbi Akiba also asked that bundles of raw flax and finely spun linen garments be brought in. Again he emphasized that the works of men are to be more admired.

Man is not left powerless by his faith in God. Man's activities are significant. A medieval mystic said, "God can as little do without us as we without Him." He may fill the hills with the precious stone, but mortal man builds His temple.

Freedom Must Be Fought For

"And the children of Israel went out with an outstretched hand." (Exodus 14:8)

THE EXODUS from Egypt is the central element in Jewish history. Had not this event taken place, the entire story of the Jew would have been different. Our people would have remained unknown, buried by the sands of assimilation. When Jews describe the experience of liberation, in most instances the reference is to *yetziat mitzraim,* "the going out from Egypt." This expression is used in preference to "being taken out of Egypt." Our people participated in their own emancipation.

Frequently, our liturgy emphasizes this theme. The most striking example of our remembrance of this singular event appears in the Friday evening *Kiddush:* "This day (referring to the Sabbath) is the first of the hallowed festivals of our people, recalling our going out from Egypt." The lesson is evident. Man must break the shackles which bind, the bonds which confine. A nation must help set itself free, going forth from slavery to liberty.

The second part of the verse, *b'yad ramah,* literally means "with uplifted hand." The meaning of this verse was subject to much speculation over the years. One commentator suggested "they went out joyfully, with songs, timbrel and harp." I would like to suggest that "with uplifted hand" means with a hand that is extended in prayer. Professor Lieberman of the Jewish Theological Seminary has drawn attention to the fact that in the Jewish mode of worship the uplifted hand and outstretched finger was a form of praise to God. There are archeological evidences of this in the remains of

152

an ancient synagogue at Dura-Europos. There are several scenes with this motif illustrated in the ceramic tile floors of the archeological findings.

The Bible reports that when the Israelites crossed the Red Sea they proclaimed, "This is my God." Rashi interprets this to mean, "God's self-revelation was so evident that the Israelite, as it were, pointed at Him with his finger." Later in the career of Moses, when our people were attacked by the Amalekites, Moses prayed for Divine help. The Bible reports, "And it came to pass, when Moses held up his hand, Israel prevailed . . ." (Exodus 17:11).

A people must be active in their own freedom. They ought not wait with folded hands and expect deliverance. When liberation comes, however, they must remember to be grateful to God, who plants the desire to be free in the hearts of men. Israel went forth from slavery to freedom with an outstretched hand, prayerfully thankful to God. Personal participation in one's own battles, with a readiness to acknowledge the true Source of our strength, should be practiced by all.

Might or Moral Consciousness

*"Amalek came and fought with Israel at Rephi-
dim. Moses said to Joshua, 'Pick some men for
us and go out and do battle with Amalek.'"*
(Exodus 17:8-9)

THE CHILDREN of Israel, newly freed from slavery, had
passed through their first major test... they had crossed the
Red Sea in safety. Almost immediately after this deliverance,
word came to the camp, warning of the approach of the
rapacious Amalekites. The camp was thrown into turmoil.
The predatory enemy would have to be repelled lest the
people lose heart and return to Egypt. Moses turned to
Joshua, then his young, untried aide-de-camp, and said, "Pick
some men for us and go out and do battle with Amalek."

The rabbis debated concerning the type of officers and
men who would be selected. Two qualities were needed for
this first defense force of Israel. According to one sage, the
fighting men had to have the primary quality of strength,
and they were also to be fearful of sin. Another sage stressed
that they had to be, first of all, fearful of sin and also possess
the secondary quality of strength.

One would never imagine that a Jewish army would be led
by men who possessed only strength and did not have a
sense of moral consciousness. On the other hand, to pick out
soldiers who had moral consciousness and did not know how
to fight would be foolhardy.

The sage who stressed the priority of strength felt that one
must have fighting men who can achieve their prime purpose,
the defeat of the enemy. On the other hand, the rabbi who
stressed the primacy of moral consciousness was touching on
the vital nerve of any struggle. Strength is important; courage, military prowess are significant. But strength in itself

can be self-defeating. "Might is right," the philosopher said, "when might is not making a mistake." Might must be blended with moral consciousness.

How modern is this lesson stressing the pre-eminence of moral consciousness over might! The prophet Jeremiah once said, "Let not the wise man glory in his wisdom; neither let the mighty man glory in his might. Let not the rich man glory in his riches." In our personal life, how often we see children who are strong, blessed with a good mind, who do not think that they have to study. Grasping a new fact comes so easily to their agile minds that somehow they forget that genius is a combination of inspiration with a good application of perspiration. There are those who glory in their strength. I shudder when I listen to the strident tone and the bellicose talk of those who see but one solution to the vexing problem of Viet Nam—"Bomb 'em." They refuse to examine the ultimate consequences of any unbridled use of America's military might.

There is a paradoxical characteristic associated with power. The stronger you are, the more careful you must be in using your strength. In our national life we are tasting some bitter results of our age of abundance. So many sensitive minds hunger for a sense of our national purpose. The strong man, the mentally bright, the military powerful, the economically wealthy, must curb their might by a highly refined sense of moral consciousness. Reliance on force alone can breed an ingrown pride that can lead to delusion and self-defeat. Smugness and arrogance can be malignant by-products of unusual endowments of capability.

As long as men live on the face of this earth, there will always be serious questions asked concerning the proper use of power. The suggestion of the rabbis that strength needs the tempering element of moral consciousness is an extension of the teaching of Jeremiah:

> *"Let not the wise man glory in his wisdom,*
> *Neither let the mighty man glory in his might,*
> *Let not the rich man glory in his riches;*
> > *But let them that glorieth, glory in this,*
> *That he understandeth and knoweth Me."*

155

How Did We Get So Forgetful?

I AM CERTAIN that many of you must have reflected, at one time or another, on the following question: "Why are we so different from our forefathers who lived in Europe?" They were devoted to prayer and to study; these activities were a vital part of their style of living. To be honest with ourselves, most of us are not as concerned about things religious as were our fathers before us. What happened? How did we get so forgetful?

An unusual rabbinic legend quoted in the miscellaneous writings of the late Rabbi Milton Steinberg may have an answer for us. The Midrash states: When Israel went out of Egypt, the angel, Sammael, began to accuse them. Boldly, he stood before God and said, "Master of the Universe, until now they worshipped idols and You are going to split the sea for them!" God answered, "Yes, they worshipped the idols of Egypt, but not willingly. They did it because they were forced to serve with rigor."

At first glance, this statement is shocking. Idolatry is one of the gravest sins a Jew can commit. Why was God so anxious to excuse His people?

The rabbinic statement offers a great observation on life. We frequently fail to live the life religious, not because of inner weakness, but because of external compulsion. Some people become irreligious on intellectual grounds. Yet, for most people, a sociological explanation for their deviation is perhaps the best. Like our ancestors in ancient times, the modern Jew becomes forgetful because of external pressures. He doesn't have the time to pray and the strength to study because of outside factors.

Recently I read a most engaging history of the early Jewish Labor Movement in the United States. Included were striking details of the way in which our forebears lived upon coming to America. The description was of Chicago's West Side, but it held equally true for the East Side of New York and other immigrant settlements throughout the land.

Some immigrants lived in small one or two-story "pioneer wooden shanties." Others resided in brick tenements with bad light, poor drainage and no bathing facilities. Some were domiciled in combination apartment-factories. They worked 60 to 70 hours a week; many of them every day of the week.

What could one expect of these immigrants who had been catapulted from the *shtetl* to the slum? In the span of a few weeks they had gone from a closed society which respected learning and tradition, to a sweatshop environment, whose only faith was worshipping the goddess of success. Only the financially successful could hope to escape and achieve a better life.

Yes, they worshipped the materialism of America, but not willingly. They did it because they were forced to "serve with rigor." Our fathers had to work on the Sabbath and could not come to the synagogue. They did not have strength at the end of the day to sit down and read a newspaper. How could they have been expected to study? They were physically exhausted and spiritually enervated.

We are grateful to this immigrant generation. They were made of stern stuff to have been able to persevere. We understand their difficulties and appreciate them all the more when we consider the trials through which they passed. We understand now how they forgot to pray and to study.

What about ourselves? Our work week is much shorter, the pressures of earning a living are not so great, the homes in which we reside are not crowded slums. There are surely areas of quiet in which we can sit down and read a good Jewish book. Our time schedule permits us to attend services and to come to adult classes. Ought we not master, once again, the habit of prayer? Should we not accept the discipline of study?

Now is the time to begin to remember what our fathers forgot.

A Discussion of Beauty

"This is my God and I will glorify Him." (Exodus 15:2)

THE SHIRAH, THE SONG of Moses and the Children of Israel, is one of the greatest poems in world literature. Its thrilling words are repeated daily in our worship service. "This is my God and I will glorify him" is one of the most impressive phrases of the song. A sage asked rhetorically, "Is it possible for mortal man to add glory to his Creator?" He declared, "This means I shall be beautiful before Him in observing the commandments. I shall procure a beautiful *lulav.* I shall erect a splendid *sukkah* in its season. I shall bedeck myself with a beautiful *tallit."* Another teacher added, "I shall lead a beautiful life, imitating God's ways; just as He is gracious and merciful, so should man be gracious in his deeds and merciful in his actions." This passage, as amplified by the sages, set the stage for the satisfaction of the impulse to realize the "beauty of holiness." Our ancestors had a keen sense for beauty. If a man beheld an object of beauty, he was to recite a special blessing: "Blessed is He who created beautiful creatures in His world." In our land hundreds of millions of dollars have been spent to satisfy this impulse to glorify and enhance the worship of the holy.

Our age lays great emphasis upon beauty. But did you ever consider that beauty is a neutral value? Beauty is related to goodness, but it is not goodness. Beauty can be applied toward good as well as evil ends.

In *Brave New World Revisited,* the late Aldous Huxley, novelist and thinker, commented on the "beauty of holiness." It strengthens our faith where it already exists. Where there is no faith, beauty of holiness may well contribute to

158

religious adherence. On an esthetic level, however, beauty alone does not guarantee the truth or the ethical value of a doctrine with which it is associated. Huxley goes on to make this striking point, "As a matter of plain, historical fact, 'the beauties of holiness' have often been matched and, indeed, surpassed by the 'beauties of unholiness.' " He relates that, under Hitler, the yearly Nuremberg rallies were masterpieces of art. Huxley quotes Britain's ambassador to Hitler's Germany, who observed, "I have spent six years in St. Petersburg before the war in the best days of the old Russian ballet, but for grandiose beauty I have never seen any ballet to compare with the Nuremberg rally." Think of it, these brutal demonic men used beauty for their own wicked ends! Huxley dismissed the well-known phrase of the English romantic, John Keats, "Beauty is truth, truth beauty—that is all ye know on earth and all ye need to know." There is more to life than the attractiveness of rhythm and the thrill of witnessing precision. Huxley stresses correctly that on some levels, "Beauty is perfectly compatible with nonsense and tyranny."

There is, as we see, the beauty of holiness and, unfortunately, there is the beauty of unholiness. We must be on guard constantly to make certain that what we regard as beautiful is committed to high purposes. Judaism appreciated beauty but warned lest it be associated with falseness and vain ends. That is why the Book of Proverbs, that practical book so full of good, common sense, ends with a tribute to woman, "Grace is deceitful and beauty is vain, but a woman that feareth the Lord, she shall be praised." Take heed that you are not fooled by outer appearances! Judaism looked for beauty in beautiful souls and beautiful deeds. That is why the Song of Songs proclaimed, "Thou art beautiful, my love," which was interpreted to mean beautiful in the good, moral life.

The Greatest Event in
Jewish History

IF YOU WERE searching for the greatest single event in Jewish history, what would you list? Many decisive moments would compete for this distinction. To help you out, may I bring to your attention the observation of Bahya, a medieval commentator. He points out that the Sabbath is central in Judaism. Then he goes on to note that while the Sabbath is mentioned 12 times in the Torah, the Exodus from Egypt is referred to 50 times.

The Exodus can be appreciated on a number of levels. It was an ancient battle for national survival. Recalling as it does an oppressed minority's struggle for freedom it inspired our people and all people to seek independence. The Exodus has to be appreciated, however, in its deepest religious dimensions. More than the satisfaction of the Jew's hunger for liberty is involved. The Exodus represents the consecration of Israel to God's service, as well as the faithful promise to obey His Commandments. We were freed from Egypt so that we could serve God.

Dr. David Daube of All Souls College, Oxford University, a great scholar and devout Jew, has tried to apply the methods of legal research to the study of Scriptures. In his latest book, *The Exodus Pattern in the Bible,* this professor of civil law analyzes the account of the liberation. The details of how the Lord delivered Israel from Pharaoh must be understood against the background of the social laws of that time. When a private individual was enslaved, it was the duty of a strong loyal relative to redeem him. Once rescued from his master, the former slave became the possession of his relative. He would, of course, have a milder and more preferable kind of subjugation at the hand of his own kinsman than from a cruel stranger. In simplest terms, the process of freeing a slave meant a transfer of ownership.

From Daube's deep insight, we now understand the expressions used by God in His efforts to free the Hebrews, and the answers of Pharaoh become more comprehensible. God identifies Himself as the relative who has the duty to redeem his enslaved kinsmen. "Thus says the Lord, Israel is My first born son . . . let My son go, that he may serve Me" (Exodus 4:22). God identifies Himself as the parent of Israel, who has the greatest responsibility of freeing his enslaved son. When Pharaoh, having been afflicted with ten plagues, in utter desperation releases the Hebrews, he uses the correct legal formula of release, "Go serve the Lord."

An ancient source records this process of transfer. "We were Pharaoh's slaves and Thou didst redeem us and make us Thy servants." (The Midrashic comment upon "Praise ye the Lord. Praise, O ye servants of the Lord . . ." Psalms 113:1.)

Modern man does not like the notion of being enslaved. There is, however, much wisdom to the traditional insight that the slavery of God is the truest freedom, "The slave of God alone; he is free." How many of us, who consider ourselves to be free men, are enslaved to our possessions and shackled to our passions. Modern man has many masters who hold him in bondage.

Annually, as we re-create the experience of the Exodus at our *seder,* different ideas and values come to mind. For some the seder and its ritual bring back recent history, modern Israel's gallant struggle for freedom. In America, some Jews use the occasion to rededicate themselves to the struggle for civil rights. We reflect on the Negro's century-old-battle for human dignity. These thoughts are precious, but the Exodus means more than that. *Yetziat Mitzraim* is the central event in Jewish experience. "For I am the Lord that brought you up out of the land of Egypt . . ." on the condition that you accept the yoke of the Commandments (Sifra). The recollection of the Exodus, through the *seder* ritual and our daily prayers, ought to remind us that we were freed by God to become His servants.

161

Advice for Our Age

OURS IS AN AGE of counseling. America abounds with vocational counselors, financial consultants, marriage advisors and management experts. Most of us seek out the wisdom of these mentors at one time or another.

One of the first counselors recorded in history was Jethro, the father-in-law of Moses. After the Israelites left Egypt and crossed the Red Sea, Jethro came to pay his respects. Moses told the breath-taking story of all that had happened since they last met, many years before. The next morning, Jethro went out to see how his son-in-law was faring as the leader of such a vast camp. He saw Moses, sitting single-handed, trying to dispense justice. Jethro summed up the situation. Moses had taken an overwhelming task unto himself. He gave the emancipator some solid advice on how to organize the camp and arrange for a properly functioning judiciary.

Jethro advised, "The thing you are doing is not right. You will surely wear yourself out ... Now listen to me. I will give you counsel, and God be with you ... and you shall enjoin upon them the laws and the teaching, and make known to them the way they are to go..." (Exodus 18:17-20).

There were two principal features to Jethro's advice. One was that Moses relieve himself of much of his physical burden, his personal involvement, lighten his work load and arrange his affairs so that things would be more tolerable for him. Judaism has always been concerned with the physical well-being of people. This is the spirit of "Take you, therefore, good heed of yourselves" (Deuteronomy 4:19). A medieval text, *Sefer Hasidim*, speaking of people who want to do it all by themselves, said: "He who sits alone is worn out quickly."

162

Dr. Eli Ginzberg, an internationally famous manpower expert who directs a project on the Conservation of Human Resources at Columbia University, has commented that our nation is not suffering from a shortage of talent, but, rather, from a shortage of talented people who know how to protect their time.

The lightening of Moses' burden had a second purpose as well. He was to have the opportunity to teach the Israelites how to lead a better and more ethical life. The idea of learning to live more efficiently in order to be better human beings is the counsel which our age needs. We have developed sufficient labor-saving devices. What our time needs most desperately are soul-saving devices.

It has been observed that leisure poses a threat. Leisure, more and more time on our hands, shows up our empty lives as lightning floodlights a darkened landscape. Our limbs are less fatigued than our fathers' but our hearts are heavier. We have overcome the debility of the tired body without developing the ability of the mind.

This paradoxical situation was discussed in a now famous letter written by the novelist, John Steinbeck, 1962 Nobel Prize winner, to Adlai Stevenson. Steinbeck described the emptiness in American life. "We have become so enchanted with material things, we have so much and yet have no real sense of satisfaction. We are like the child at holiday time who having received more presents than he can ever use, tears off the wrappings, throws down the gifts and says, 'Is that all?' "

Steinbeck writes mournfully, "Having too many things, Americans spend their hours and money on the couch searching for a soul. The strange species we are, we can stand anything God and nature can throw at us save only plenty . . . If I wanted to destroy a nation, I would give it too much and I would have it on its knees, miserable, greedy and sick." Steinbeck finished his letter by saying, "What we have beaten in nature we cannot conquer in ourselves."

America needs counsel. We are hungry for meaning in life.

163

Is ours not the age predicted by the prophet Amos, "Behold the days come, sayeth the Lord God, that I will send a famine in the land, not a famine of bread nor a thirst for water, but of hearing the words of the Lord." God's words, when heard, are the counsel which we must hear and understand.

The Lesson of the Eagle

"And I bore you on eagle's wings..." (Exodus 19:4)

THIS BIBLICAL EXPRESSION is a most familiar one. The image that its words conjure up in our mind suggest great majesty and power—the mightiest of birds taking its young aloft.

Martin Buber speaks of this verse, which likens God, in His historic relationships to Israel to the eagle. The giant bird stirs up his nest and hovers above it, in order to teach its young how to fly. The great eagle spreads out his wings over his young. He takes up one of them—a shy or weary one—and bears it upon his wings until the fledgling attempts to fly by itself and follows the father. Buber concludes his description, "Here we have election, deliverance, and education—all in one."

The eagle is a familiar emblem. It is used as the symbol of America, and in ancient times, was a symbol of Imperial Rome. One legend speaks of the eagle being identified with the Jewish people. An ancient despot spoke of Israel, saying, "The great eagle, Israel, had spread out his pinions over the whole world; neither bird nor beast can withstand him."

There is a deeper meaning to the expression "I bore you on eagle's wings." Man is compared, a sage once said, to a bird. What enables a bird to fly? His wings. The bird can soar to the heights only by moving his wings. The moment he stops flapping his wings, the bird begins to coast and then must crash to the ground. This is true of the spiritual life of man as well. Man can rise only by activating himself. Man can soar aloft only through his personal, strenuous efforts.

165

Our faith, to be sure, is one which takes a hopeful, cheerful, optimistic attitude toward life. Nevertheless, we are realistic enough to realize that things don't happen in the physical world or the spiritual realm by themselves. "I bore you on eagle's wings" may mean "I have given you the ability to rise above the ordinary, the earthy and the mundane." It is incumbent upon you to exert yourselves. The power to fly, to rise spiritually, does not come from yourself. It comes from a Source greater than yourself. "They that wait upon the Lord will renew their strength. They shall mount up with wings as eagles."

Each of us has the power to fly very high. The rabbis expressed this in a quaint saying, "The ear is only asked to hear that which it is able to hear." If a man strives to do that which is in his power, God will aid him to accomplish what is beyond his power.

Let us exert ourselves, realizing that the more valuable the goal, the more effort it demands.

How to Greet Your Father-in-Law

JETHRO, THE FATHER-IN-LAW of Moses, was astounded
to hear what had happened to Israel in Egypt. Together
with Moses' wife, Zipporah, and her two sons, Jethro went
out to meet the emancipator. (During his mission to Egypt,
Moses' family had been left behind.)

They met in the wilderness near Sinai. The Bible gives us
some illuminating details about the dramatic scene. "Moses
went out to meet his father-in-law, he bowed down, kissed
him, and each asked after the other's welfare" (Exodus 18:7).

Implicit in this description is a most profound understanding of the levels of human confrontation. In stage one,
we bow down, we greet, we smile. With how many people
do we have this nodding acquaintanceship in the elevators
of our apartments and office buildings? We may even call
out a saccharin "Good Morning" or a cheery "Good Night."
There is, however, no real engagement of personalities.

At times, we get closer to other human beings. We embrace them, we shake hands. If the occasion is joyous, as at a
social gathering, a wedding, or a Bar Mitzvah function, we
become "kissing cousins."

The Bible emphasizes that the most significant level of
our encounter is when we ask after each other's welfare,
when we concern ourselves about the other man's peace and
well-being. This is the test of real involvement and genuine
interest.

A Hasidic rabbi astounded some of his faithful followers
by declaring that at times a man must deny God. Recovering
from the initial shock, a disciple asked, "How is it possible?"
The answer was brief. "When someone comes over to you

167

begging for help, don't parry his request with the sanctimonious declaration 'God will help.' It is better that you help."

We live in a world where too many of us are content with the first two levels of greeting. I remember reading this phrase about urban life. "People tend to live externally crowded but internally lonely, morally isolated lives. We each know more people and fewer persons."

Two men, it is told, were employed by the same firm. They appeared to be very close. After many years, one of them was transferred to another city. People came over to commiserate with the remaining man on his losing a friend. The answer that came back was interesting. "He was not my friend. He was only an acquaintance." "But you laughed together, you shared so many good times." The man pondered for a moment and answered, "But we never cried together."

The rabbis were impressed by the fact that in recounting the reunion, Moses first inquired after the peace and welfare of his father-in-law and then told him of what had happened in Egypt. "Great is peace, it precedes our praise of God." How delicate is this insight of Jewish ethics! We must concern ourselves with the welfare of man before we proceed to proclaim the greatness of God.

Cooperation Means Existence

NINETEENTH CENTURY naturalists presented a vivid picture of nature. They went out and observed jungle life at its rawest. Darwin, Huxley and others wrote of a "survival of the fittest." Tennyson, in a poetic view of the struggle in the jungle, spoke of "nature, red in tooth and claw." This brutal picture of the animal kingdom was used to justify the cruelest forms of competition in the business world. The argument ran that just as in the natural order, survival is merited only by the strongest, so, in the economic and social order "the race is to the swiftest." They reversed the Biblical teaching, "The race is not to the swift" (Ecclesiastes 9:12). Only the strongest merit and can survive. The weakest, by natural selection, go to the wall.

With the passing of the years, considerable revision has taken place in our understanding of the animal kingdom, as well as in our appreciation of the true nature of the social order. Beginning with the findings of Prince Peter Kropotkin, laboratory science has demonstrated most adequately that cooperation is a more vital factor among animals than competition. The University of Chicago scientist, Professor Warder C. Allee, summarizing this information, gave us a new picture of the jungle. The isolated animal is retarded in growth and suffers death more quickly than an animal that lives in association with others. Those animals that live group lives increase in size, tend to recover quickly from wounds, and survive longer. Allee concluded that the co-operative forces are biologically more important. (These observations have been summarized in Ashley Montague's *On Being Human.*)

That which science has discerned was sensed by the rabbis a long time ago. They emphasized that nature itself demonstrates that mutual concern and cooperation are more important than fierce competition. Commenting on the verse, "If you lend money to My people, to the poor who is in your power, do not act toward him as a creditor: exact no interest from him" (Exodus 22:24), they said, "Observe how all God's creatures borrow from one another." Day borrows from night and night borrows from day. In the summer, when the day is long, it borrows from the night. In the winter, the reverse is true. At the spring and fall equinox, day and night are in balance, as if they had repaid one another. The moon borrows from the stars and the stars from the moon. When the moon is at its brightest, the light of the stars seems to be dimmed, as if the moon had borrowed light from them. But, when the moon is waning, the stars shine more brightly, as if borrowing from the light of the moon. The heavens borrow from the earth and the earth from the heavens. The clouds of heaven draw water from the sea, and the earth, in turn, receives much from the heavens.

The homily which stresses the interdependence of the elements of the natural order ends by teaching a moral lesson: God's creatures borrow from one another, yet make peace with each other. Man ought to learn from this experience in relating to his fellows.

The spirit of our Midrash is reflected in a medieval Arabic source. That nature itself seems to bespeak cooperation was expressed by the mystic poet, Rumi:

"No sound of clapping comes from one hand without the other.
Divine wisdom is destiny and decree made us lovers of one another.
Without the earth, how should flower and tree blossom?
What, then, would Heaven's water and heat produce?"

Nature is still man's best teacher, if he but study her lessons well. The law of life is one which demonstrates our mutuality and dependency. "What is the nature of life?" a scholar was asked. He answered in one word—"Cooperation." "Without cooperation it is not possible to live. At best, it is only possible to exist."

170

The Slavery of Security

"But if the slave declares 'I love my master . . .
I do not wish to be freed.'" (Exodus 21:5)

ONE OF LIFE'S most pleasant experiences is to hold a baby.
Normally, the infant wiggles and tries to work his way free by
moving both arms and legs. This instinctive reaction, according to some students, demonstrates that, by nature, man
yearns to be free. Yet everywhere we find so many men enslaved.

Our Torah reading suggests a reason for man's loss of liberty. In ancient times, under specific circumstances, a Hebrew
could be enslaved. He was to work for six years, but in the
seventh year he was to be freed. However, a slave could refuse
his freedom by declaring, "I love my master . . . I do not wish
to be freed." He was then to remain a slave for life.

The language which the slave used, "I love my master,"
seems to suggest that the slave preferred his material security
to his personal liberty. The reassurance of the familiar was
more desirable than the threatening unknown. The struc-
tured setting of slavery was preferable to the unstructured
future of freedom. The burdens of responsibilities were too
much for him to bear. Many men, to borrow Erich Fromm's
title, seek an *Escape from Freedom.* All too frequently, this
flight is motivated by material considerations.

Our over-concern with material comforts has affected our
life on several levels. Think of what has happened to our col-
leges as they change from centers for cultivating the intellect
and have become career preparatory schools. A college di-
ploma is more than a signed guarantee of a higher lifetime
income. It should be an admission card to a better life. A

171

school, to be sure, has to train a person in skills which will enable him to earn a living, but a school is also an academy for the refinement of character. Will our college graduates, in years to come, be prepared to surrender their freedom for their material security?

Our abundance has affected our lives as Jews. For the first time in Jewish history, we have become the defenders of the status quo. Think of it, the children of the prophets have become so concerned with profits that we find Jewish members in the John Birch Society. This past year our press reported that two Birchers "announced the formation of a Jewish Society of Americanists composed of members of the John Birch Society." They claim that the Jewish membership is about 1,000. How pathetic it is to realize that Jews are prepared to give up their birthright to ensure their property rights. The John Birch Society rallies round it some of the most extreme rightwing elements in our nation. Robert Welch, their leader, alleges that Chief Justice Earl Warren of our Supreme Court is "the idol of the Communists." Welch attacks the civil rights movement as being "a Communist-perpetrated rebellion." Welch's thesis is a simple one: "The United States is an insane asylum and the worst of it is that the patients are running the place." Some observers believe that Welch himself is paranoiac, suffering from delusions of persecution. One must question the real motives of a Jew who seeks the fellowship of such a rabble-rouser.

The story is told of a man who was aboard a sinking ship. Together with all the other passengers, he was given a life preserver. This traveler had some gold bars with him and was so anxious to save his fortune that he slipped the precious objects into his belt. Unfortunately, when he hit the water, the weight of the gold treasure dragged him down. In the course of our lives, the decision as to whether or not we will be free depends upon us. A wise man, I would suggest, will not sacrifice his freedom for his material security.

The Half-Way Mark

IN DESCRIBING the first ark in the Tabernacle, the Bible recorded its dimensions. They were to be "two and a half cubits long, a cubit and a half broad, and a cubit and a half deep."

An old commentator, looking at the dimensions stated in halves of cubits, made an interesting suggestion. "This is to teach you that the heart of a wise man is broken (*shavur*), never complete. The wise man should know that his work is only half done. He is only at a half-way mark on the road to perfection in the study and service of the Lord."

Every wise man realizes that he and his tasks are only half done, and that there is many an uncompleted duty in one's life and in our society.

During his second inaugural, only a month before his assassination, Lincoln spoke these immortal words: "With malice toward none, with charity for all, with firmness in the right, as God gives us to see the right, *let us strive on to finish the work we are in*." Lincoln realized that his task was only "half done." Our 16th president had only partly completed the structure of the better society.

Lincoln had had a most trying life. He had been tested in the crucible fires of personal defeat and disappointment. He had buried his young sweetheart and had had a trying marital experience. He had stood at the grave of his own young. Yet, in spite of his broken heart, he won for himself a supreme place in American consciousness and world memory.

Lincoln exemplified the power of building out of his own disaster. He had the spirit which was captured by the medieval poet who said, "*Mizbeach evneh b'shivron libee. Out of the fragments of my broken heart, I will build an altar to*

173

God." His life reflected the moral essence of his being, and was an altar upon which there burned a continuous offering of service to the highest purpose, a united America in which every man would be free and equal.

Lincoln was a deeply moral personality who wanted to breach the gap between the North and South. Motivated by a deep love for all men, he tried to prevent a brothers' war. At the end of his first presidential address to the American people, he said, speaking particularly to the South, which was preparing for secession, and to all America: "I am loathe to close. We are not enemies, but friends. We must not be enemies. Though passion may have strained, it must not break our bonds of affection."

Lincoln, in his way, expressed that which the rabbis taught two thousand years ago in answer to the query, "Who is mighty"? "Mighty is he who makes of his enemy a friend."

We are, as in Lincoln's time, only at the half-way mark to the better life. As Lincoln drew his strength from Scripture, we, too, may draw our courage in rededication to his high principles from the very words of Isaiah which he quoted at his second inauguration. "None shall be weary nor stumble among them . . ." May we finish, in our time, the building of the better society.

What Do You Look At?

*"Make two cherubim of gold...Make one
cherub at one end and the other cherub at the
other end...The cherubim shall have their
wings spread out above. They shall face each
other."* (Exodus 25:18-20)

SYMBOLS PLAY a very important role in life. They represent an ideal or a value taken from abstract thought and fixed in concrete form. Symbols are important, for they communicate important messages to us. What we look at is important. What we are willing to face and to confront is an acid test of the nature of our personalities.

We are all familiar with the symbol of our American nation. The British have their lion, the Russians their bear, the French their rooster. We Americans have our eagle.

Since 1782, the seal of our nation has displayed the American eagle as its central figure. In the bird's right (or dexter) talon, there is an olive branch. In the left (or sinister) talon, there is a bundle of arrows. The beak is turned towards the right, facing the olive branch, symbolic of man's quest for peace, rather than towards the arrows, emblematic of war.

During the last 180 years there were occasions when the position of the arrows and the olive branch was reversed. This occurred on coins and even on the President's seal. To prevent any misunderstanding of America's intention, a recent American president re-affirmed that the eagle's beak must always face right and toward the olive branch.

An early Jewish symbol was the pair of cherubim, placed on top of the Ark. We have legends as to their appearance. One of these accounts tells that they bore the faces of children.

175

In Exodus, the Bible requires that their wings be outspread, lifted above. What is most significant is that they faced each other.

The suggestion that the cherubim's faces were childlike seems to convey an important lesson. The childlike face was selected because children are innocent. They are yet unspoilt by the world, and for a long period of time, remain unblemished and untarnished. We need this childlike simplicity of faith. "Man," a contemporary theologian observed, "is aware of his weakness. He is overwhelmed by the mystery of the Divinity which simultaneously attracts and repels him, and is resentful of his own impotence. In the inner sanctum of his personality, man is reduced to childlike innocence . . . Only by admitting his childish innocence can man open his heart to God." We need childlike faith and a purity of appearance.

The wings of the cherubim were "spread out above." This seems to suggest that we must lift our thoughts above the transient, and hope that we will be able to examine things in the light not merely of the hour but of eternity. We need not only a purity of appearance but a purity of attitude. Let our thoughts be heavenbound.

The last characteristic of the cherubim is perhaps most significant. The Bible tells us that they shall confront each other, which meant literally, "and man looked at his brother." They must turn to one another. Man's attitudes may be heavenbound but his responsibilities are brother-bound. Faith and values ought to be translated into positive terms. The position of the cherubim is an invitation to purity of action. Bonds of love and cords of friendship should bind us together.

During the days of Solomon's Temple, the Bible reports that the orientation of the cherubim was changed. They no longer looked at each other but faced inward toward the house. Our sages were puzzled by this direction. They resolved this difficulty by saying that when Israel obeyed the will of God the cherubim turned toward each other, but when Israel disobeyed the will of God the cherubim turned from each other. The nature of the disobedience can be understood

176

from the text itself. The Hebrew reads, "And their faces were inward toward the house" (II Chronicles 3:13). Men concerned themselves with selfish interests. They were not prepared to look at other human beings. They were unconcerned with the wellbeing of others.

What we look at is important. It tells much about us, for goals are the measures of our soul.

The Free Deed vs. the Forced Act

OUR ANCESTORS were instructed to build "a sanctuary that I may dwell among them" (Exodus 25:8). The tabernacle served as the focal point of worship for the children of Israel as they marched through the wastelands of the desert.

The establishment of the sanctuary meant that God could be worshipped wherever the children of Israel dwelt. Unlike other ancient religions that restricted their worship to the deities at a sacred spot, the God of Israel was to be worshipped in each Jewish community.

The first tabernacle was built through the efforts of our people alone, as opposed to Solomon's temple, whose construction depended greatly upon foreign craftsmen. The two structures differed too in the mode of financing their construction. The desert tabernacle was built solely through the free will offerings of the children of Israel. So great were their gifts that Moses was compelled to cut off their contributions. "The people bring much more than enough for the service of the work, which the Lord commanded to make."

In the case of Solomon's temple, the situation was completely different. The king's edifice was built by a corvee, a forced levy of personal service. "Solomon raised the levy out of all of Israel and the levy was 30,000 men." The men were compelled to go to neighboring Lebanon, to work a month away from home, with a respite of two months back with their families.

It was hard for a population which was basically a farming community to lose a full third of its production. This forced labor project sowed the seeds of the ultimate destruction of Solomon's temple and the splitting up of his kingdom after his death.

A simple lesson may be learned from these contrasting accounts. Religion is at its best when it is the free expression and voluntary deed of men. That which is forced can never attain the same degree of religious intensity as the freely chosen act.

Parents, for example, who want to have their children continue the tradition, ought not demand or insist that their children follow the faith. Parents should rather set a proper atmosphere, prepare the mood for their children's acceptance of Judaism. It has been wisely said, "Religion is caught rather than taught."

The greatness of American Judaism, perhaps its most distinctive character, is that it is built on the solid bedrock of voluntary association. No one but ourselves and our inner conscience compels us to participate in the affirmative aspects of Jewish life.

We will build a sanctuary of American Judaism like our ancestors of old, based upon the element of our free choice, and may our gifts of service be as great as those of our ancestors in the desert.

Foresight and the Golden Calf

"And I said unto them: Whosoever hath any gold, let them break it off; so they gave it to me; and I cast it into the fire, and there came out this calf." (Exodus 32:24)

AFTER AARON had made the golden calf, he tried to defend his actions by rationalizing that he did not realize that a calf would come out of the fire, as it did.

Aaron, it would seem, revealed a great measure of moral weakness. His lack of courage to admit his wrong incurred the wrath of God, and he would have been destroyed, were it not for the prayers and intercessions of his brother Moses.

A teacher of mine once made an interesting observation: "If one strips himself of his gold and casts it into the seething cauldron of life without plan and without purpose, an idolatrous calf emerges."

There is much to be said about this "homey" yet profound insight. Many of us commit the sin of giving our money away without inquiring as to the nature of the charity which we have helped. Some of us cast off our own children by exposing them to difficult or unsuitable environmental situations. We permit our young to join clubs and organizations without inquiring as to the nature of these activities. We may ignore the character of our children's friends and the company they keep. We are unconcerned about the groups that command so much of their time and attention.

Some of us cast away the most precious of our possessions. We throw away our time. We take this limited gift, which we can use only once, and throw it into the consuming fires of a hyperactive schedule marked by a constant whirl of activity.

We fritter away our time and we ask not whether it is being consumed in a false fire or by a holy flame.

The Pennsylvania Dutch have an expression, "We grow old too soon and smart too late." At the end of our careers, we lament that our choicest possessions, our children and the days of our lives have lost their real meaning. Idols that we cannot control have emerged to haunt our very existence and to taunt our sense of real achievement.

To build a proper life, one must have a proper plan. Like the sanctuary of old, which was described in intimate detail in the Bible, we, too, must build a sanctuary of our lives, the tabernacle of our careers, with good sense and good purpose. Then our gifts of money will lead to purposeful ends. Our children will indeed be a blessing, and the brief span of time allotted to us will be hallowed by our creative deeds.

The Vestments of Aaron

FREQUENTLY, AFTER A SERVICE, some kindly people come over and observe, "How warm your robes must be." I am grateful to those who feel for the rabbi and who are genuinely concerned with his comfort and discomfort. If their hearts go out for me, how much more would they sympathize with Aaron, the High Priest. The Bible tells us there were two stones embedded in the garment that covered Aaron's shoulders, as a symbol of the Israelite people. Not only did he bear this weight upon his shoulders, but he also carried on the breastpiece of decision the *Urim* and *Thummim*, twelve mounted stones—one for each of the tribes. The Bible goes on to state, "Thus shall Aaron carry the instrument of decision for the Israelites over his heart before the Lord at all times" (Exodus 28:30).

Aaron bore the symbol of the physical burden upon his shoulders and the sign of the moral decision upon his heart. These weights surely were heavy in both a physical and a spiritual sense. But the High Priest carried them proudly. There are some weights which seem to be heavy, yet really are uplifting!

Some years ago I read a poem whose words impressed themselves upon me. As this thought of the buoyant burden came to mind, I remembered its message. Called "The Porter of God," its author used an unusual simile for our people, speaking of Israel as one given over to the carrying of a burden.

> *"Heavy, heavy is the burden*
> *Heavy, heavy is the load*
> *Which is placed upon my back . . .*
> *My knees are bent, but I shall never*
> *Throw off the load.*

I shall continue to bear it
For I am a porter of God."

Assigned with this heavy task, our people, as the porter of God, have carried the burden of His Word through every type of environmental situation. The road has been tortuous, full of twists and turns; nevertheless we have continued on our way.

> *"I shall walk forever*
> *I shall stand firm in every trial*
> *For I am the porter of God."*

Even when the world whipped us for nonconformity, we persisted in carrying the precious gift of God which was entrusted to us.

> *"I shall not be ashamed or abashed*
> *For I shall bring that load more*
> *Perfect unto the living God . . ."*

This idea is a splendid one. The burden we carry has been heavy, but it has also been ennobling. Our charge did not demean us, but gave dignity and purpose to our acceptance of it.

A remarkable thing about the Hebrew root *nasso* is that it means both to carry and to lift up. In our prayer book we speak of God as *El Ram V'nissa,* which means High and Exalted God. God places burdens upon us. The acceptance of these weights helps to exalt Him and to uplift us. Marriage is called *nissuin.* Here, too, we accept burdens which enhance our life and our love.

To those who wish to throw off the load which we have carried through the ages, may I quote the splendid observation of Joshua Loth Liebman—"Take away the burden from the shoulder of Israel, there is no weight . . . there is nothingness."

These weights are like the Ark of the Covenant which was carried through the wilderness. Legend had it that the Ark "carried its carriers."

This is the paradox of life. The burdens which we carry really carry us. Let us remember that ours is a wonderful destiny. We are the carriers of the Covenant.

> *"Look my God and see how dear and precious*
> *This burden is to me.*
> *I am your firm and faithful one,*
> *the porter of God."*

The Pagan and the Prophet

WHY DO MEN STUDY HISTORY? What is the purpose of rereading the accounts of previous generations? History lengthens our perspective and helps us to understand that our existence is more than the swift moment, the fleeting hour, the passing year. We are sustained when we study the continuous challenges that have been mankind's. History helps to shield us from hysteria in moments of anxiety and guards us from a failure of nerves in trying times.

We live in an anxious era. Mighty and diametrically opposed philosophies compete for the souls of men. There is some strength and comfort in studying the past and realizing that life has always been a struggle between good and evil, light and darkness, right and wrong.

Recently, I reread a play based upon a Biblical theme, telling of a struggle similar to our own which took place some 3,000 years ago. The work by Mattitiahu Shoham, was called "Tyre and Jerusalem." The principals were Queen Jezebel and Elijah the prophet. Jezebel represented the temperament of Tyre. Tyre, symbolizing the pagan world, declared that man is weak; a human being is nothing but dust and ashes. Man cannot be summoned to mighty deeds. Why try to move anyone? Let human beings remain in darkness. Don't teach your young people to dream great dreams or your old men to hope for renewed glory. Why place ideals before humanity and why call upon men to sacrifice? Satisfy the senses, enjoy yourself! Things will never really be better, so live for today! This was the spirit of paganism.

Elijah taught the message of Jerusalem. The prophet, who is a beloved figure in Jewish folklore, believed in the future redemption of mankind. Man is blessed with the will to as-

185

cend and to become better. Elijah's teaching was the vision of Jerusalem—the glorious picture of man's innate spiritual greatness, an inner desire to make the world about him a better place in which to live. He believed that the will to ascend must be developed in man—human beings can and should be educated and improved.

Elijah often walked alone in solitude along this path of faith in man. So great was his trust in the potential goodness of human beings that he challenged even the mightiest with this belief. Always, Elijah taught, you must pray that people may be stimulated to become more than themselves and to reach out for perfection. This is the vision of Jerusalem, of man's growth, uplifted by the spirit of faith.

The struggle between Tyre and Jerusalem, between Jezebel and Elijah, is not ended. The reverberations of this ancient clash can still be felt today. There are still those who look at the world in the most pessimistic of ways. Thankfully, there are those who have faith that a better future is possible for man. Man wants to be ennobled and improved. Mankind may yet be redeemed.

More or Less?

THE INCIDENT OF THE GOLDEN CALF creates many
opportunities for reflecting on what happens to people when
they come into money; when goods and services becomes more
readily available to them. An interesting commentary exists
on the plea which Moses made to God on behalf of His people. He appeared and said, "This people is guilty of a great
sin in making . . . a god of gold, and yet, if You would only
forgive their sin!" (Exodus 32:31). Moses, like a devoted defense lawyer whose client had been caught red-handed, was
looking for a mitigating excuse. Legend had Moses declaring,
"O God, You have caused them to sin, for You gave them
gold in abundance and everything they wished. What else
were they likely to do if not to sin!" (Rashi)

This type of thinking seems to ring a most modern note.
So many people blame the shortcomings of our contemporary
society on the fact that we are materially much better off than
were our ancestors.

A recurring theme concerning the ethics and economics of
American life asks, "Can we stand abundance?" This question
implies that the root of many of our modern problems can
be found in the soil of our improved way of living. To be
sure, there is always an implicit danger when additional
wealth is placed in the hands of people. Some individuals become what my teacher, Dr. Mordecai M. Kaplan, once la-
belled as "self-made men, who worship their own creator."
Others delude themselves with the type of thinking about
which the Bible warned us, "When you have eaten . . . and
built fine houses . . . your silver and gold have increased and
everything you own has prospered, beware lest your heart
grow haughty . . . and you say to yourself, my own power and

187

the might of my own hand have won this wealth for me . . ."
A few modern thinkers speak with great contempt about our age of abundance. Their approach recommends, in essence, that we might be better off if we turned the clock back. They argue that if there is an abuse of wealth perhaps we will be better off if we lived simpler and more austere lives.

Judaism appears to me to be a very wise religion, with a profound appreciation of human nature and man's needs. Our basic approach to life stresses that man is constantly given new opportunities in every age. These opportunities are challenges. They can be used for a better life, but if misused they can lead to despair. Judaism was concerned with the abuse of wealth, but also emphasized that there could be a proper use of man's possessions.

Twentieth century man moves faster. Much of our life is interwoven with the automobile. Autos not only move man about more quickly, but, unfortunately, they are involved in accidents. Shall we be like the Plain people, a sect in Pennsylvania, who refuse to drive a car and insist upon using the horse and carriage? Or shall we rather say that men ought to use automobiles but to try to drive them safely?

We produce more goods with less effort these days than our ancestors ever dreamed of in their fondest flights of fancy. Some students are disturbed that machines now permit a laborer to work a much briefer work week. They question what a man is to do with so much time on his hands when he can earn enough income in a twenty-hour work schedule. Here, again, we may ask, shall we regress to a longer week, or shall we rather try to create those types of opportunities which will permit men and women to make proper utilization of their increased leisure time?

Whenever I read the legendary statement of Moses, "O God, you put wealth into their hands. What did you expect them to do?" I am reminded of the story of a little boy. He was engaged in a forbidden sport, playing ball in his bedroom, bouncing it along the wall. Everything went well until one bounce went beyond his reach and cracked a window. When his father came running in to see what had happened, the little man protested in self-defense, "If you had only been stricter and taken the ball away from me when I started to play, this never would have happened."

The moral of the story seems obvious. What is put into our hands is not as important as our moral decision to use our possessions properly.

The Leader and the Led

AFTER THE TEN COMMANDMENTS were given to Moses at Sinai, he remained for another forty days on top of the mountain. This delay in returning to the camp disturbed the former Israelite slaves greatly. They gathered about Aaron and demanded, "Make us a god who shall go before us, for that man Moses who brought us from the land of Egypt—we cannot tell what happened to him." Aaron weakened and instructed them to bring the gold rings that were on the ears of their wives, their sons and their daughters. The jewelry was brought. He took the rings and cast them into a mold and made a molten calf. The people exclaimed joyfully, "This is your God, O Israel, who brought you from the land of Egypt." When Aaron saw this he built an altar before the calf and proclaimed, "Tomorrow shall be a feast to the Lord." The next day the people offered sacrifices. They sat down to eat and drink and then rose to make merry.

This earthly scene disturbed God. Legend fills in the details of the Biblical account. When the people turned from God, the Holy One, blessed be He, said to Moses, "Go get thee down, for your people whom you brought from Egypt have corrupted themselves." The instruction to Moses, "Go get thee down" was not merely a statement that it would be best for Moses to go back to his people. The sages understood God's statement to mean that Moses had to go down, for his stature had been diminished. He was no longer worthy of remaining in such serene surroundings. The impact of God's words can be understood from this statement: "Moses, descend from your greatness. Have I at all given to you greatness save for the sake of Israel?" (Berakot 32a).

To understand Moses' predicament we need but think of

him and compare his position to that of a leader of a state or an ambassador of a nation, who has come to another country to negotiate on behalf of his people. Things are moving quite smoothly. Suddenly, while away from the homeland, a revolution takes place. No longer is the envoy the spokesman for a constituency. Figuratively, the props have been pulled out from under him. He represents no one but himself. We have seen this happen frequently in recent years at the United Nations, where ambassadors suddenly find that there has been a radical change of government at home. Moses had to go down, for his stature had been reduced by the actions of his people.

A leader's ultimate position and authority depend upon the character of the group which he represents. One of the greatest dangers to any leader is that of his ideals and values being watered down by his followers. The leader may go far and wide, acting as a spokesman for great causes, yet his people may not appreciate the ideals which their leader represents. The actions of those led make or break their leaders.

When I think of this Biblical story as it was extended by the rabbis, I can't help but reflect that what happened to Moses frequently occurs in the relationship between parents and children. When children behave properly or correctly in the presence of their parents, that is to be expected.

Father and mother are there and can, if need be, discipline them on the spot. Their very physical presence communicates to the child the possibility and the reality of correction. The acid test of the influence of elders upon children is not what happens when the parents are there, but rather what takes place when the folks are away. How do young people behave in their parents' absence? This is the most probing determination of whether or not parents have had a positive influence upon their children. We might also note how offspring conduct themselves when parents have gone away on that most permanent of voyages, the eternal one, is a splendid gauge of parental training.

A leader's stature depends upon the actions of the led. A parent's position is most directly related to the behavior of his children.

191

Missing the Point

*"Moses did not know that the skin of his face
was radiant . . ."* (Exodus 34:29)

THE HEBREW LANGUAGE is known for its terseness and
brevity of expression. Many Hebrew words reflect a complex
of ideas and values. Read in translation, we lose the nuances
involved. For example, the word *yada,* means more than the
English "to know." It connotes to learn, to understand, to be
aware, to experience intimately. A simple word "to know" is
summum bonum, the chief good of human existence.

It is related that Moses went up to Mt. Sinai on two occasions to receive the tablets of the law. His first experience was
frustrated when the children of Israel, in his absence, began
to worship the golden calf. When Moses came near the idol
and saw the people dancing, he became enraged. He hurled
the tablets from his hands and shattered them at the foot of
the mountain. Fortunately, there was a second chance. Moses
received another set of tablets and came down from Mt. Sinai.
The Bible reports "Moses did not know . . . that his face was
in a glow." He did not comprehend the serenity of his own
spiritual experience.

In another exciting Biblical account, the story of a powerful man is told. Samson, in a moment of weakness, revealed
the secret of his strength to the treacherous Delilah. She
played upon his sympathy. "How can you say 'I love you' . . .
and you have not told me the source of your great strength?"
Foolishly, Samson revealed that he was a Nazarite, and that
from birth he had pledged himself to God. As a Nazarite, he
would not cut his hair. Apprised of this intelligence, Delilah
had his hair shaven while Samson was asleep. Then she

shouted, "The Philistines are upon you, Samson." The Bible then completes the account of Samson's denouement: "But he did not know that the Lord had left him." The Philistines took advantage of his weakness. They gouged out his eyes and he become "Eyeless in Gaza, at the mill with slaves" (John Milton in "Samson Agonistes").

These two passages and the use of a common phrase "did not know" can surely be compared and contrasted. The mighty Moses, our most beloved spiritual guide, did not know the heights to which he had risen. Samson, physically the most powerful of men, did not know the depths to which he had fallen. This is the great tragedy of life. Men, both in the spiritual and physical realms, are often ignorant of their powers and are not aware of their failings!

What a paradox! We miss the point of life. We do not know who we are. We do not understand ourselves. We are not aware of our real potentialities and our true responsibilities.

We go through all of the motions of life but we miss the point of our mortal existence. All too frequently we fail to carry out the basic purpose of our being. It is pathetic, for example, to re-read the account of a great master who learned the value of a colleague too late. Rabbi Johanan had fallen out with his brother-in-law, Resh Lakish. He only discovered, after the latter's passing, what he had lost (Baba Mezia 84a).

Edwin Arlington Robinson, a Pulitzer Prize winner wrote of the tragedy of our failure to know the truth in time.

AN OLD STORY

"Strange that I did not know him then,
That friend of mine.
I did not even show him then
One friendly sign;
I would have rid the earth of him
Once, in my pride.
I never knew the worth of him
Until he died."

To know, to become aware, to appreciate, to understand the point of life is indeed a great attainment.

193

And Moses Went Up to God

A Eulogy of Rabbi Morris Adler

*"When thou takest the sum of the children of
Israel according to their number, they shall give
every man a ransom for his soul unto the Lord
when thou numberest them."* (Exodus 30: 12)

THE *SIDRAH* "Ki Tissa" provides us with a most penetrating observation on Jewish leadership. The words *Ki Tissa*
can be translated as "when you take the sum," or "when you
conduct a census." It can also be translated as "when you lift
up." When you want to take the sum of a people, you must
first lift up their leader. If the head of the leader is high, the
entire people is elevated. This idea is almost self-evident. The
Zohar, the *Book of Splendor,* comments that if the head of
the people is worthy, the people are protected through him.
The people can take shelter in him. The *Book of Splendor*
goes on to say: "If the head of the people is unworthy and
unfit for his responsibilities, woe to the people!" Tragically,
in the case of Rabbi Morris Adler, a young Bar Mitzvah boy
found his spiritual leader becoming his physical protector.
According to the newspaper accounts, Rabbi Adler threw his
own body over the body of his young student to shield him
from the bullets of the assailant.

Rabbi Morris Adler was a most worthy leader of our people. Like Moses of old, whose Hebrew name he bore, Rabbi
Adler merited the comment on the closing verse of the Book
of Leviticus, the Book of Sacrifice. "These are the commandments that the Lord gave Moses for the children of Israel."

194

It is good when the messenger is worthy of his message and the message is truly a fitting one for the messenger to carry.

Rabbi Adler was an American rabbi. The modern 20th century rabbi is actually a fusion of two earlier types of Jewish leaders. The traditional representative of rabbinic Judaism was the *Talmid Hakham,* the disciple of the wise. He was the living embodiment of Torah scholarship. The more recent Hassidic *Zaddik* was an individual whose leadership depended upon the charisma of his religious personality. The *Talmid Hakham* was a master of Torah. The *Zaddik* was a master of the righteous life. Professor Gershom Scholem explained this quality of the Hassidic saint: "Personality takes the place of doctrine." The quality of the leader's life was all important. "I did not go to the Maggid of Meseritz to learn Torah from him," a disciple said, "but to watch him tie his boot laces." Learning, the mastery of the Torah, was important, but the character of a man's life was equally significant. The ideal American rabbi is a fusion of these two qualities of the older rabbinic scholar and the more recent charismatic leader. Rabbi Adler was a gifted scholar, and he was also blessed with the attributes of a warm and charming personality.

Ki Tissa can be translated as "when you count." Morris Adler was the head of one of the most significant congregations in the world. His synagogue numbered some 1600 families. Morris Adler did not deceive himself. He did not merely count the number of his members but asked: "How many of my members really count? Are they merely entries on our membership roster? Are they statistical items or are they individuals whose lives I have touched, inspired, raised up and uplifted?" Much of his seemingly boundless energy was given to building a fine school system for young people and an equally outstanding adult education program. Teaching was his *forte.* One of the most gifted preachers in the land, he delighted in direct classroom teaching. He tried to teach both young and old alike. "Therefore my heart is glad and my soul rejoiceth," says the psalmist. The rabbis interpret this to mean "My heart is glad"—when young people study the Torah; "My soul rejoiceth"—when their elders study, too.

Ki Tissa means to forgive. As his mad assailant, his own student, moved toward him during that eventful tragic moment four weeks ago to this very day, Rabbi Adler shouted to his people: "Leave him alone! I know the boy." He tried to reassure the terrified congregation who saw a young man brandishing a gun, that he would be able to handle the demented young man. *Ki Tissa* means to forgive. That is what we must ask now. May God forgive the young man, himself now dead.

Our verse instructs that each man give a ransom for his soul to the Lord. A good leader is the man who is prepared always, every day, every hour, to give up his own life as a ransom and as an atonement for every other individual in the community of Israel. Morris Adler, a great rabbi, a courageous chaplain and a masterful teacher, gave up his own life as a ransom for the life of others.

Finding Your Other Half

WHEN MOSES was commanded to conduct the first census of our people, every man was to contribute a half shekel. This gift was regarded as a "ransom for the soul." Rabbi Hanokh of Alexander, one of the later Hasidic masters, made an interesting observation. He noted that the Hebrew word *shekel* has the same numerical value as the Hebrew word for soul (*nefesh*). Every man, the teacher went on to say, receives only half a soul from Heaven. It is man's duty to complete the other half through the worship of God and the practice of good deeds.

This interpretation calls to mind an ancient Greek custom known as the *tessera hospitalis*. When a man took leave of his friends and went to distant places, he faced the problem of future identification. How would this man and his descendants be able to prove, after the passage of time, that they were connected with friends or even relatives who remained in Greece? As a token of mutual hospitality and friendship, a small coin or die, was given by the host to his guests at the time of departure. It was broken into two parts. Half remained with the host's family and the other half was given to the traveler. Each party retained half a coin, in order that if either of them met in the future, or if their descendants should again meet after many years, they might recognize each other. Putting the pieces together would serve as sufficient identification for the renewal or the repayment of their ancient family obligations.

A similar practice is recorded in rabbinic literature. In the *Pirke de Rabbi Eliezer,* a twelfth century work, there is a report concerning Isaac and Abimelech, King of Gerar. The King said to Isaac, "We see that the Lord is with you. We would like to make a covenant with you . . ." What did Isaac do? He took a piece of the bridle of his donkey and broke it off. He gave the section to Abimelech as a sign forever that there was a "sworn covenant" between them and their descendants. This report, the professor believes, was actually an echo of the Greek custom of the *tessera hospitalis* that had been adopted by the Greek-speaking Jews of the ancient world. A thousand years later, the nature of the covenant arrangement was forgotten. In transmission, the details were garbled and changed.

Getting back to our half *shekel* coin, after this brief excursion into the rarified atmosphere of scholarly parallels, would it be too much to suggest that every man possesses only half a soul? The great search of life is for the other half of our soul which will match the half that is already in our possession, and will then make our life and soul complete. Some of us find the other half of our soul in a good marriage. This is what was meant by the Elizabethan expression concerning true friendship, "One soul in bodies twain." Some of us find fulfillment, our completion, in dedication to a great cause.

Man has only half a soul. It is incumbent upon him to complete it.

Mask to Mask

"IMAGINE! MOSES with horns!" This was the shocked report of a Jewish lady who had just seen the famous statue of Moses in Rome's San Pietro in Vincoli. Michelangelo's sculpture and painting have always been great tourist attractions, and Irving Stone's best selling novel, *The Agony and the Ecstasy,* have heightened public interest in the great Italian artist.

Michelangelo knew the Bible only in the Latin translation. In describing Moses the original Hebrew text was mistranslated. The Torah reports that when Moses came down from Mount Sinai with the second set of the Tablets, he was not aware that the skin of his face was radiant, *"Ki karan or panav"* (Exodus 34: 30). The word *karan* can mean "radiant light" or "horn." The Hebrew was understood by the Latin translators to mean "horns" in this case. When Michelangelo executed his magnificent statue of a seated Moses in 1513, he portrayed the great emancipator with horns coming out of his forehead.

The Biblical account describes what happened when the people saw Moses descending from Mount Sinai. They were afraid to approach him. At first Moses didn't realize what had happened. When he became aware of the radiance attached to him, Moses put a veil over his face. Thereafter Moses followed this practice. Whenever he faced the people he put the veil over his face; whenever he went in before the Lord, he would take the veil off.

Biblical scholars are not certain what the Hebrew word for veil, *masveh,* means. Some Bible scholars think that the *masveh* was a type of mask. The English word which we use for "person" comes from the Latin *persona,* which means "a mask." In the ancient theatre, different characters wore special wigs; a white wig meant an old man; a red one meant a slave. Later, in the development of the Roman theatre, each character had a distinctive mask.

How suggestive is the thought that we put on a mask when we stand in the presence of men. We must strip ourselves of the mask when we stand before God.

Attending a social gathering is often being set adrift in a sea of conversation. Social discussion is all too often not an encounter between two people, but a case of mask speaking to mask. The speakers never really get to talk to one another. They are rather stereotypes of non-communication engaged in conversation. Ask yourself candidly: when I speak to other people, do I really confront them or do I talk from behind a mask? Shakespeare said, "All the world's a stage, and all the men and women merely players." Too many of us are content to play-act out our lives. We hide behind a mask. We shield our real identity. We camouflage our intentions.

This is not always an improper procedure to follow. There are times when we cannot permit our faces to reveal the concern of our hearts. A poker face is necessary at times. After Pearl Harbor, President Roosevelt had to don a mask lest the American people become terrified. Could he, on December 7, 1941, reveal the full extent of the damage done to our fleet by the Japanese surprise attack on Pearl Harbor? A physician, at times, must put on a mask when he speaks to a patient afflicted with a terminal illness. But even if necessity compels us to wear a mask when we face men, let us never forget that when we stand in the presence of God, we must strip ourselves of all pretense. He is the Great Examiner of hearts. He understands our innermost thoughts.

To See Ourselves as Others See Us

ALL OF US have become accustomed to the abundance of mail that comes from publishers seeking subscriptions. The announcements become ever more attractive and intriguing. In some cases, we subscribe; in most instances we dispose of the announcements. The other day, a little piece from the Manchester Guardian in England caught my eye. It depicted Uncle Sam in a stars and stripes covered top hat. The symbol of America, wearing striped pants and tails, was being painted by John Bull dressed in a morning coat, gaiters and festooned in a Union Jack colored vest. The inscription under the illustration read "To see ourselves as others see us." The copy inside went on to say, "A portrait painted by an alert and accomplished artist can be most interesting, informative and amusing to the subject."

"To see ourselves as others see us" is important. This motto brought to mind something which I read in connection with the furnishings of the first Jewish house of worship. The children of Israel built a temporary tabernacle which went along with them as they moved through the desert. A copper laver was installed between the Tent of Meeting and the Altar. Aaron and his sons were to wash their hands and feet in water drawn from it. According to tradition, the copper was contributed by the women, who gave up their burnished mirrors as part of their contribution to the sanctuary. Some commentators (who may have had a male bias) stressed that the mirror which had been used to satisfy female vanity was transformed into an object used for ritual purity.

A much more profound observation was made by Rabbi Ya'akov Yosef of Polnoy, an early Hasidic teacher. He sug-

201

gested that the purpose of the laver was to help the priests purify themselves. Fashioned from a mirror which was originally used to see a reflected image, the teacher reasoned that a person can only purify himself when he sees himself as he appears to others. A good friend, for example, is one who restores our humility rather than feeds our arrogance, who loves us for our best and does not cater to our worst.

It is important for us to know what others think of us, to see ourselves as others see us. In this way we gain an understanding of our life as reflected in the eyes of others. This does not mean that we must depend completely upon what other people tell us concerning the conduct of our affairs. We are still the masters of our own fate, the captains of our souls.

"The Big Man"

"And Moses reared up the Tabernacle . . . and he spread the tent over the Tabernacle." (Exodus 40: 18-19)

THE RABBIS ATTRIBUTED great physical strength to Moses. They imagined him to be strong enough to erect the Holy Tabernacle by himself. Knowing of Moses' strength and also of his modesty, our sages taught: "The Holy One causes His Presence to rest only upon him who is strong yet modest, who is of great physical stature yet humble" (Nedarim 38a).

This value judgment seems to have a unique message for our own generation. We are accustomed to "big men." Our society is a fast-moving one. We are accustomed to seeing individuals move from dire poverty to great wealth within the span of a lifetime or even a generation. Our age has seen men doing big things, building our material society, invading even the heavens of the Lord and reaching for the moon and the stars.

The rabbinic insight that described Moses as a strong individual and yet a humble man, provides a useful observation for our generation. We have enough "big men" in our time. What we really need are men of great spiritual stature.

It is told of the Hasidic master, Rabbi Simcha Bunam, that when his wealthy disciples would come to his home to spend the holidays, the rabbi had a most unusual custom. He would have the great men, the men who were the leaders of communities, do simple chores and humble tasks in the kitchen and about the house. When asked why he had "big men" do little things, he responded, "You don't have to teach humility to a poor man, but you have to impress modesty upon men who think that they are strong, wealthy and powerful."

Another sage would express his love for his neighbor most strongly in his relationships with the poorer elements of the community. When asked about this practice, this teacher responded, "It is easy to love an important person. We must demonstrate our concern for those who are weak and need our sympathetic understanding."

When Moses completed the building of the sanctuary, legend has it that he wrote the 90th Psalm—the psalm which begins, "A Prayer of Moses, the Man of God . . ." He asked, ". . . And let the graciousness of the Lord be upon us. Establish Thou also upon us the work of our hands."

As our generation does big things with the effort of our hands, as we acquire more wealth, more physical strength and material power, let us retain our proper perspective toward ourselves. Let us retain the mood of modesty and the spirit of humility.

Count Me In!

DURING TEMPLE TIMES every adult Jew contributed a half shekel coin to the Sanctuary. An announcement was made on the eve of the month of Adar alerting the people to their responsibility. Throughout the ages this Sabbath has been used to remind our people of the needs of our central Jewish institutions. Then, as now, this day was the occasion to stress the importance of community development.

Several years ago the president of Barnard College spoke to her students. She dealt with some of the problems that face a modern school administrator. The educator concerned herself with "privatism," the attitude of "count me out." "Privatism" is the mood of being uncommitted to anything, of taking no part in anything, of being primarily devoted to personal ambition.

"Privatism" may be a modern word but it reflects a frame of mind that is as old as time. In most traditions there was a stress upon community participation. An old rabbinic passage taught, for example, "When the community is in distress, one should not say, 'I will go home, eat and drink, and peace will be upon my soul.' " Other sages added, "If an individual separates from the community when the populace is in distress, the two ministering angels that escort every man place their hands upon his head and say, 'Such a man who separated himself from the community merits not seeing the ultimate comfort of the community.' "

Judaism did not divide men into participants in the arena of life and bystanders. Our faith stressed that bystanders are not innocent. "Let the well-being of your neighbor be as dear to you as your own." We react when we are hurt and our flesh is maimed, but do we respond when the hurt comes to another?

205

It is reported that Solon, the Greek jurist, had a maxim which said, "It seems to me that the community that does the best and preserves democracy the most, is the one in which those who are not wronged prosecute and punish the criminal no less than those who are." We achieve a civilized society when those who are not hurt directly are as indignant as those who are. This sense of being concerned for others, of taking part in affairs, of being committed to communal needs, of proclaiming proudly, "Count me in!" is a basic Jewish notion.

We do not ask to be counted in solely because it helps to bind the community together. Our decision to be a participant is an answer to our ethical sense of duty.

There are, to be sure, legitimate differences of opinion as to how a community ought to be run. These disagreements cannot be used as convenient excuses for non-participation. Judaism has always taught that we are "a community of action," rather than "a community of belief."

The Bible advises us concerning the *Tefillin*, "Bind them as a sign upon your hand and let them serve as reminders upon your forehead." The memory devices on the forehead, the symbol of the mind, are stated in the plural. The sign upon the hand is given in the singular. We may have differing thoughts about Jewish communal life but when it comes to giving, let our hands join together in becoming one.

Two Freedoms

THE SABBATH which precedes Purim is known as the Sabbath of Remembrance (*Shabbat Zakhor*). A special section of the Bible is read: "Remember that which Amalek did to you . . . Do not forget."

Annually the Jew is reminded that on his road from Egyptian slavery to the freedom of Israel, as he moved through the wastelands of the desert, a bitter and implacable foe attacked him.

The early teachers of our people tried to expand this mood of remembrance. In place of a negative emphasis on primitive vengeance, they taught that Jews ought to remember a number of different things. These remembrances were included in the Prayer Book and were read daily after the conclusion of the formal services. Among the remembrances were:

1. Remember the Exodus,
2. Recall the attack of the Amalekites,
3. Reflect on the gift of the Torah,
4. Think of what happened to Miriam when she abused her sister-in-law, the wife of Moses, through slander and gossip.

At the outset, these events which we are to remember seem to be a listing of unrelated episodes. However, if one probes a little deeper, one can see that they fall into two distinct categories: remembrance of physical freedom, and recollections of spiritual freedom.

The redemption from Egypt and the fight against the Amalekites are part of a common pattern. Man must struggle to become free; he must break the ancient bond. Yet in his movement to liberty, he finds enemies seeking to restrict his independence. This was true in ancient days and it is true even today. No people have found a smooth high road on the way to liberty.

In every generation, a free nation is called upon to defend its right to self-determination. The Jewish people must remember the ancient struggle for our people's freedom and rededicate ourselves to this ideal in our own generation.

Physical freedom is a blessing, but it is not complete without the element of spiritual liberation. The Jew must remember that "only a servant of God is truly free." Only a person who accepts the words of the Ten Commandments, which spell out man's responsibility to God as well as to his fellowman, is truly free. Yet, in our quest for personal freedom, we must always remember the next man's needs. That is why stress was placed upon recalling that which happened to Miriam. The Jew, as evidence of his personal spiritual liberation, must respect the integrity of other free human beings. He must guard his tongue from misuse in relation to other people.

The sanctity of words is something which we must guard every day. The ultimate meaning of man's freedom is tested in the inter-play of our personal relations. It is on this level of our being that we determine whether we remember the true meaning of freedom for ourslves and for all people.

Leviticus

On Leadership

*"When a ruler sins and does through error any
of the things which by the commandment of the
Lord . . . ought not to be done . . . once the sin
of which he is guilty is brought to his attention
he shall bring as an offering . . ."*

(Leviticus 4:22-23)

THE BOOK OF LEVITICUS does not receive much attention from the modern reader. Although there are extremely significant passages like "Love thy neighbor as thyself" or "Proclaim liberty throughout the land unto all the inhabitants thereof," most of Leviticus, the Book of the Priesthood, remains uninviting. Twentieth century men are not excited about rereading the laws of sacrifice.

Only a few centuries after the destruction of the temple and the suspension of the sacrificial system, the rabbis brought another level of appreciation to Leviticus. They used its texts to understand some of the basic values of Judaism. They projected their sensitive appreciation of human nature against its background, seeking an understanding of the strength and weakness of people, particularly those in power.

The rabbis observed that the chapter under discussion lists different categories of people who unwittingly sinned, through error. In each case the preposition "if" is used. For example, "If the anointed priest sins . . ." However, in the case of the ruler or the leader, the preposition "when" is used. The Bible, itself, seemed to indicate that a leader, by the very nature of his position, was bound to make mistakes, knowingly and unknowingly. For this he ought to ask forgiveness.

"A prince's heart is uplifted because of his error," the Book

211

of Splendor stated, and therefore he is almost bound to sin. The rabbis seemed to capture the spirit of Lord Acton's epigram, "Power corrupts and absolute power corrupts absolutely." The leader, possessing great power, is tainted by pride of heart.

Rabbi Johanan ben Zakkai taught, "Happy is the generation whose ruler brings a sacrifice for a sin he committed unwittingly." (The Hebrew *asher*, "when," was rendered *ashray*, "happy.") Happy is the community whose leader is self-critical and is willing to make a visible demonstration of his act of atonement.

Rabbi Israel Salanter, the founder of the Mussar movement, added his thoughts on this theme. He asked, "Why is a generation to be regarded as fortunate and happy if its leader brings a sacrifice for his sins?" He observed that the leader's action was in response to the community's reaction. The generation was a happy one because it did not bow down indiscriminately. The leader's contemporaries did not flatter him. They were courageous, willing to be critical. Happy is the age when leaders acknowledge their shortcomings and those led are mature enough to exercise their responsibilities.

Back in 1898, a United States Supreme Court Justice stated, "It is a mistake to suppose that the Supreme Court is either honored or helped by being spoken of as beyond criticism. On the contrary, the life and character of its Justices should be the objects of constant watchfulness by all and its judgments subject to the freest criticism."

Criticism is good when it is constructive and helpful.

Hot-House Children

ONE OF THE EARLIEST records of the educational history of our people tells of a child's first lesson. After the pupil had mastered the alphabet and was able to read with some fluency, he was initiated into the study of the Bible. At that juncture in the child's development, a most unusual thing happened. Instead of introducing the student to the fascinating stories of Genesis—the creation of the world, Noah's ark, the flood—he was taken to the difficult passages to be found in Leviticus.

A possible explanation for this practice was offered by Professor Louis Finkelstein. He thought that the first schools in Israel had been established by the priests, to train their young in the art of the temple ministry. As future officiating priests, it would be logical for them to get an early start in learning the difficult laws of sacrifice.

Another explanation for the educational practice is given by the Tradition itself. Rabbi Assi observed, "Why do young children start with Leviticus and not with Genesis? Surely it is because young children are pure and the sacrifices are pure; so let the pure come and engage in the study of the pure."

Although the Hebrew word, *tahor*, means "pure" in a general sense, it connotes "innocent" when used concerning children. Heine, the German poet, captured this mood of childlike innocence when he said, "Child, you are like a flower; so sweet and pure and fair . . ." The implication of this educational practice is that the innocent, pure child ought to come and study those laws which can teach a person how to draw nearer to God. The preservation of the innocence of our young people is a central concern of our time. Our youngsters are rocketed from childhood into the status

213

of young adults. The maturation which normally would come during the years of adolescence has been forced upon childhood years by the adult pressures upon young people to grow up quickly.

The problem is not a new one. The Jerusalem community of 2,500 years ago also had difficulties with its young people. This is evident if one reads the book of Proverbs. The opening chapter offers this advice: "Hear, my son, the instruction of thy father, and forsake not the teaching of thy mother . . . My son, if scoundrels would lead you astray, never agree to it; if they say, 'Come along, let us trap honest folk, let us ambush the innocent . . . we shall get all sorts of precious stuff and cram our houses with booty. Cast in your lot with us, we will have all one purse'—my son, never join them, keep clear of their course . . ."

Perhaps most parents do not face the problem of dealing with juvenile delinquency. But there are other difficulties lurking ahead. The impact of the early loss of childhood innocence has concerned sociologists. They are worried about the current marriage explosion among youngsters who would have been considered children a generation ago. These early marriages are regarded to be less durable, acknowledged to impede educational growth. It has been proven that the risk of the marriage breaking up is greater as the age level spirals downward. Sadly, we can say that our jet-propelled youngsters too often are *"get"*-propelled.

Dr. Margaret Mead, the noted anthropologist, believes that this trend toward early marriage is wasteful, not only because of the high separation and divorce rate, but because of the emotionally stunting effect on the young couple. These youngsters, if they had waited, might have developed into different and more mature human beings.

How do our youngsters lose their innocence? Much of the blame rests at the feet of parents. To cite a recent report, "Today's parents push a child toward an earlier marriage when he is about 10, which is when debonair youngsters take dancing lessons. At 12 he has been on his first date. Many

214

parents are seriously worried about a girl if she is not dating steadily by the time she is 16 . . ."

The responsibility for training our young is essentially a home-centered activity. We ought to deal with our children as children, rather than as premature adults whom we have to rush through a hot-house of maturity. We owe them the legacy of a sense of values. Our children, who are pure and innocent, ought to be brought up in an atmosphere that encourages a normal, balanced process of moral and emotional growth. Let us not rush our youngsters, for the children of today will too soon be the parents of tomorrow.

Be a Builder

"The Lord spoke to Moses saying, 'Command Aaron and his sons.' " (Leviticus 6:1)

"Listen to my voice and I will be your God and you shall be My people and live exactly as I command you that it may be well with you." (Jeremiah 7: 23)

THE BOOK OF LEVITICUS does not make for exciting reading. While it does contain one of the Bible's greatest teachings, "Love thy neighbor as thyself," most of its passages deal with sacrifices. The destruction of the Jerusalem Temple and the abrupt break-up of the sacrificial cult brought about an intellectual crisis. How should the Book of Leviticus be taught? To make the dry text live again, the ancient rabbis applied the midrashic method. They used Leviticus as a springboard for ideas. They drew them out by re-interpretation of ethical implications of the original text. Applying their method, let us deal with the *sidrah* called Tzav. In its verb form, *tzav* means "command"; in its noun form it means "a precept."

Significant use of this word is made in the book of Isaiah. The prophet sought to teach God's word to the debauched court of the Northern Kingdom of Israel. In a most dramatic encounter, he enters the royal palace. To his dismay, the throne room is heavy with the fumes of liquor; the false priests and the prophets are reeling and unaware of his entrance. When they finally realize that he is present, they start to mock him, "Look who's here! Whom is he going to teach? Are we babes in arms that he keeps repeating his infantile

216

lesson, *tzav la'tzav* (precept by precept)?" The prophet is undaunted and repeats his admonition, "Precept by precept, precept by precept; line by line, here a little, there a little." The prophet kept hammering away at the key word *tzav*.

Implied in Isaiah's words is the great lesson that anything worthwhile must always be done bit by bit, precept by precept, line by line. We must appreciate this necessarily slow pace of building whenever we apply ourselves to any worthwhile undertaking. It is only by patient building that a firm and lasting structure can be erected. Just as we must have patience in our construction, so must we have forbearance in our criticism. It is hard to build up; it is easy to tear down.

I remember some anonymous lines of mediocre poetry that made good common sense.

> *"I watched them tearing a building down,*
> *A gang of men in a busy town;*
> *With a Ho-Heave and a lusty yell*
> *They swung a beam, and a sidewall fell.*

> *"I asked the foreman, 'Are these men skilled,*
> *As the men you'd hire if you had to build?'*
> *He gave a laugh and said, 'No indeed!*
> *Just common labor is all I need;*
> *These men can wreck, in a day or two,*
> *What BUILDERS have taken a year to do.'*

> *"I asked myself, as I went my way,*
> *'Which of these roles have I tried to play;*
> *Am I a BUILDER, who works with care,*
> *Measuring Life by the rule and square—*
> *Am I shaping my deeds by a well-made plan,*
> *Patiently doing the best I can,*
> *Or am I a WRECKER, who walks the town*
> *Content with the labor of tearing down?' "*

Are you a BUILDER or a WRECKER?

Some time ago, a five-year old son of a rabbi saw the steel work of a half-finished building and asked, "Mother, is the building going up or down?' This child's question, asked in

217

all innocence, inspired a holiday message that was later published by the Jewish Theological Seminary:

"How Young The World Is"

"A five-year-old boy, riding with his mother,
saw the steel work of a half-finished building
and asked her:
'Mother, is the building going up ... or down?'
To a child the clutter of construction
looks like the debris of destruction.
Clearly, to the precise eyes of childhood
half a building is only half a building.

How, then, can he know
in which direction the building is going?

Looking at the world around us
we are often as confused as the child.
We see a world
in which some people want to tear down
what others are building up."

Everyone's world is built up precept by precept, line by line, command by command. It takes a long time to build. Ask yourself this question—"Are you a BUILDER, or a WRECKER? Are you trying to tear down or build up?"

218

God's Glory and Man's Kinship

"And Moses said, This is the thing which the Lord commanded that you should do; that the glory of the Lord may appear upon you." (Leviticus 9: 6)

MOSES, SPEAKING to the Congregation of Israel, assembled at Sinai, the first Jewish place of worship, asked our people to carry out God's word. He assured them that if they would do what the Lord had requested, the "glory of the Lord" would appear upon them.

How does one attain the blessed state of having God's glory rest upon him? How does a human being achieve a greater sense of awareness of God and a feeling of closeness to Him?

One scholar suggested that our ancestors felt God's presence as a vital force in their lives through a simple process. This sage called attention to the fact that the verse immediately preceding our text stated that "all the Congregation drew near and stood before the Lord." When people draw nearer to one another, when they feel a little closer to one another, when they sense a spirit of kinship for one another—then they really stand before the Lord. They feel His presence.

It is comparatively easy to draw near to one's flesh and blood; this is no real achievement. A child loves his parents because he needs the affection of father and mother. Parents love their young because their children satisfy an indescribable urge in their lives. To draw closer to people who are not related to us by blood, and from whom we expect no material or social gain, is, in a sense, a higher achievement. The rabbis spoke of this type of affection for other human beings as "love which does not depend upon some selfish or material end."

219

Men can get closer to one another by learning to give of themselves. When a person gives of his own personality, he is not really sacrificing. We draw closer to people by trying to share that which is vibrant and alive within us, and by seeking to stimulate that which is created within them.

If we learn to look for the strong points in other human beings, if we master the art of accentuating the positive in their behavior, we can draw a little nearer to them. Wisely, a great medieval teacher wrote, "Man is in need of others in acquiring his virtue." If we really want to feel God's presence, we have to draw nearer to one another, feel closer to other human beings.

The Same Old Thing

C. S. LEWIS, a professor of literature at Cambridge University, writes delightful popular articles on religion. In one of them, he speaks of the dread of the familiar which many modern people have. He labels it "the horror of the Same Old Thing." Whether it is children who turn up their noses when they see their dinner: "What! The Same Old Thing?" or adults who change vacation resorts from years to year—so many of us seem to be obsessed with this horror. We have to do something new! We have to change our style!

In light of this background, it is interesting to reread that portion of the Bible which discusses the altar fire. Sufficient wood was to be present on the altar at all times, to keep the fire continually burning. In a sense, the priests who kept the fire going were doing the same old thing, over and over again. Yet, this commandment—"And the fire upon the altar shall be kept burning. It shall not go out." (Leviticus 6:5) found the priests vying with one another for its daily observance.

The concept that maintaining the flame of religion must be a constant activity is highly significant. We cannot live by spiritual spurts and starts. Religion is a matter which requires daily devotion and attention.

Only on rare occasions do we have deep religious experiences. These revelatory moments come infrequently in the lives of men. We retain a memory of these inspired moments in the daily deed, which heightens, celebrates and recalls the transcendent moment. Unless we practice the repetitive daily deed which reminds us of a great spiritual moment in our lives, or in the collective lifetime of our people, the inspiration of that hour is dissipated and lost. Like water, it can either be spilled upon the ground or saved in vessels which retain it.

A basic difference between the Christian and Jewish ap-

221

proach to religious stimulation can be seen through studying the effects of Billy Graham. His great evangelical campaigns stir the hearts of his listeners. However, after a while, in most instances, his would-be converts lapse back into their old ways. Judaism, on the other hand, tries to bind its people closer to the faith by weaving a strong bond with the filaments of constancy.

To be sure, all high purposes require enthusiasm and spark, but we must also have the ever-present element of effort. You surely remember the description of genius as being 10% inspiration and 90% perspiration. The pianist must have many years of practice preceding the occasional hour of performance.

All of us derive pleasure and joy from a great achievement. We overlook the fact that it is achieved only with thousands of little acts and an abundance of detail. We abhor the dullness of detail, the tedium of the seemingly trivial, the horror of the same old thing.

It would be good to remember that gathering wood for the Temple altar fire was, perhaps, a boring task, yet for those who did the work it was more than a menial duty. There was a holiday, observed in ancient times, which was regarded as one of the two happiest days of the Jewish calendar. The 15th of Ab, coming during the driest part of the summer, was the time when people celebrated with great festivity the gathering of the altar wood.

There is a mystic notion that man should acquire enough strength during the moments of the uplifting of the soul, those occasions when his faith seems very real, to carry him through his daily tasks when there is littleness of the soul. There is much that can be said for the converse. We must keep alive the possibility of the occasional illumination, the spiritual flash, by continually feeding the flame.

The ancients had an expression: "If a man says, 'I have found and not searched,' do not believe him. If a man says, I have searched and have found,' trust his word." Only the many hours of effort in any good cause, the abundance of detail, the "same old thing," permit us the ultimate breakthrough in a grand burst of religious ecstasy.

The Eloquence of Silence

"And Aaron was silent . . ." (Leviticus 10:3)

THE BIBLICAL STORY of the death of Aaron's sons is full of pathos.

After much preparation, the Tabernacle in the desert was erected. Aaron and his sons were consecrated for worship. Then, a terrible thing occurred. Two of Aaron's sons "offered strange fire before the Lord." The Bible goes on to say that "There went out fire from the Lord . . . and they died." Moses tried to console his brother, and the account concludes "And Aaron was silent."

The Bible tries to teach us that in the face of irrevocable tragedy we must keep our peace and say nothing. How different is this action of Aaron compared to the manner in which we moderns meet grief! Think of how many people conduct themselves during the *shivah* period. The conversation is as incessant as it is trivial. We think that we help the mourners by talking to them about every banality. Yet, let us ask ourselves. "Do we really help them to pass through their anguish?"

"The best medicine," the Talmud said, "is silence. If a word is worth a *sela,* silence is worth two."

Recently, my attention was drawn to the account of a terrible tragedy where a father lost his son and two grandchildren in an aircrash. A writer wrote to the bereaved, and said in Yiddish, "I must come to see you and we will sit down *auschweigen* (to sit out in silence) the tragedy."

What did Job's friends do when they came to comfort him in his despair? After a while they spoke with him and debated his affliction. But before that, the writer tells us, "They sat

223

down with him, seven days and seven nights, none spoke a word unto him, for they saw his grief was very great" (Job 2:13).

We are silent in the face of irrevocable tragedy because God, in a sense, is silent. At times, nature speaks out to us in the most meaningful ways. In the Spring, when nature renews itself and throws a flag of green to the skies, we are reassured of rebirth. On other occasions, however, nature is quiet, almost mysterious. The sages, commenting on "Who is like unto Thee among the mighty (*elim*) ones" suggested that we understand "Who is like unto Thee among the silent (*illemim*) ones."

At times God is silent. His ways remain inexplicable and inscrutable. Much remains in life which we cannot explain. When the Temple in Jerusalem was destroyed, the author of Lamentations spoke forth these words: "It is good that man should quietly wait for the salvation of the Lord . . . let him sit alone and keep silent . . ." (Lamentations 3: 26).

Nonetheless, Judaism did not think of silence as being our permanent reaction, for Judaism reaffirms life. Thus the Psalmist cries out, "What profit is there if I am silenced." (Psalms 30:10)

Trying to pass through our tragedy, we proclaim "so that my glory may sing praise to Thee and not be silent." With the Psalmist, we sing forth, "I shall not die, but I shall live and declare the glory of the Lord."

The Danger of Haste

"And Moses diligently inquired." (Leviticus 10:16)

THE TORAH, as we have it, has been copied faithfully from generation to generation. The scribes were very careful to make certain that their transcriptions were exact. Every letter of the Torah was counted. Our ancestors knew the Torah so well that they could tell you the exact middle point of the *Humash*. They observed that the verse *darosh darash Moshe*, "And Moses diligently inquired . . ." was the midway point of the Bible in terms of words. It was the very heart and core of the Pentateuch, halfway between the beginning and the end.

A commentator suggested that Moses' careful inquiry represented an example that we ought to emulate. This should teach you that one of men's shortcomings is rushing into matters. We do not search out most questions. Ours is a harried generation and a hurried one.

There is a tendency in American society to do things quickly. At times, swift action is of supreme importance. In the case of a blockage in the windpipe, an emergency tracheotomy has to be performed, if necessary even with a kitchen knife at home, without the benefit of a sterile operating room.

There are times, however, when acting too precipitously leads to great difficulty. As Bishop Fulton J. Sheen said, "You can never love in a hurry." This is true, and not only in terms of love between two people. "You can never love in a hurry" is a correct insight into the relationship between God and man. One cannot love God in a hurry. One cannot develop a proper relationship to God in prayer if one's attitude is that

225

of rushing to get the service over. A wedding ceremony is not a 100-metre dash, nor a *seder* a four-minute mile.

Psychiatrists will tell you that if one wants to establish a psychologically meaningful contact with people it requires time. When a psychiatrist or psychoanalyst meets with his patients, the key to his mode of treatment is to function as if he had all the time in the world. He advises his younger colleagues, "Do not suggest that you are in a hurry. Do not act as if you are a hurried man."

A piquant expression has come down from our immigrant days in this land. Our people were very poor and there was a shortage of bed-space. Members of a family slept in shifts. Frequently a sleeping relative was told, "Sleep faster. We need the bed."

Some things must be done quickly. Others require all the time and patience in the world. Let us, like Moses of old, inquire diligently before we act.

With Open Eyes

EVERY SO OFTEN the newspapers carry a story similar to the following one. A desperate man is perched on a high roof determined to jump to his destruction. Among the mob that assembles, are those who yell, "Jump, jump." Someone screams, "Chicken," when the would-be suicide wavers and does not proceed to destroy himself. Men make wagers with one another as to whether or not their thirst for blood will be satisfied. Finally, the man is persuaded not to go down to his death. The crowd is disappointed.

I thought of such suicide incidents as I read the Biblical passages dealing with the duties of the priests. In ancient Jewish society the priest was the health officer. It was his duty to examine the variety of skin diseases that are recorded in Leviticus (chapter 13). The law was very explicit. Concerning the priest, it said, "A priest that is blind in one eye or the light of whose eye is dim, may not inspect skin disease signs." Nor was the examination to take place when there was insufficient light. The priest had to be able to see well and the area of his study had to be clearly lit up.

So many of us see the world with only one eye open. We ought never make judgment without evaluating the whole. We should view events with both eyes wide open. Yes, life is at times sordid, frequently cruel. However, if we see the whole, in perspective, we are forced to make a positive judgment and thank God that we have had the privilege of being alive.

When our ancestors were delivered from Egypt, Balak, King of Moab, was alarmed that the Israelites would over-run his land. He went to a distant place to fetch Balaam to put a curse on them. Balaam, however, was so impressed by the Is-

227

raelites that instead of cursing them he blessed them. The disappointed king tried another gambit. He said to his seer,
"Come with me to another place from which you will see
them; you will see only a portion of them; you will not see all
of them; and curse them for me from there."

When examining the ills of our people the priest was supposed to carry out the judgment by the full light of midday.
When we study our world and judge our fellow men, let us
do so in the clearest of circumstances. Let us see the world
with both eyes wide open, and we will declare it to be good.

Write on the Horn

JEWISH SOURCES include only a limited number of references to the Syrian Greek occupation of the Holy Land prior to the Hasmonean Revolt. One of them is found in the commentaries on the portion of the Bible dealing with various skin conditions that were to be examined by a priest. Among them is a "bright spot." The Midrash comments that this "bright spot" alludes to Greece who made herself conspicuous, who drew light upon herself by her decrees. What were some of the decrees? Th decree against Israel instructed and compelled the population to "write on the horn of an ox that you Jews have no share in the God of Israel."

What was behind this Greek demand? The horn was the symbol of pride and strength. When Job wanted to describe his pitiable state, he lamented, "I have sewed sackcloth upon my skin, and have laid my horn in the dust." His mood was the reverse of the Psalmist who, in a moment of triumph, proclaimed, "But my horn hast thou exalted like the horn of a wild ox."

Several years ago a book called *The Horn and the Sword* appeared. The author, Jack Randolph Conrad, traced the cult of the bull in the history of religion from the Stone Age to our own time. Explaining the symbolic use of the bull, he observed that man responded strongly and reverently to the fundamental qualities of the bull—his tremendous strength and great fertility. Indeed, he noted that man has always reacted more to the bull as a symbol of these two qualities than to the bull as an animal. "It was as a symbol that man worshipped the bull in all the early civilizations on earth. And today, millenia later, it is still as a symbol that the bull is slain in the modern Spanish *corrida*."

We can now understand what the Midrash was talking about in telling us of the Greek demand. The Jews were to write on the very horn of the animal which symbolized strength and brute power that they had no share in the God of Israel, that they were consciously rejecting the spirit of Judaism.

Many learned articles have been written contrasting and comparing the Hellenic and the Hebraic views on life. Perhaps the most famous of these articles was by Matthew Arnold, but an Italian Jew, Samuel David Luzzatto, had pointed out this distinction between the two world outlooks many years before. There are fundamental differences between the Greek and the Hebrew outlook. In more recent years, Erich Auerbach, in his book *Mimesis,* stressed the difference between the Greek and the Hebrew spirit even when it came to the use of language. The Greek loved to describe beauty, grace, charm. His language was filled with adjectives. The Hebrew was committed to action, and his language is one of verbs. Similarly the spirit of Jewish prophecy emphasizes man's response of action. This is in sharp contrast to Greek philosophy which held that action was a weakening of contemplation, that doing was an attenuation of vision. The Jew insisted upon the deed, the translation of the conceived ideal into practice. Unlike the Greek philosopher, Professor Shalom Spiegel observed, the Jewish prophet could never rest until the gap between contemplation and action was bridged.

Behind this difference in world view we may find an explanation for one of our most important observances. In Jewish practice, the horn of any kosher animal can be used for the shofar except the horn of a cow or an ox. The Talmudic explanation is that the horn of a cow or an ox ought not to be used, for it reminds us of the incident of the Golden Calf. Let me suggest that perhaps this use was forbidden because the bull's horns represented a pagan element, the adoration of power.

The theme of the Jew has always been "Not by strength nor by power but by My spirit."

Outside the Camp

THE BIBLICAL LAWS dealing with the leper were usually interpreted in a moral sense. In the case of an outbreak, the afflicted one was to be isolated for seven days. After that period, the priest-physician was to go "outside the camp" to examine the blemishes and to conduct an elaborate ritual of purification.

The Bible's description is extremely suggestive. In a sense, every man, at one stage or another of life, is afflicted by a spiritual blemish. Some form of moral malaise touches him. Periods of isolation and withdrawal become very necessary. We leave our normal routine to examine our wounds and to cleanse ourselves.

At first hand, this approach may sound very un-Jewish. We have long heard the loud clamor urging community participation. We are a people, to be sure, who have always admonished, "Do not separate yourself from the community." However, if one examines Judaism's philosophy of life closely, one must admit that historically, deep concern for the group existed side by side with a healthy regard for the emotional stability of the individual. There has always been a dynamic tension between community involvement and personal withdrawal.

The philosophy of withdrawal was emphasized by many nineteenth century teachers of Hasidism and the Mussar movement. They urged *hitbodedut,* occasional withdrawal. Man ought to go into spiritual retreat, go off for a while, get away from the outer pressures to be able to understand the inner self.

These teachers would practice moments of reflection, periods of silence and hours of meditation. They would

231

demonstrate, by example, the benefits of slipping away from their villages to walk in the woods, or to be alone in the field and to engage in silent contemplation.

Rabbi Nahman of Braslov extolled the virtues of this approach. "If a man learns the correct art of withdrawal as he goes through the woodlands, he tastes at each step the succulence of the fruit of the Garden of Eden."

A 19th century writer claimed that "A man will satisfy his spiritual needs not in the crowd but while alone."

Judaism, as a religion of balance, did not stress this mode of conduct as a steady diet. It recognized the dangers of going to extremes. Just as absolute involvement in the community can destroy the self, complete withdrawal may lead to the destruction of the community.

The purpose of isolating the patient was that he become fit once again to return to society. This is our goal, too. We withdraw, we go off for a while, so that we can return refreshed to our total responsibility.

Morals and Medicine

"This shall be the law of the leper." (Leviticus 14:2)

IN THE EARLY HISTORY of medicine, the religious personality of the community was also the physician. For many years, the partnership between morals and medicine continued. As late as the eighteenth century, some of the Sephardic rabbis were also medical men.

With the increase in specialization and the advancement in medical knowledge, a division of labor arose between the teacher of morals and the practitioner of medicine. Yet the relationship between the two callings remains. A case in point can be seen in the comment of the sages upon the laws of leprosy: "This shall be the law of the leper." The Hebrew word for leper (*metzora*) suggested itself as a springboard for moral teaching. Instead of reading "leper" (*metzora*), the teachers suggested, "This shall be the law of him who spreads evil talk (*motzi shem ra*)."

This is a most courageous re-interpretation and moral application of the Biblical laws of medicine. There are, thank God, few cases of leprosy today. Yet moral leprosy is prevalent.

A person must guard himself against succumbing to the moral leprosy of improper talk. The sages understood human nature very well. They were keen students of behavior. They were concerned about *lashon ha-ra,* the "evil tongue." They spoke of *lashon ha-ra* as being the "third tongue."

When a man slanders another, three symbolic deaths take place. Slander annihilates the personality of the slanderer. Calumny reduces the inner worth of the listener who hears

233

the tale. Gossip hurts the reputation of the individual about whom the story has been told.

Slander—spreading evil in words—is more than a bit of vapory breath issuing forth. Slander is a grievous failing of character. The ability to speak is the one quality that differentiates man from the rest of the animal kingdom. Speech is a precious gift. How thrilled we are when a baby utters its first understandable syllable. When the Bible, in the Genesis story, spoke of the fact that "Man became a living soul," the old Aramaic translation paraphrased this to mean that "Man became a speaking being." The power to speak is the distinctive mark of the uniqueness of man. "One who bears evil tales denies God," the Talmud taught.

Judaism can be defined in a host of a different ways. Yet I would like to regard our faith as a constant call to a career of dignity and purpose. A life of moral holiness is marked by self-control in a man's actions and generosity of thought in his relationship to others. If moral impurity is a mirror of our passions, moral holiness, reflected in proper speech, is a sign of control of our lust. The temptation to gossip is ever present in man, but we must learn to curb ourselves.

We must turn away from the gossipy word and the obscene remark. In a diet-conscious age, when we weigh so carefully the calories which go into our mouths, we ought also to learn to weigh the words which issue from our lips.

"Guard my tongue from evil" is our closing prayer as we finish our silent devotion before God. In the guarding of our tongue lies the path to our personal holiness and to our moral health.

When Religion and Medicine Meet

"Heal me, O Lord, and I shall be healed;
Save me, and I shall be saved;
For Thou art my praise." (Jeremiah 17:14)

IN 1963, THE American Medical Association formed a Committee on Medicine and Religion, reflecting a growing awareness of physicians that there is an intimate relationship between their profession and the clergy. Ten physicians and ten clergymen were assembled to explore jointly the possibilities of meeting the spiritual and emotional needs of the patients they served.

This approach is not new. A distinguished Swiss physician, Paul Tournier of Geneva, has for some time emphasized that the patient must be treated as a person rather than merely as a medical case. Tournier, who is a devout Christian, deals with the problems of the patient in terms of his personal life, his relationship with his family, friends, and what is most important, with God. Dr. Tournier has made many contributions to synthesizing modern psychology and religious faith. He insists that there is a need to incorporate faith into one's professional work—"One must apply all one's scientific knowledge, but must realize that it is not enough."

In 1964, Professor Abraham J. Heschel spoke before the American Medical Association's Annual Convention and stressed that, "A patient is a person in crisis and anxiety." He continued with the statement that the doctor in treating the patient is not just a dispenser of drugs ... "he is morally involved."

Much of modern medicine reflects the secular, humanistic image of man as the master of nature; many physicians,

235

products of their century, emphasize the "material manipulation of life." Fortunately there is a growing recognition that there is more to man than mere matter. Medicine is beginning to move away from treating the patient as if he were a physical mechanism and not a person.

The Committee on Medicine and Religion has begun to deal with some difficult questions. Shall one tell the truth to a patient suffering from a terminal malignancy like cancer?

What should be our position on therapeutic abortion? Some members on the committee believe that this is a cardinal sin. Others have a more understanding attitude.

A more perplexing question for the clergyman is the attitude toward the childless woman who has been advised to participate in an artificial insemination procedure. There are dozens of ethical and moral questions that can be raised within the realm of medicine.

One of the areas in which the clergy and the physicians have been involved is that of mental health. A survey of the Joint Committee of Mental Illness and Health found that when people sought assistance for their emotional problems, 42% went first to their clergymen, 29% went to their physicians, 18% to psychiatrists and psychologists, and 11% to social agencies. Sadly it must be reported that despite these many requests for help, only a very small percentage of clergymen in this country have adequate training for dealing with any deep-seated mental or emotional problems.

Yet another exciting example of the relationship between religion and psychiatry involves a group of psychiatrists working at the University of Chicago, who have developed a most imaginative approach to their patients. They utilize religious data to make a symptomatic and character diagnosis of the person who needs help. The rationale for this technique is that a person's current religious interests are determined by his whole life's experiences. The method which they use is to give the patient a religious interview. They ask him about his early religious memories, they inquire about his favorite Bible verse, they question him about his favorite Biblical character, they ask him, "What does religion mean to you?" and, "If God would grant you any three wishes, what would they be?" "What would you consider to be the greatest sin one could commit?" This novel approach has enabled the physicians to establish a good rapport with their patients and reach a meaningful diagnosis. In some cases when a patient was guarded in the usual psychiatric interview, when asked to speak about his religious activities and beliefs, he was able to talk more freely.

One of the new frontiers of modern medicine involves the basic genetic processes which govern life. Human genes are the basic units of heredity. Has man the right to consciously direct the evolution of the human species by correcting genetic errors? When asked about this one rabbi was quoted as saying that "an artificial control of man's genes would run counter to the whole philosophy of Judaism; it robs the act of procreation of its personal element." One might suggest that before offering an opinion, more research and a deeper examination of our tradition is needed.

Yet another area of interest which touches the life of so many of us concerns our relationship to the cancer patient. A psychiatrist of my acquaintance claims that "the development of cancer is influenced from the beginning to the end by psychological factors." The clergymen, he adds, can be of great help in reconciliating the patient to the world in which he lives.

A patient with organic diseases needs more than physical therapy. He needs spiritual support in order to benefit from the progress of physical medicine. It has been recognized that with the intensification of therapeutic techniques, physicians, nurses, and others on the medical team have less time to devote to the moral support of the sick which is so essential.

A long time ago, God said, "For I, the Lord, am your Healer." Here on earth, clergy and doctors can do much by working together to help His children.

Micah to Malachi

*"Behold I will send you Elijah the prophet be-
fore the coming of the great and awesome day of
the Lord; and he will turn the heart of the
fathers to the children and the heart of the children to their fathers."* (Malachi 3:23-24)

ON THE VERY SUNDAY prior to *Shabbat Hagadol,* I was
completing an analysis of the prophet Micah with my high
school class. The reading was a disturbing one. Jewish society
had reached its lowest point. Micah bewailed the corruption
of his land and bemoaned the conduct of his countrymen.
Things had reached the most pathetic state. Immorality had
so corroded the conscience of man that Micah advised, "Trust
ye not in a friend." He went on to warn that a man was to
guard himself in speaking to his own wife. Sons insulted
their fathers; daughters defied their mothers. The passage
ended, "A man's enemies are the men of his own house."

I explained to my students that the lament of the prophet
was a pathetic description of what can happen to a community. This was the nadir, the low point, of degeneration. One
may develop, I continued, a simple historical law—one of
the surest signs of the moral collapse of a people is in the
dislocation of the family unit.

The Talmud describes the collapse of Jewish society after
the year 70, when the Romans destroyed the Jerusalem
Temple. The decades that followed were very trying ones
for our people. Calamity after calamity plagued our ancestors.
There was physical hunger in the land. People went begging
from place to place without anyone to take pity on them.

An ancient text describes how young people put old men

238

to shame. When the editor of the Mishna wanted to describe the sad state of affairs, he wove the prophecy of Micah into the pattern of his words. He coined the phrase. "The face of the generation was like the face of a dog," i.e., impervious to shame.

I spoke to my students about family life and the importance of keeping this central unit of society together. This is the reason why, on Passover, we stress the reunification of families. We try to bring the family together to heal the breach, if it exists, between the generations. On the Sabbath prior to Passover we read the hopeful words of Malachi, the last of the prophets. We remember ancient events and hope for future redemption.

All of us are concerned that an age of peace come to this world. It is my feeling that the road to world peace will start in the home, when parents and children embrace one another, when the generations learn to live together in a spirit of mutual understanding and, what is perhaps more important, mutual respect. Malachi emphasizes that fathers must understand their children, and then children will understand their fathers.

Where do we stand now? Are we on the steps of the descending spiral described by the Mishna, reflecting the words of Micah, or are we on road pointed out by Malachi? Let us hope that the latter position is our lot.

Twin Loves

"Reprove your neighbor . . ." (Leviticus 19: 17)
*"Love your neighbor as yourself, I am the
Lord."*   (Leviticus 19:18)

THE COMMANDMENT, "Love your neighbor as yourself," is a central teaching of Judaism. This verse was interpreted by Martin Buber to mean, "Look upon your neighbor as a person like yourself." Do not regard him as a thing.
Man is not to be manipulated and used for one's own selfish
ends. "As you are a person, so, too, he is a person."

The mystics, who emphasized the element of love between
man and man and love between man and God, cherished
this teaching. One of them explained that in everyone there
is something of his fellow man. "Love your neighbor as yourself, for he is really you, yourself." Coming from a common
ancestor, Adam, there is part of him in you and part of you
in him.

I have had one difficulty in understanding this concept.
Immediately prior to its citation in the Bible there is another
doctrine—"Reprove your neighbor." The two passages seem
to be contradictory. On the one hand, the Bible commands
us to rebuke, to reprove, while the subsequent statement
bids us to love.

An 18th century source provides an explanation of this
paradox. There are two types of relationships which we
establish in life. One is more personal than the other. The
phrase, "Reprove your neighbor," speaks of *amiteha* (your
neighbor). This was interpreted to mean *im-itha* (he who is
with you). The person who is with you is one with whom
you have established a real relationship. You are called upon

240

to criticize such a person in the hope of correcting him. "Faithful are the wounds of a friend." This action is the fulfillment of a religious responsibility.

However, in the case of a casual relationship, one without true understanding—towards that person we must follow the advice of Hillel: "Be of the disciples of Aaron, loving peace and pursuing peace, loving mankind and bringing men near to the Torah." This is our responsibility, to establish a loving relationship with those people with whom we have no real sense of relatedness. It is our responsibility to love them as ourselves.

One might consider reproof to be a manifestation of a higher type of love. Our father, Abraham, developed a good rapport with Abimelech, King of Gerar. One day an incident occurred between them. The Bible reports, "Then Abraham reproved Abimelech." A sage commented, "Reproof leads to love." Ultimately, we are cherished by those whom we correct. Love unaccompanied by reproof is not love. "Reprove a wise man," the book of Proverbs teaches us, "and he will love you."

It is a positive act to chastise, to rebuke, when we have a true sense of relatedness. If this relationship does not exist, then we must content ourselves with love.

Love Thy Neighbor

*"Thou shalt not take vengeance, nor bear any
grudge against the children of thy people, but
thou shalt love thy neighbor as thyself: I am the
Lord."* (Leviticus 19: 18)

THIS VERSE, or, at least part of it, "Love thy neighbor as
thyself," is one of the most familiar Biblical expressions. It
is important to read the statement in its full context. Viewed
in the original setting, a much deeper significance may be
appreciated.

We normally think of "Love thy neighbor as thyself" as a
relationship between two persons. In reality, however, there
are three principals involved: man, his neighbor, and God.
To love one's neighbor as oneself means to have a proper
appreciation, not only of one's neighbor, but also of oneself.
There are those who are prompt to regard the correct assess-
ment of self as self-love. They are quick to remind us that
self-love is dangerous, for it borders on what the psychologists
call "narcissism." You will remember that Narcissus, in
Greek mythology, was the youth with whom the nymph,
Echo, had fallen in love. Narcissus repulsed Echo's affections,
and for his cruelty, the goddess of love punished him by
making him enamored of his own image in a fountain. His
fruitless efforts to approach his beautiful reflection led to
frustration, despair and death. He was changed into the
flower that bears his name.

Self-love is not selfishness. The Jewish view toward a
proper appraisal of oneself differs sharply from the attitude
of the Protestant reformer, Martin Luther, who said, "To
love is the same as to hate oneself." Luther thought that a

person must have contempt for himself before he could develop a correct attitude toward others. Judaism, on the other hand, stressed that for a person to have proper regard for others, he must affirm his own capabilities and potentialities. "Be not wicked in thine own esteem." In a sense, Judaism mirrored the statement of a German mystic, who wrote, "If you love yourself, you love everybody else as you do yourself."

To guard against improper self-love, the last part of our verse is of great import. "Love thy neighbor as thyself: I am the Lord" was amplified by Israel's teachers to mean, "Love thy neighbor as thyself, because I, the Lord, have created him."

We cannot be selective in our love of mankind. An example of this selectivity is given in the statement of Rabbi Joshua, a 2nd century teacher, that "hatred of mankind puts a man out of the world." What is the meaning of that unusual teaching? He teaches that "No man should think of saying, 'I love the scholars but hate the disciples, or I love the disciples but hate the ignoramus.' On the contrary, love all these, for God has created all." "Hatred of mankind puts a man out of the world . . ." does not mean that man's life is shortened. It means that one's worthwhileness on earth is diminished when he submerges his humanity, the capacity to love others, that is within him.

Realizing that God has created both you and me, my neighbor and myself, places both of us in a completely different light. The love given to the living, Martin Buber observed, is the love of God and it is higher than any other service. A teacher asked his student, "You know that two powers cannot take possession of the mind of man at the same time. When you rise from your bed in the morning, there are two ways before you: love of God and love of man: which is the more important?" The student thought and finally answered, "I do not know." Then the teacher said, "In the prayer book which is popular with the people, the opening instruction is 'Before you pray, say the words, Love thy neighbor as thyself.' Do you think that this was suggested without forethought? If anyone says to you that he has love of God but no love of the living he speaks falsely, and pretends he has that which it is impossible to have."

Cultivating love of one's neighbor calls for our constant reflection that all of us are the children of one Creator.

Aspiring to Holiness

"You shall be holy, for I, the Lord your God am holy."
(Leviticus 19:2)

THE FIRST HALF of Leviticus deals with the laws of the priests and the order of sacrifices. The priests were holy men by status, having been born of the seed of Aaron, the first High Priest.

The Jewish people, on the other hand, were to be holy by aspiration. Their lives were to represent a constant effort to climb the ladder of personal sanctification. As a holy people, Israel was invited to imitate the ways of God.

How can man imitate the ways of holiness? The method recommended by Judaism was to match God's ways. "The Lord of hosts is exalted through justice and God, the Holy One, through righteousness" (Isaiah). When justice is uplifted and righteousness is practiced, God's holiness is made manifest. Philo wisely said, "Holiness towards God and justice towards man go together." In the Hebrew language the word "just" meant "straight" (*yashar*). "He leadeth me in paths of righteousness" actually means "He leadeth me in a straight path." To do a holy act means to do an act that is morally straight.

The commandment of righteousness, the sages taught, outweighs all the commandments put together.

Man, in the course of his existence, can never equal God's activities in the natural realm. Yet functioning in the ethical realm, where he can exercise moral holiness, man can complete the work of God.

The cosmic being depends upon the Almighty, but ethical life depends upon mortals. God is hallowed by the ethical

245

behavior of a people dedicated to personal holiness. That is why Amos, looking at those who oppressed the poor and the needy, said that they offended the holiness of God. Those who "pant after the dust of the earth on the head of the poor," those "who turn aside the way of the humble" ... those "who profane My holy name," will be punished. When there is wickedness in the world, when there is injustice between man and man, there is defilement. The labor of the Lord is negated.

We ought not consider the invitation to pursue a life of moral holiness as being beyond our reach. Judaism understood the limitations inherent in our human situation. Menahem Mendel of Kotzk interpreted the verse, "And ye shall be holy men unto Me," to mean, "You shall be holy unto Me, but as men you shall be 'humanly holy' unto Me." We are expected only to be holy men and not to be holy angels. Each of us can hallow his existence within the framework of men living with other men. It is for us to follow the advice "that thou mayest walk in the way of good men and keep the path of the righteousness." Walking in the ways of the good, living a life of righteousness, we can attain the life of holiness; we can achieve true blessing for ourselves and mankind.

Care for the Common Deed

*"You shall not coerce your neighbor. You shall
not commit robbery. The wages of a laborer
shall not remain with you until morning."*
(Leviticus 19:13)

WHY IS THE BIBLE so exercised over the principle of
prompt payment of wages? What if a man's pay is delayed
over-night? Does this merit the use of such strong language
as "coerce your neighbor" and "commit robbery?" We
moderns know that few employers pay their employees
before the end of the week. In the case of some great corpora-
tions with thousands of men, the payment date may be
delayed for a full week or more. There is so much book-
keeping that has to be done.

The Bible, it is apparent, uses strong language to stress
that any delay was a form of oppression and of robbery. If
the laborer, who lived from hand to mouth, would have to
go to bed hungry, his children unfed, the Bible was concerned. If his night's sleep might be disturbed by the anxiety
that he would not be paid in the morning, the moral teachers of Judaism cared about his emotional discomfort.

In Abraham Joshua Heschel's collection of essays entitled
The Insecurity of Freedom, he makes the exciting point that
Judaism has a basic moral message which differed completely
from the outlook of the pagan world. Their philosophers
believed that "The gods attend to great matters; they neglect
small ones." Our religious tradition, however, is involved in
the welfare of every man. In Judaism, "God Himself is described as reflecting over the plight of man, rather than as
contemplating eternal ideas."

247

Judaism emphasizes "the theology of the common deed." The test of life is not only how we manage our major affairs, but how we handle what might outwardly appear to be minor things. The prophets were concerned not with "the mysteries of heaven, the glories of eternity, but the blights of society, and the affairs of the market place." The teachers of Israel did not neglect great affairs, but they also did not permit themselves the luxury of forgetting the significance of little things.

Professor Heschel points out that "the predominant feature of the Biblical pattern of life is unassuming, unheroic, inconspicuous piety, the sanctification of trifles, attentiveness to details."

We are all aware of the paradox involved in finding it relatively easy to urge people to accept a responsibility, to lead a great effort, to be the banner-bearer. But how hard it is to convince men to assume the responsibility of routine tasks and the so-called minor duties and drudgeries. Everyone wants to be on the dais; few want to stand in the kitchen.

Over and over again, in every possible didactic experience, the teachers of Judaism emphasized, "Run to fulfill the lightest detail even as the weightiest"; "Be heedful of a light precept as of a weighty one, as you do not know the reward of each precept."

When the Bible cited the instructions to the priests, we read, "Say to the priests, the sons of Aaron, say unto them." Why the repetition of the verb "say?" This was to emphasize that the elder priests must warn their young sons to obey the law.

A nineteenth century commentator interpreted the Hebrew words *l'hazhir hag'dolim al hak'tanim* to mean that the elders must admonish their young sons in another sense. When man is engaged in study and prayer, said the sage, he attains a grandeur of the mind and of the spirit. Unfortunately, after he has reached the pinnacle moment, he descends into the pit of pettiness. "That the elders warn their young sons" might be understood in the sense that the ecstasy of our great moments should carry over into our lesser occasions.

248

A Sense of Significance

"And they shall teach My people the difference between the holy and the common." (Ezekiel, 44: 23)

IN DESCRIBING THE duties of the priests, Ezekiel speaks of them as the great teachers of religion who were to instruct the people in all religious matters. The modern rabbi takes on the functions of the ancient priests in this regard. He too must teach his people to distinguish between the holy and the ordinary. The holy is to be approached with reverential awe; the commonplace may be encountered with familiarity. Every social system has a pattern of separation between the holy and the ordinary. Every society has its sancta and its saints.

To be sure, it is difficult at times to draw a border between the holy and the common, American culture is affected by a leveling-down process. We approach even the greatest of men on a first name basis; a distinguished physician or scientist is greeted with, "Hello, Doc." We have lost what David Daiches called "a sense of significance." We have lost the skill of making proper differences. Everything in our way of life is deemed holy. Every cause is labeled great.

From time to time I shudder when I read the ads of some of our resort places in the East or in the South. These hotels are brazen enough to advertise in one piece of copy that they have religious services followed by night club entertainment. Other ads feature what one quipster called an invitation to "God and golf." Here is a confusion between the holy and the common; between liturgy and leisure.

In the more sensitive area of fund raising for Jewish causes,

249

we have also forgotten our "sense of significance." We have lost the art of differentiation. All too frequently the claim is made that some particular charity is the "holiest" of all, although in any carefully thought-out priority scale of Jewish survival, the rating of that cause would be relatively low.

The "sense of significance" of drawing a boundary between the holy and the profane existed in the past. It was present in the mind and action of every Jew because we had a community of belief. We shared common religious attitudes and responses. We knew how to draw a distinction between what was sacred and what was secular.

Our failure to equip ourselves with the common share of knowledge which was the possession of our ancestors has contributed to our loss of this "sense of significance." The Talmud wisely points out, "If there is no knowledge, how can there be differentiation?"

To restore dignity to Jewish life, to recapture a "sense of significance" in what we do, we must work towards developing an informed and discriminating American Jew who will know and appreciate the difference between the holy and the common.

A Time to Keep Silence—A Time to Speak

I. A TIME TO KEEP SILENCE

AT A RECENT Board of Education hearing on "shared time," I grew curious about an unusual microphone held by a TV technician. The object was some two feet long, encased in foam rubber. The technician explained that if he pointed his device at a group in private conversation many feet away, he could pick up the words of each discussant distinctly.

These last years have witnessed the invention of more and more gadgets to intrude upon our privacy. There has been an almost total annihilation of a precious possession—the right to be alone with one's thoughts and with one's words. When the High Priest entered the Holy of Holies on Yom Kippur the Bible instructed, "When he goes in to make expiation in the Shrine, no man shall be in the Tent of Meeting until he goes out." "No man shall be with him" was understood to mean that no human concern was to intrude upon his spiritual consecration. As the High Priest needed his splendid hour of sacred service, so we desperately need our moments of silence when no man is with us. We must live in this world yet we must be able to develop for ourselves those meditative moments, those contemplative periods which make human existence possible.

Hans Bethe, one of the world's outstanding physicists, and a leader of our atomic energy program, was once asked, "Can't a determined person carve out for himself some zones of silence, some period in his life, despite the obstacles?" Bethe answered, "It is difficult because the pressures against

251

it are so tremendous. Our educational system has failed to develop in the average American the habit of thinking before acting. We are so caught up in a perpetual whirl of activities that we fail to develop our capacity for contemplation." Each of us needs the opportunity to lead our separate lives for limited periods. When you read works like Packard's *The Naked Society*, or Brenton's *Privacy Invaders*, you realize that there are those who are determined to intrude on our most intimate moments.

"Many are the opportunities for public speech: where are the occasions for inner silence?" my teacher, Professor Heschel, once asked. "It is easy to find people who will teach us to be eloquent, but who will teach us how to be still?" It was Dr. Heschel's feeling that the synagogue permits us to develop this sensitivity which is reflected in our periods of silence. Our houses of worship with their assemblages of people ultimately teach us a sense of inwardness, of being alone with our thoughts. "Speak to the community and say to them, ye shall be holy," was interpreted to mean, "Holy shall you be, separate shall you be."

There is much wisdom in the ethical teaching of Rabbi Simeon who said, "All my life I grew up among the wise and found nothing better for a person than silence." There are times when man must separate himself from the tumult and turmoil of society. "Let us be silent," Emerson said, "that we may hear the whispers of God." Like the High Priest of old, each man must, for a moment, enter the quiet stillness of his private sanctuary to refresh his soul.

II. A TIME TO SPEAK

There are times when man must be silent; there are times when to speak demonstrates our humanity. In commenting on the untimely death of the two sons of Aaron, the sages quoted Job, "At this also my heart trembles." Why did Job suffer from great anguish? To appreciate his mood, we must rely on an obscure legend. When Pharaoh saw the children of Israel increase, he said, "The children of Israel are too many and too mighty... come let us deal wisely with them lest they multiply and . . . when war occurs they will join our enemies to fight against us." "Come let us deal wisely with them," was interpreted to mean that the monarch sought the advice of several leaders of his time. They were Balaam, Job and Jethro. Balaam said, "Kill the baby boys, the future fathers." For this advice he was ultimately punished and killed. Rather than advise the king, Jethro ran away. In merit of this action he received a great reward. Job kept silent and because of that was doomed to great suffering. This, then, is why Job said, "At this also my heart trembles." He remembered the fact that he had been mute in an earlier tragedy.

Why are men silent? Dr. Martin Luther King, Jr. asked a group of Reform rabbis at convention assembled to participate in "prophetic witness against the social evils of our time." To his invitation to demonstrate in the South, one of the rabbis said, "Silence has been one of the great sins of the 20th century; hence, when a call comes for help on a clear and present moral danger, how can we stand idly by? We are taking this small step less to help our Negro brothers than to help ourselves by reaffirming our sense of right."

We are silent when action is called for, because we refuse to get involved. We are silent because we suffer from the sickness of apathy. We are silent because we lack courage. We are silent because we are afraid of adverse publicity.

Recall the tragic beating suffered by some Yeshiva students and their teachers at the hands of hooligans in Brooklyn. People stood by and watched in silence as the ruffians did their dirty work. All of us were appalled when a young woman was knifed to death by a night-time marauder in Queens, New York. The police discovered that 38 of her neighbors had seen her stabbed or heard her desperate cries. Not one of them called the police during the half hour prior to her brutal murder for fear of "consequences and getting involved." A newspaper asked editorially, "What kind of people are we?" When the famed *Saturday Review* analyzed Rolf Hochhut's play, *The Deputy*, the review was captioned, "Cry Against the Decision of Silence."

Ezekiel has taught us that man has the moral duty to speak out, whether or not he will be heeded. The duty of the prophet is to warn the people as to the potential dangers which face them. It is his responsibility to sound the alarm, to cause the warning *shofar* to be heard. We may not be prophets but we are the children, the sons of prophets!

Charles Morgan, Jr., a courageous southern lawyer who had the strength to take on civil rights cases of Negroes in Birmingham, wrote of his experiences. He knew fear and heart-break, suffered harrassment and finally was forced to leave his community. His book, *A Time To Speak*, has been called a "trumpet call to conscience." One reviewer titled his article, "When A Man Stands Up To Be Counted, He May Be Counted Out." The man of conscience, however, must express himself despite the risks. Was it not Oliver Wendell Holmes who said, "I think that as life is action and passion, it is required of a man that he should share the passion and action of his time at peril of being judged not to have lived."

Sun and Shadow

"You shall live in booths seven days . . ." (Leviticus 23: 42)

"A Sukkah which has more sun than shade is not valid." (Mishnah, Sukkah)

OUR CENTURY has witnessed the vast expansion of public concern with art. Museums report ever-increasing numbers of visitors. Reproductions of the works of masters are to be found in many homes; those who can afford them display originals.

Among the first elements of art appreciation introduced to the neophyte is the use of light and shadow. This technique, developed during the Renaissance, reached a high point in the works of Rembrandt. Great attention was directed to the play of light and shadow. Art, if it is a true reflection of life, must be able to mirror the elements of sun and shadow, of light and darkness, of satisfaction and sorrow, in man's existence. Against this background, let us understand the law that there was to be some sunlight in the *sukkah,* but that there must be more shadow than sun.

Shadow is a most expressive symbol which occurs over and over again in the Bible.

SIGN OF DANGER

If one goes in for a medical or dental examination, an X-ray is frequently taken. If a shadow is seen, it is a warning to the examiner to probe deeper.

The shadow symbolizes man's mortality. Job said (8:9), "For we are but of yesterday and know nothing, because our days upon earth are as a shadow." Man realizes, when he sees a lengthening shadow, that his days are coming to an end, "for we are strangers before Thee, sojourners as all our fathers were. Our days on the earth are as a shadow and there is no abiding."

The sundial was used by ancient men to tell time. The longer shadow was the sign of the waning of the day. The Bible records the experience of a king who asked of the prophet Isaiah that the shadow go back. A shadow can be a sign of danger. The *sukkah* shadows remind us of the limited nature of our lives.

SYMBOL OF SHELTER

The first reference in the Bible to "shadow" is in the case of Lot, Abraham's kinsman. We read how two messangers came to visit him. Schooled by the example of Abraham's hospitality, he invited the sojourners to stay with him. During the evening, the men of Sodom surrounded the house and demanded that the guests be turned over to them. Lot said to them, "Don't do anything to these men, for they come under the shadow of my roof."

Just as men are sheltered by other men, the shadow is used as the symbol of God's protection. Isaiah speaks of "in the shadow of His hand hath He hid me." The Psalmist proclaims (36:8), "How precious is Thy lovingkindness, O God, and the children of men take refuge in the shadow of Thy wings." The *sukkah* shadows promise us the protection of God.

SONG OF JOY

During this season of the year, as the circuit of the sun appears lower in the heavens and the shadows lengthen, we enter our *sukkah*. It reminds us of the limited span of our moral existence. The shaded *sukkah* causes us to reflect that in all of our days we look to God as our Protector. Yet, the holiday is a time of joy. Man, alerted to his mortality, reflects, "Life may be fragile but it is not futile; existence may be

256

frail but it is not ephemeral; life's days may be measured but man's activities have meaning."

During Sukkot, when we are reminded so vividly by the law of the *sukkah* that in life there is more shadow than sun, we nevertheless delight, "for Thou hast been my help and in the shadow of Thy wings do I rejoice." Though our existence appears to be transitory, man's life is, in effect, eternal. The shadow below testifies to the sun above. The *sukkah* shadows summon us to festival gladness.

Numbers

The Mystery of the Holy

"When Aaron and his sons have finished cover-
ing the sacred objects and all the furnishings of
the sacred objects at the breaking of camp, only
then shall the Kohathites come and lift them, so
that they do not come in contact with the sacred
objects and die . . ." (Numbers 4:15)

THE BIBLE continues to instruct that the Tabernacle's vessels were not only to be covered, but that the members of the Levite tribe were not even permitted to see the holy objects during the time when they were being covered.

The holy vessels were not to be regarded simply as material things. An air of mystery was to be placed about them. They were to be shielded from the eyes of the Levites, who might, through the familiarity of constant sight, grow to be less respectful of them.

A medieval commentator probed deeper in his interpretation of our verse. Abarbanel wrote, "The soul of man longs in his approach to the holy to see more than he is permitted." The commentator struck upon a note of life which was true not only of man in his day but in our own also. One of the cardinal problems of modern man is his attempt to grasp the imponderable. He tries to remove the veil which shields the holy from us. Modern man attempts to touch everything. He has even uncovered the holy vessels. He stamps everything in creation with the label of the mundane and the commonplace. He has secularized the holy and made ordinary the sacred.

For the Jew, this secularization of the holy began in the 19th century in the analysis of Jewish ritual. Every age-old

261

custom was placed under the scrutiny of would-be scholars. With a limited knowledge of anthropology and comparative religion they devaluated the worth of every ceremonial. They forgot how Judaism enriched each custom, even those that were borrowed from other peoples.

In the realm of thought we have been guilty of stripping away the coverings of the holy. To be sure, a Jew is supposed to search out his faith. Maimonides regarded the study of theology, the knowledge of God, as the noblest form of human experience. He quoted Moses' request to God: "Now, if I have truly gained Your favor, pray let me know Your way, that I may know You and continue in Your favor."

A Jew is supposed to search for a deeper knowledge of God. He is taught to seek a better understanding of nature. Yet Maimonides stressed that we must recognize the limits of human reason. There are, he emphasized, matters which are beyond the mind of man. In the realm of faith we dare not tread upon dangerous ground. Surely we are to use our minds, but we must also appreciate that human reason has a limit. There is a residuum of unknown in the world.

In Howard Singer's wonderful text book for young people, *With Mind and Heart,* there is this splendid quotation from Albert Einstein: "The mind can proceed only so far upon what it knows and can prove. There comes a point where the mind takes a leap—call it intuition or what you will—and comes out upon a higher plane of knowledge, but can never prove how it got there. All great discoveries have involved such a leap." There are impassable boundaries across which we cannot go. We must cleave to God with complete trust even in the face of incomplete knowledge. The Ethics of the Fathers spoke wisely—"It is not within our power to understand why the way of the wicked prospers and why the righteous are made to endure sufferings."

The limitations of religion in the matter of faith are comparable to the limitations of science. Modern science and mathematics are based upon the undemonstrability of certain propositions. Though we cannot understand the origin of electricity, of magnetism, we nevertheless can try to comprehend their operation. We cannot plumb the depths of faith yet we can appreciate the working of God's laws in the universe. Though there is the boundary of the unknown, there is still room for man to act.

It is wise that the Bible taught us, through the symbolic covering of the vessels, that in life the holy should be shielded from the gaze of man. We ought to heed the word of the poet who advised:

> *So I go on, not knowing,*
> *I would not if I might.*
> *I would rather walk in the dark with God,*
> *Than go alone in the light.*
> *I would rather walk with Him in faith*
> *Than walk alone by sight.*

Prayer and Peace

IT IS A WONDERFUL coincidence of the calendar that on
the Sabbath preceding Memorial Day the Torah reading includes the words of the priestly blessing: "The Lord bless
thee and keep thee . . . The Lord lift up His countenance
upon thee and give thee peace" (Numbers 6: 25 ff).

The quest for peace is an age-old aspiration of our people.
Other nations may have longed for the glories of war and vic-
tory. The Jewish people has always been in a constant quest
for tranquility. Many important Jewish prayers end on the
note of *shalom*, peace. This meaningful word marks the conclusion of our silent devotion and the grace before meals.

A most unusual rabbinic comment notes the fact that the
Mishna, the code of Jewish law, began with the letter *mem*
and ended with the letter *mem*.

This observation may mean little at first. Upon closer examination, we see that the first *mem* beginning the Mishna
is the letter of the word *me'emati*. (From what time may one
recite the *Shema* in the evening?) The final *mem* in the Mishna is the last letter of the word *shalom*, peace. The Mishna
concludes with the hopeful verse: "The Lord will bless His
people with peace" (Psalms 29).

What is the link between the opening *mem* prayer and the
final *mem* of peace?

In reality, the life that begins with prayer is a career which
ends in peace. Proper prayer does not guarantee that we will
be saved from all of the possible dangers which may come into
a man's life, or that we will be spared all difficult situations
that are present in the experience of living. Prayers are not
magical incantations which set up an automatic barrier to the
dangers and difficulties of life.

264

Prayer does, however, give us a more assured understanding and a confident acceptance of our existence. Prayer permits us to examine our hearts, to challenge our deeds and to set ourselves aright.

All of us anxiously look for peace. We want harmony in the universe and we want tranquility in our inner world. Wisely, a sage once said, "You cannot find peace anywhere save in your own self." An earlier teacher found a Biblical source for his attitude. Commenting on the verse, "The Lord will give strength unto His people; The Lord will bless His people with peace," he interpreted that passage to mean that peace is the fruit of inner strength.

If we learn to pray, if we begin our lives from the starting point of prayer, our existence will surely be a more peaceful one.

The Blessing of Love

"And the Lord spoke unto Moses, saying: Speak unto Aaron and unto his sons, saying: On this wise ye shall bless the children of Israel; ye shall say unto them: The Lord bless thee, and keep thee; The Lord make His face to shine upon thee, and be gracious unto thee; The Lord lift up His countenance upon thee and give thee peace." (Numbers 6: 22-26)

THE PRIESTLY benediction, the *Birkat Kohanim,* is a most beloved blessing. Whether one prays in a synagogue or visits a church there is a great likelihood that these words will be used during the service.

Rabbi Levi Yitzhok of Berditchev explained that, "ye shall say unto them . . ." meant, "speak to them with love." The medieval commentator, Rashi, noted that "say unto them" meant "speak with a full heart."

In the Orthodox Prayerbook, when the priestly benediction is introduced, it is always preceded by a formula to be recited by the *kohanim.* "Blessed art Thou, O Lord our God. King of the Universe, who has sanctified us with the holiness of Aaron and commanded us to bless Thy people Israel in love."

One can trace this magnificent concept, that to bless a person one must love him, back to the mystic Book of Splendor, the *Zohar.* There, a most significant doctrine was developed: "A priest not beloved by the people ought not to take part in blessing the people . . . A priest who loves not the people or whom they love not may not pronounce the blessing."

The priest actually was transmitting God's word: he was

266

conveying God's blessing. Dr. Evelyn Garfiel, in her significant study of prayer, *The Service of the Heart,* expressed this quite succinctly when she said, "In Judaism only God can bless as only God can forgive. No man, layman or priest, ever acquires these powers."

To be able to pronounce God's blessing requires an understanding nature. The rabbis interpreted the phrase, "he that hath a bountiful eye shall be blessed" as meaning "he that hath a bountiful eye shall bless." It is important for any man whose life's work is the ministry to extend his blessings with love. There are times when one must be understanding of the frailties of every man.

Once I saw a cartoon which showed a sad-looking figure being fitted for glasses. He said, "I'd like to see things a little less clearly, please." This may cause us to smile, but there are occasions when we can relate to people only if we cloud our vision somewhat and view them through the dimension of love. Love for people is important. A brilliant theologian, whom I heard recently, spoke of "the paralysis of analysis." If we keep analyzing the habits of those we know, dissecting what they do, at times we are stymied and come to a dead end in our relationships with them.

Perhaps the greatest contribution of the hassidic impulse in Jewish life was that it stressed the doctrine that the love of God must always be preceded by a love for His creatures. Aaron, the high priest, who was the first to bless our people, was the symbol of love. It is said of him that he loved his fellow human beings and tried to bring them closer to the Torah. It is told that Aaron had a most unusual habit. He, the high priest of Israel, who tried to live a life of physical purity and moral excellence, had the unusual habit of associating with evil people. He maintained contact with them until they grew embarrassed and said to themselves, "Woe unto us. If Aaron really knew what we are like he would resolve never again even to look upon us. He must think we are worthy people. We at least ought to try to match our conduct with his thinking."

In the very same spirit of Aaron, the poet, Yeats, said, "I

have believed the best of every man and find that to believe the best is enough to make a bad man show himself at his best, or even a good man swing his lantern higher."

The priest who loves gives strength to those who have gone astray. He mirrors the Divine attribute mentioned in our culminating *Neila* prayer: "Thou stretcheth out Thy hand to transgressors."

Our hope and prayer is that during the coming year all of us may feel only love for one another, and be able to bless and be blessed.

Mankind's Favorite Blessing

"Aaron lifted his hands toward the people and blessed them." (Leviticus 9: 22)

"The Lord spoke to Moses . . . Speak to Aaron and his sóns . . . Thus shall you bless the people of Israel . . . Say to them: The Lord bless you and keep you! . . . The Lord make His face to shine upon thee and be gracious to thee! The Lord lift up His countenance . . . Thus they shall link My name with the people of Israel, and I will bless them." (Numbers 6:22-27)

THE BIRKHAT KOHANIM, the priestly blessing, is one of mankind's favorite prayers. While we share this benediction with other religious communities, we can be justifiably proud that it was first pronounced by Aaron, Moses' older brother.

After the ceremony of the induction of the priests, the sanctuary was set up and an elaborate ceremony was conducted. Upon the completion of the service, the Bible reports, Aaron lifted up his hands toward the people and blessed them. Some commentators envisaged Aaron pronouncing the priestly blessing: "May the Lord bless you and keep you." The rabbis studied this text carefully and learned several important principles concerning the posture and procedure of the priest while conveying this benediction. "Aaron lifted his hands." This seemed to indicate that the priestly blessing must always be given with uplifted hands. The sages went on to add other instructions. "The priest must be standing while he is blessing the congregation. He must bless them, face to

269

face." They added one last requirement, "The prayers must be recited in the Hebrew," or to use their exact language, "in the holy tongue."

The *Birkhat Kohanim* is more than a prayer for the well-being of the congregation. Its words mark the occasion when the priests of old proclaimed and modern rabbis pronounce a spiritual charge. The fullest blessing, the most meaningful blessing, is when we have peace, when we live our personal lives in a tranquil world in which men are united and are able to fulfill their human destiny. The procedures involved in the priestly blessing can teach us how to achieve fulfillment and peace.

When there is a great cause which seeks our help and summons us to participate, *one must stand up* for it. One must be prepared to *lift up his hands,* to participate in the work and to partake of what has to be done. Great causes need more than well-wishers; they need people who are prepared to roll up their sleeves and to pitch in.

When Martin Luther King attempted to give his blessing, the charge of building a truly united America, to Governor Wallace face to face, the Alabama executive avoided a direct confrontation by closing down his office on that eventful day. Face to face meeting is important; without it no blessings can accrue.

My psychologically oriented friends tell me that in the most advanced methods of mental health, the patient and the therapist *face each other*. The old Freudian technique of the patient prone on the analyst's couch with the physician behind him is now on the way out. In dialogue, men must face each other, not only to hear their words but to understand the message of their eyes and the responses of their facial muscles.

The priestly blessing was to be given in the *holy tongue*. This meant, of course, Hebrew. Would we be far off base to suggest that the holy tongue means, in the language of holiness. Although we may disagree, we must seek to express ourselves in that language which reflects the best in ourselves and helps to draw out the finest in others.

When the priestly blessing was given its final form later in the Bible, the commandment expressly stated, "Thus shall you bless the people of Israel. Say to them . . ." The late Chief Rabbi of Israel, Dr. Isaac Herzog, once observed to me that while "Thus shall you bless" is stated in the plural, the remainder of the verse is given in the singular. When the priest blessed even the greatest of multitudes, he had to feel that he was speaking from out of his heart directly to the heart of each individual human being. May we ever be mindful in these trying days that every one of us is personally and individually involved in building the better world.

The Price of Pride

ONE OF THE MOST pathetic stories of the Bible is the account of Jephthah and his daughter. Jephthah, an early leader of Israel, was about to engage the enemy in battle. He vowed to the Lord and said: "If Thou wilt indeed deliver the children of Ammon into my hand, then it shall be, that whatsoever cometh forth of the doors of my house to meet me, when I return in peace from the children of Ammon, it shall be the Lord's, and I will offer it up for a burnt-offering." Upon his return from a successful encounter with the enemy, the first person to come out of his door was his daughter, an only child. According to the terms of the vow, the girl would have to be sacrificed.

The account of Jepththah's daughter has become a frequently treated theme in world culture. Handel composed an oratorio about the vow; Shakespeare, who rarely treated Biblical personalities, wrote of Jephthah, his daughter, and the oath in several passages.

The rabbis tried to understand this horrifying incident. As they interpreted Scripture, there was a way out. The vow could have been rendered void. A priest could release Jephthah from his oath. Yet, that was not done because two men stood on their pride. The high priest, who could have annulled the vow, said proudly, "What, I the high priest should humble myself and go to Jephthah!" The military hero, on the other hand, said, "What, I the chief of the tribes of Israel, the first prince of the land, should humble myself and go to him!" The false pride of these haughty men sealed the daughter's tragic fate and ultimately brought grief to the others concerned.

All too often we stand on our pride and remain slaves of

protocol. Instead of jumping into the breach and offering to help when we are needed, we hesitate, we wait too long.

In another unusual passage, the rabbis tell the story of King Jeroboam. Though he had been an evil king, God offered him a last chance to repent and enter the Garden of Eden. In a richly meaningful legend, the sages relate how God, Himself, spoke to Jeroboam, and urged him: "Repent. Then I, you and David will walk in the Garden of Eden." Jeroboam responded with a question. "Who shall be at the head?" God answered, "David will be at the head." "If so," Jeroboam replied, "I do not want it." Think of it! To sacrifice the peace of eternity for the vanity of the moment.

In more recent times, we have the instance of Russian-born Waldemar Haffkine, offering his services to his mother-land during a serious epidemic. His offer of help was rejected by the Tsarist minister, who arrogantly said, "Better that a million Russians should die than Mother Russia be indebted to a Jew."

Wisely, the Book of Proverbs advised, "A man's pride shall bring him low; but he that is of a lowly spirit shall attain to honor." Pride goeth before destruction, and a haughty spirit before a fall. The vanity of men, their pride and presumption, is odious to God and to man.

Deuteronomy

Christian-Jewish Encounter

"Lo! It is a people that shall dwell alone."
(Numbers 23:9)

"The Lord alone did lead him." (Deuteronomy
32:12)

*"And Israel dwelleth in safety, the fountain of
Jacob alone."* (Deuteronomy 33:28)

SINCE WORLD WAR II, Christian leaders have been reassessing and recasting their attitude towards Judaism and the Jewish people. A number of factors have led to this re-evaluation.

There has been a deep sense of guilt concerning Christendom's inaction in the face of the annihilation of six million Jews. Great clerics, lesser clergy, as well as the rank and file, stood by and never lifted a finger during the period of Hitler's brutality.

There is also the growing realization that all religions live in a pluralistic society. The re-establishment of the State of Israel in 1948 caused a profound theological dilemma within Christianity. For almost 2,000 years, the Jews were regarded as the rejected of God. We were doomed to be eternal wanderers for our failure to accept the founder of Christianity. Medieval Christian artists frequently depicted the Synagogue in defeat by the side of the Church triumphant. At the Cathedral of Strasbourg there are two statues. The one of the Synagogue is of a woman blindfolded and her crown slipping from her hand. The establishment of the Jewish State shook the very spiritual foundations of the Christian theological position, and in Roman Catholicism, particularly during the reign of Pope John XXIII, new liberalizing trends developed.

277

More recently, Jews have been involved in consultations with the World Council of Churches in Geneva. The Jewish response towards these religious encounters varies among different groups.

A PEOPLE THAT SHALL DWELL ALONE

There are those who follow the words of Balaam, in his analysis of the Jewish people, and proclaim, "There is a people that dwells apart . . . *Hen am l'vadad yishkon.*" There is a segment of Jewry identified mainly with right-wing Orthodoxy which has avoided or minimized contact with the non-Jewish world. Even in this country, we have witnessed an attempt to set up small, isolated communities where encounter with the non-Jew is barely minimal. There is no attempt to influence the world and there is a conscious emphasis upon keeping the outer world from affecting the thought processes of the Jew. This is a difficult posture to maintain in our type of society. Isolation freezes one out of so much in life.

THE LORD ALONE DID LEAD HIM

The word *badad* (alone) occurs again in Scriptures. A second approach to inter-religious encounter bases its position on another Biblical text. "The Lord alone did guide him . . . *Adonai badad yanhenu.*"

The preponderant majority of Orthodoxy subscribes to the position of Rabbi J. B. Soloveitchik of Boston and Yeshiva University. His thesis has been carefully articulated in a major position paper published in *Tradition,* the organ of the Orthodox Rabbinical Council of America. Dr. Soloveitchik spoke of confrontation and addressed himself to such questions as: On what basis can a Jew relate to other religious communities? How much and what kind of interfaith activity can religious groups take and survive? This brilliant rabbinic scholar, the unchallenged intellectual leader of American Orthodoxy, argues against religious dialogue. He feels that a harmonious relationship among all religious faiths is imperative, but he avers that this relationship can only be of value if it will not be in conflict with the uniqueness of each religious community.

Dr. Soloveitchik and his disciples will participate in discussions on sociological problems. They will join in conversations on political, economic and moral issues. They do not believe that it is possible to conduct discussions with any other faith on religious doctrine and theological dogma. They insist that any such conversations will be misunderstood. Dr. Soloveitchik emphasizes over and over again that we are "members of the community of the few." He insists that we speak a language of faith which is totally incomprehensible to a community of a different faith. One must note that Rabbi Soloveitchik is not alone in his position. Dr. Steven Schwarzchild of St. Louis' Washington University maintains a similar position. He believes that Jewish-Christian theological accommodation is impossible.

ISRAEL DWELLS IN SAFETY

American Conservative and Reform elements have had considerable experience in interreligious communication. They would appear to subscribe to a third emphasis found in the use of the word *"badad"* (alone), in the closing verses of Deuteronomy, "Israel dwells securely alone. *Vayishkon Yisrael betah badad."*

We Jews draw our strength from the Well of Jacob. But the waters of the Well of Jacob are abundant; they can quench the thirst not only of the Jew, but can help slake and satisfy the thirst of other peoples.

Theological dialogue between Jews and Christians on a respectable level of intellectual exchange was pioneered by the Jewish Theological Seminary of America and its Chancellor, Dr. Louis Finkelstein, almost 30 years ago. Long before ecumenism and interfaith discussions became fashionable, an effort was made to conduct intelligent dialogue between different religions.

The Conservative movement has since sponsored and participated in inter-religious dialogues within various frameworks. Their guideline might well be expressed in the splendid words of the prophet Malachi (Chapter 3), "Then those who revere the Lord speak to one another."

279

Give to Get

*"And it shall be righteousness unto Thee before
the Lord thy God."* (Deuteronomy 24:13)

ONE OF THE MOST fascinating accounts in all of Jewish
history is the conversion to Judaism of an entire royal house.
Headed by Queen Helene and King Monobaz I, the regal
family of Adiabene, a small state on the Tigris, embraced
Judaism.

It is related that their heir, Monobaz II, in a year of famine,
started to distribute relief to his subjects using royal treasury
funds. His family became quite agitated; they protested his
action to him and said, "Your fathers put these resources
aside; generation after generation added to the wealth, and
you are squandering them." The king answered, "My fathers
stored up below and I am storing above . . . my fathers gathered treasures of money, and I have gathered treasures of
souls."

Monobaz had an enlightened attitude toward the use of his
wealth. His position on money was comparable to that recently expressed by a modern millionaire, who had made an
extremely large gift to a public institution. He said, "My
father created an organization for the making of wealth. I
regard it as my responsibility to see that the vast amount of
money he accumulated is used for the good of humanity."

Some eight centuries ago, a Georgian poet developed a remarkable formula: "What you keep is lost, what you give is
yours forever." At first reading, this verse seems to be paradoxical. Only weigh its words and see if they are not true! The
expression soon became the common possession of an entire

people. Potters scratched the verse on unglazed clay; smiths engraved the lines on metals; women embroidered the words of wisdom on their shawls. The poet's words were memorized and often repeated. Why was his idea so invigorating?

Men are no different today from what they were 800 years ago or in the lifetime of Monobaz. What gnaws at men? We have our possessions and we are afraid to lose them. We are anxious to guard our treasures from thieves, our wheat from rot, our cloth from the moth, and our iron from rust. Yet, the only way to preserve our wealth is to give it away. "The wise man," Lao Tsze once wrote, "does not lay up treasure. The more he gives to others, the more he has for his own."

The giving of charity is a joyous occasion. Extending an act of hospitality is to perform an act of delight. We have to learn to give—not only of our substance but of ourselves. We must give others of our affection, our concern and our time.

The Bible was always anxious to guard against a double standard in life. A merchant was forbidden to have two types of weights, so that he could measure out cheaply for himself and dearly for others. Biblical ethics declared that it was wrong to expect more than we are prepared to give. Let us learn to share our talents, our counsel and our sympathy. Doing all of this, we will be like the ancient Monobaz, the medieval poet and the modern millionaire, "And for thee it will be righteousness."

May I close these thoughts with some words of John Masefield—

> "All lovely giving is a Heavenly seed
> Dropped to the chosen heart as glittering corn,
> That everlasting gladness may be born,
> Bread never-spent, Beauty that never ends."

Till the Heart Take Fire

"Now Mount Sinai was all in smoke, for the Lord had come down upon it in fire . . ." (Exodus 19:18)

"The mountain was ablaze with flames to the very skies." (Deuteronomy 4: 11)

THE REVELATION at Sinai was the greatest moment in human history. There "we received both the word and the spirit to understand the word" (Abraham Joshua Heschel).

The event at Sinai has served and will ever serve as the most profound of mankind's experiences. The account of the giving of the Ten Commandments is recorded twice in the Torah. In Moses' final address, he relives the serenity of that greatest day. He describes that the mountain was ablaze with flames to the very skies. "To the very skies" can literally be translated as "to the very heart of heaven." Rabbi Mendel of Kotzk, with typical brilliance and insight, offered this interesting interpretation. The mountain of man's spiritual aspiration must become aglow with fire until man's heart becomes like the heart of heaven.

Ours is a "cool age." Our lives lack enthusiasm. Frequently our posture is one of detachment and unconcern. The very observance of some of the most precious moments of life are perfunctory. There is no burning, no ardor of ecstasy, no *hitlahavut,* to borrow the familiar hassidic phrase. We do not become engulfed by fire; we do not become ablaze with spiritual flame. There is no burning within. Professor Buber once wrote, *"Hitlahavut* unlocks the meaning of life. Without it even heaven has no meaning . . ."

282

Emma Lazarus, in one of her poems, demanded of her generation:

> "Clash, Israel, the cymbals,
> touch the lyre,
> Sound the brass trumpet, and
> the harsh-tongued horn,
> Chant hymns of victory till the
> heart take fire."

How important it is to become exhilarated until the heart takes fire!

We need religious enthusiasm. We have a desperate need for "peak experiences," those "moments of great awe . . . moments of the most intense happiness or even rapture, ecstasy or bliss . . . moments of great insight and discovery." We need these "peak experiences" when we are so aglow with the flame of fervor that our heart becomes like the heart of heaven. We need the flame of enthusiasm, a flame which does not consume but which rather energizes our life. The years may wrinkle one's skin, but it is losing enthusiasm that wrinkles one's soul.

"Nothing great," Emerson once said, "was ever achieved without enthusiasm." Unfortunately, there are some men who have burning enthusiasm but have no great goals. They spend their lives scrambling to reach the top, expending great energy as they climb the mountain of personal aspiration. An entire lifetime is frequently given up in this pursuit. Finally, they arrive at the peak and they find that their lifelong quest was for objectives that were meaningless and empty. The insight of Rabbi Mendel was sound. May our climb up the mountain of personal experience be full of enthusiasm, but let us make certain that the goal which we attempt to reach is to get a little closer to the heart of heaven.

The Urge to Join

"Ye are the children of the Lord your God: ye shall not cut yourselves . . ." (Deuteronomy 14: 1)

THIS IS THE SEASON when the membership committees of our American organizations move from their summer lethargy into the year's activity. Somehow, we Americans are given to joining groups. Over a hundred years ago, Alexis de Tocqueville, the French man of letters, came to our country. After studying our people and their different customs, he wrote down his reflections in his classic *Democracy in America* (1835). He observed that "Americans of all ages, all conditions and all dispositions constantly form associations." He went on to say that America is blessed with these organizations of a thousand kinds, "religious, moral, serious, futile, extensive, restricted, enormous or diminutive." What was true in his time is true in our own.

It would be worthwhile to pause for a moment and reflect on this phenomenon. A long time ago, the sages were concerned with people breaking themselves into many groups; they were particularly anxious about the smaller units. In commenting on the verse "Ye shall not cut yourselves . . . ," referring to the pagan custom of cutting one's flesh in bereavement as a sign of grief, the rabbis, in a play on words, interpreted *'don't cut yourself,' lo tit-god'du,* as *don't divide yourself into many groups, lo ta'asu agudot agudot.*

This concept ought to be examined critically. There are positive aspects to small groups. A small, select fellowship supplies its members with the warmth and intimacy which can only be found with those people who are closest to us in aspiration and outlook. We feel comfortable in their presence; they help to lighten our personal burden—give encouragement when it is needed and correction when it is timely.

Jewish history is marked by a long line of small groups that played decisive roles in the emerging pattern of our people's development. The early Hasidim, mentioned in the Mishna over 2000 years ago, were small groups of deeply dedicated, highly ethical people who tried to enhance Judaism. They took upon themselves special observances and limited their worldly pleasures. In more recent times, the Hasidic movement that developed in Central and Eastern Europe consisted of small groups of devotees consecrated to the revival of the joyous aspects of folk religion. Prior to the establishment of the Zionist movement, Ahad Ha'am, the famed Jewish philosopher, organized small units called *B'nai Moshe*. Scattered throughout Russia, they nurtured the idea of restoration of the homeland and the revival of Hebraic culture.

The establishment of small groups has its advantages. Yet, at times, there are disadvantages. If the group serves as a fragmenting force in society, if it tends to make its members insular or "cliquish," concerned only with their own well-being, that association tears the fabric of society; it cuts the bonds which bind people together. If our membership in a small group prevents us from seeing the greater needs of the rest of society, then that body is of the type that concerned the rabbis when they said, "don't make many groups."

The Bible gives this advice to our people immediately after the reminder, "Ye are the children of the Lord your God." Let us join hands with those forces which keep that reminder ever in the minds of men.

Here and Now

*"See, this day I have set before you a blessing
and a curse."* (Deuteronomy 11:26)

TODAY, ROSH HODESH ELUL, we begin our prepara-
tions for the "Days of Awe." We open our penitential season
with the sounding of the Shofar during each weekday morning service, and our religious fervor increases as we move
closer to the New Year. We begin to recite the Selihot, the
expression of our moral deficiency and the confession of our
sins, and finally, on Rosh Hashanah and Yom Kippur, our
prayers end on the grand note, *"This day mayest Thou
strengthen us—this day mayest Thou bless us."*

Notice that the Torah speaks in the present tense; the word
hayom is used. The Bible does not say "I gave you the opportunity of choosing the blessing or the curse." Its very words
emphasize "I give you *this day*." Man has a choice given to
him every day to reject evil and to choose good, to return in
repentance and to renew himself.

Frequently men and women ignore the demands of the
present and seek their peace of mind elsewhere. They fly
off into the fantasy of dreams. The realities of life are too
harsh for them and they try to run away, at least in their
minds, to find a haven in the world of illusion.

There are those who fly away into the past. We are grateful
for prior generations and are always thankful for the wonderful memories that are ours. But many people look only
backwards. They try to recapture what they consider to have
been their most wonderful and most creative days. They
rush away from the problems of the here-and-now which they
feel they cannot solve.

Some fly away into the future. They seek to escape from the imperfections of the present by awaiting the next opportunity. The future is important, but it must begin with action—here and now.

It has been said that man should not look back in anger nor forward in fear. Man should look around him in awareness. For the religious person, living with God means living in this moment of opportunity, in the present hour which God has given us. We must learn to put our entire being into what God expects of us in this hour and in this day. The past and the future belong to Him. It is the present which waits to be hallowed by us.

The Paradox of Abundance

"Things are in the saddle and they ride mankind"

HOW TO LIVE — WHAT TO LIVE FOR

THE BOOK OF DEUTERONOMY represents the great last address of Moses to the children of Israel. He reminds them, "For you are not as yet come to the rest and to the inheritance which the Eternal your God gives you" (Deuteronomy 12:9).

Rabbi Simeon explains that "inheritance" referred to the city of Shiloh, and "rest" alluded to Jerusalem. Shiloh was an early center of religious devotion, but it never attained the spiritual significance of Jerusalem. The Holy City, Jerusalem the Golden, represented then and remains now the quintessence of mankind's religious experience.

I would like to think of the Jew coming to his inheritance and to his rest in another dimension. Materially, most American Jews have come to a fine state of financial security. In sober reflection, we must grant that there has been no generation that has been so well off materially as our own. Truly, we have our inheritance, our lines have fallen in pleasant places. Let us bluntly ask ourselves a forthright question—have we reached the rest, the haven, the point of spiritual satisfaction? Have we attained that inner spiritual serenity which every man aspires to reach some day?

If we examine our lives, we are faced with a paradox. We share with most Americans in an age of abundance, yet we are unsatisfied. David Riesman used a most striking expression as the title of his last book, *Abundance—For What?* A French magazine features this engaging subject,

288

"Learning To Live With Prosperity." Our paradox haunts and troubles us. We live in an age of abundance, yet we are horrified at our inner emptiness. Our riches have left us in a unique predicament. We have satisfied stomachs and empty souls. We have succeeded in the business of making a living but have failed in the art of making a life.

Abundance and affluence affect us. Living, thank God, in a rich and physically powerful land we realize how different our own life is from the lives of our grandfathers. They carried on under the shadow of the sword. They persevered, agonized by hunger. Their existence was marginal at best, and often precarious. "The Jew in the ghetto," one observer noted, "had nowhere to turn so he was obliged to go upwards." How different is our situation!

How can we teach our people to love God when each man thinks that his personal success depends upon his own ability. "My own power and the might of my hand have gotten me this wealth," was a mistaken notion in Biblical times and is reflected in the attitude and action of modern man.

We must learn a basic lesson. The real status of every people is measured by their spiritual life. Power, physical goods, are not ends in themselves. Material things alone cannot truly satisfy us.

The accumulation of worldly goods, the acquisition of more and more of our inheritance, has left the world all the poorer. Mankind is able to wage costlier wars because we have greater strategic resources. This was not the case in centuries gone by. Then, faced with a scarcity of goods, the farmer had to lay down his arms, go back to his field, and take up the plow again to make certain that his children would not go hungry. The smithy laid down his sword and returned to his forge because there was no warehouse filled to the rafters. Our wars are costlier in human lives because we have become wealthier. This is modern man's challenge.

We should remain grateful for this age of abundance, for having come to Shiloh, to our inheritance. Judaism has never made a fetish of poverty. Let us, however, pray that some day there will come into our lives the spirit of Jerusalem, the spiritual serenity of that city of our hope. Man needs more than the physical goods of the world. Peace and tranquility in our personal lives will come only when we learn that faith alone can truly satisfy us. More than ever before, our age must master the lessons which the prophets and sages of Israel articulated centuries ago. The most satisfying gifts of the world are the gifts of the mind. The most sustaining elements in society are the works of the spirit.

The Lesson of a Bird's Nest

THE RABBIS LIKED to categorize the various commandments that a Jew was to observe. In their scale of values
they would rate different observances according to their
significance. Concerning the commandment that if one came
upon a bird's nest with young ones and the mother bird
was there, the finder was not to take away the mother bird
along with her brood; the mother bird was to be set free,
the sages considered it to be a *mitzvah kallah,* a simple commandment, one with lesser religious significance.

It is remarkable that in discussing this commandment, two
teachers described it as having awesome implications. "If you
fulfill this precept you hasten the coming of Elijah." " . . . you
hasten the coming of the Messiah," his colleague added. At
first glance, this far-reaching consequence seems to be a bit
of extravagance. With deeper probing, however, we realize
that there was much more implicit in the teaching.

The rabbis were saying that what you do in the realm of
nature ultimately affects the historic order. There is cosmic
significance to even a simple deed. Seemingly insignificant, a
simple occurrence may have the most profound effect. What
you do in the animal order affects the human order.

It might appear, at the first thought, that the underlying
reason for sending the mother bird away was to be kind to
her, to spare her the anguish of witnessing the fate of her
young. More important, however, than sparing the mother
bird, was training oneself in mercy.

If a man teaches himself to be compassionate toward a bird,
he conditions himself to be compassionate toward men. He
trains himself to be compassionate toward men if he realizes
that the ultimate source of compassion in this world is God

Himself. "He who is merciful to others, mercy is shown to him by Heaven."

The sages have said that "whoever is merciful to his fellow-man is certainly of the seed of our father, Abraham." Samuel David Luzzatto, a 19th century Italian Jewish philosopher, contrasted the way of Abraham and the way of Aristotle. Aristotle's mean sought to teach man to make self-centered, calculated decisions, aiming to achieve his own good. The way that Abraham taught his descendants is the way of love, and its aim is to seek the good of others and to find favor with God. "Whoever is merciful to his fellow men is certainly of the seed of our father, Abraham," means that he is truly a Jew.

As a people, we have trained ourselves in compassion, for we feel that when a man does kindness on earth and performs a deed of mercy he gives a better tone to the world. We think that cruelty is only the work of our enemies. "They are cruel and have no compassion" (Jeremiah 50:42). Yet, we live in a world marked by the callousness of would-be friends and the cruelty of so-called companions.

The more concerned we become about the inconsequential, the more sensitive we shall be about the significant. Life is a school which we attend every day. There we must train ourselves in developing attitudes of mercy and kindness. We may well start with our own immediate circle of family and friends, of business associates and co-workers. Ultimately, these attitudes will affect mankind. A world at peace—and this is the true meaning of a Messianic age—can only come about through a society that has learned that compassion and mercy ought to replace cruelty and inhumanity.

Only on the Testimony of Two or More

I WRITE THIS on the eve of our New Year. This is a season of soul-searching, a time of judgment. Our ancestors viewed God as sitting in His great court on high, examining the ledger of life, making decisions on the activities and deeds of men.

The Bible states specifically that all judgment had to be established on the minimum testimony of at least two witnesses. No matter how strong the evidence there must be at least two men who were prepared to corroborate what transpired. Legend has it that Kohelet, who is identified with Solomon, wanted "to make judgments concerning the laws of the heart without witnesses and without warning." He sought to pronounce verdicts based upon his own insight alone. Though he was truly a brilliant man, perhaps the wisest of all men, a heavenly voice called out, "Just are the words of truth. Only through two or three witnesses ought judgment to be rendered."

How frequently do we make judgments concerning others! How often do we play God! We pass judgment on our neighbor's deeds. We crystallize our opinions about others upon hearsay and unfiltered information, all too often taking our stand on the shifting sands of rumor and half-truths.

According to Biblical law, even a single person is competent to try certain types of cases. Thus the sages interpreted, "In righteousness shall you judge your neighbor," as referring to a single judge. As Jewish law developed, however, it required a court of three whose members had these basic qualities—wisdom, humility, hatred of gain, love of truth, love of one's fellowman, and a good reputation.

Beginning with the Ethics of the Fathers, the emphasis of Jewish ethics was that man ought not to judge alone. "Do not act the judge's part by yourself," said Rabbi Ishmael, "for none may act the judge's part by himself alone, save One." "He is by Himself," the medieval prayer manual, *Mahzor Vitry*, tells us, "who can controvert Him" (Job 23:13). Though God Himself can render judgment alone, we find a delightful legend in the Palestinian Talmud which teaches that God never does anything in this world below before He consults His court on high.

Even though the evidence is strong and circumstantial, we need the corroboration of others. There is a remarkable story told about Rabbi Simeon ben Shetah who said, "May I never see comfort, may I always be afflicted, if I did not see a man pursuing another man into a room. When I ran after him and saw him, sword in hand, with blood dripping from it and the murdered man writhing in pain, I exclaimed to the sword-bearer, 'Wicked man, who slew this man? It is either you or I! But what can I do, since your life does not rest in my hands, for upon the testimony of two shall he (the murderer) be put to death.' "

How often do we see character assassination based upon one man's evidence and one man's personal judgment. A contemporary of Rabbi Simeon, Judah ben Tabbai, once sentenced a perjured witness to death on the word of a single individual. Simeon told him that he had caused the blood of an innocent person to be shed because the testimony of two witnesses is always required. Realizing his error, from that time on, Judah ben Tabbai refused to pass sentence without an extra judge by his side, without the presence of his learned contemporary, Rabbi Simeon.

The story continues that Judah ben Tabbai would visit and prostrate himself on the grave of the executed man; then a weeping voice would be heard, which ordinary folk believed to be the cry of the executed man.

How wise are the words of Maimonides, "Though every judge has the right to act alone, the rabbis enjoin upon him the duty of associating himself with others. Although a court

294

of three constitutes a full court, even so the larger the number of those who participate in deliberations the better. It is more desirable that judgment be rendered by a larger number of people than by a smaller number of people."

When something is misplaced in our home, my wife will call me and say, "Lend me a pair of eyes." It is good to have an additional pair of eyes to help seek out the truth. All of us can use the counsel of an additional mind to examine what happens in the lives of people. A single person, just like a single judge, ought not judge alone, for there is a greater possibility of error. Wisely did the Bible say, "A case can be valid only in the testimony of two witnesses or more" (Deuteronomy 17:6).

The Limits of Judgment

*"Judges and law officers shalt thou make thee in
all thy gates."* (Deuteronomy 16:18)

THROUGHOUT THE CENTURIES, our people, inspired
by Scripture, have contributed to many judicial systems. We
have enriched mankind not only through the application of
our own religious law, but also through contributions to the
various systems of jurisprudence of the nations.

Some of the 19th century moralists considered the appoint-
ment of judges spoken of in the Bible in a more personal
vein. They said that beyond the judges who sit in courts,
every man, in a sense, is a judge, in that he sits continually
in judgment upon life. He may not be draped in a judge's
robe, yet each individual makes decisions every hour of the
waking day. These judgments on life are not limited to their
maker, but have direct impact upon others.

These moralists read the Biblical text in a symbolic sense.
They stressed the use of the Hebrew word "thee" in the
expression "Judges and law officers shalt thou make thee in
all thy gates..." A man must appoint himself as his own
judge; he must understand the essence of his nature, try to
evaluate his world properly, and what is more important,
know who he is and what he is.

While we are reluctant to appoint judicial guidance over
our own moral behavior, this inhibition does not extend
to our judgment of others. Here we really let go. We pass
critical judgments on others in the strictest manner while
we are most lenient concerning our own shortcomings. We
have eagle's eyes to detect failure in others, but we are blind
as bats to our own limitations.

296

It was once said, concerning a truly pious person, that a saintly man is not one who watches his own body and someone else's soul; rather he guards his own soul and someone else's body.

The Bible, as these moralists understood it, was very concerned with men designated as personal judges over their own behavior. They added, however, a note of caution. Here, again, they turned to our Scriptural source. The Bible, in describing the system of justice, went on to give additional admonitions. In ancient times, the courts of law were either in the temples or close to the houses of worship. Thus, the section on setting up the court system is followed immediately by a warning against any idolatrous practice within the temple of the Lord: "Neither shalt thou set thee up a pillar."

One commentator suggested that just as the previous word "thee" hinted at our role as supervisors of our conduct, so the word "thee" has significance here. It meant that a man ought to be careful and watch that he did not set up the "thee" of his own personality as a form of idolatry.

Certainly, we have to judge ourselves. We ought to be careful in whatever we do. But we cannot permit ourselves to become so self-critical that we are paralyzed with fear. There are some people who cannot act because they are afraid that their actions will be judged wrongly in the eyes of others. It is good to appoint judges; yet let us be heedful that we do not set up our self-judgments as idolatrous pillars. Let us not become worshippers in the cult of hypercriticism.

Passive Spectator or Participant

*"When you enter the land that the Lord your
God is giving you as a heritage, and you occupy
it and settle in it, you shall take some of every
first fruit of the soil, which you harvest from the
land that the Lord your God is giving you, put
it in a basket and go to the place where the Lord
your God will choose to establish His name,"*
(Deuteronomy 26:1-2)

THE BEAUTIFUL and impressive ritual of the *bikkurim*,
the bringing of the first fruits, is well known to us. At the
Passover *seder,* we recite its formula of acknowledgment, just
as it was recited by the farmer. Like him, we pray, "My
father was a wandering Aramean. He went down to Egypt
with meager numbers and sojourned there..." Ever present
in our minds is the recollection, "He brought us to this place
and gave us this land, a land flowing with milk and honey.
Wherefore I now bring the first fruits of the soil which You,
O Lord, have given me."

Studying the laws of the bringing of the *bikkurim* is most
instructive. Every farmer, rich and poor alike, would come
up to Jerusalem. Entire communities went up in splendid
processions, singing, "Let us rise and go up to Zion, to the
house of the Lord our God." Led by a flutist, they entered
Jerusalem joyfully. When they reached the temple grounds
every man placed a basket on his shoulders. The king did
this so that he, with his own hands, could present the first
fruits to the priest.

I think that this particular action on the part of the king
is all important. Kings, as a rule, do not do menial work. The
monarch could have watched the ceremonies, which were

298

extremely moving. The ruler could have been stationed on a podium or a balcony. He could have remained a passive observer of the pageantry. Yet, the king chose to be a participant.

In June 1963, Dr. Louis Finkelstein was a member of a five man delegation representing the President of the United States at the Papal coronation. Afterwards he described his reactions. "This was my first experience of a religious ceremony in which I was outside looking in. For the first time I realized fully how different a ceremony appears to participants who understand its symbols and believe firmly in them, and to an outsider."

For the passive spectator, a ceremony can be stirring, the symbolism may represent an esthetic experience. There is, however, a vast difference between being an onlooker and a participant. The king demonstrated that he chose the more meaningful role.

In an article on "Prayer," Ruth F. Brinn writes, "There are three types of worshippers who can be found in almost every Jewish congregation: the genuine *daveners;* the artistic kind; the spectator variety." The spectator comes to a service (and I witness this every week), has a prayerbook given to him by a dutiful usher, but will not open it. The spectator type believes that the *siddur* is a "sealed book." Why should he break the seal?

The artistic kind comes over at the end of the service and tells you how beautiful everything was. He liked the appearance of the structure, the stance of the officiants, the personality of the *Bar Mitzvah* boy.

Only by being a *davener,* by participating in the service, can one truly have a religious experience. Every service requires the application of both heart and mind, of intellect and emotion. For a service to have meaning we must become part of it by learning the language of prayer, by studying the meaning of its words. Each one of us can bring the first fruits—the gift of our spirit— to the sanctuary. Let us learn from the king, who was not too proud, and partake of the service in the most personal and intense fashion.

The Sensitive Soul

"Lest there should be among you some man or woman . . . whose heart is even now turning away from the Lord, our God . . . when such a one hears the words of this curse he may fancy himself immune, thinking, 'I shall have peace.' " (Deuteronomy 29:17-18)

As I was rummaging through some papers I ran across this little poem:

Your bowl is empty little brother,
Your hands are blue from the cold,
Your face is a map of terror and pain,
Old as mankind is old.
Men launch their miracles, little brother,
They send their rockets up.
But should it not be their first concern
To fill your empty cup?
Men try to reach the moon, little brother,
To lasso outer space.
But would they not come closer to God
If they wiped the pain from your face?

I DO NOT REMEMBER where I clipped this poem from, but the impact of its lines has remained with me. As the verses raced through my mind, I began to wonder, how is it that so many individuals are insensitive and do not feel the pain of others.

An accident happens and people just walk by. Someone falls to the ground and lies prone; pedestrians keep moving along. Tourists go to India and see abject poverty and the worst forms of human misery; entire families sleeping on the

300

streets at night. This shocking experience becomes one of the curious things which they tell about their trip.

Within our own affluent country, the evils of our society have been with us for a long time. The curse of segregation has been an American malady for a hundred years. Blighted slums have scarred the beauty of our cities for decades. Stark poverty has long stared us in the face. How is it that we act as if we never saw it? How is it that there are so many evils in the world and men do not seem to care?

The theory has been advanced that people fail to develop a sense of injustice because they have anaesthetized themselves. They react to violence taking place before their very eyes as if it were an incident which they were watching on the television screen. The drama of life unfolds before their very eyes, but they do not feel that they are involved in it or a part of it. "I am but a bystander," they say. Surely our educational system has as one of its purposes the development of sensitive human beings who are able to feel the shock of tragedy taking place thousands of miles away. Should they not also be able to feel for the tragedy that takes place on our very street?

Sometimes men accept an evil just because it has been going on for so long. As our rabbis taught, when Adam experienced darkness for the first time he said, "This is the way of the world."

While American spokesmen were traveling around the world preaching human equality, Negro and white staff members ate in segregated dining rooms in our own State Department in Washington. While we were struggling to defeat Hitler with his perverted notions of Nordic supremacy, American soldiers were segregated into white and Negro units and were sent to segregated churches. "This is the way of the world."

Men sometimes accept the status quo because they feel impotent to change it. How can we be strong enough to correct the accumulation of centuries of inequities? If earlier generations could not undo the ills of society, what will give our generation the power to improve man's lot?

The most shameful of excuses for inaction is offered by the individual who accepts the evils of society not because of their

301

antiquity or because there is no course of action open to him, but because of his self-centeredness. As long as the tragedies of our society do not affect him directly, why should be get involved?

The Bible warned man about this. Scripture was concerned about those men and women who fancy themselves to be immune from all the hurts of life and say, "I shall have peace." It does not directly hurt or touch me, why worry about it? In the Biblical spirit, the rabbis repeated the warning, and spoke out against the self-centeredness of a man who, witnessing his community in distress, says to himself, "I will go home, eat and drink, and peace be upon my soul" (Ta'anit IIa).

We stand before a new year. One of the purposes of our liturgy is to sensitize us, to teach us that tragedy anywhere in the world touches every man. If the status quo is undesirable, it must be changed. We must be courageous enough to accept the idea that through our creative activities it can be changed. We must accept the commitment that you and I can change it.

To Number Our Days

MOSES, COMING to the end of his career, spoke to the children of Israel. Having lived a long and eventful life, spanning many decades, he said unto them, "I am 120 years old this day" (Deut. 31:2).

The Talmud asks about the emphasis on *this day*. The purpose of the verse, the explanation goes, is to teach that God completes the years of the righteous from day to day, for it is said, "The number of thy days will I fulfill" (Exodus 23:26). The basic lesson is that *this day, every day* counts!

Men think of their lives and measure their careers in terms of years and the span of decades. These are important, but the true measure of our existence is what happens to our individual days. Perhaps that is why we conclude our *Mussaf* service on the stirring note, "This day do Thou strengthen us; this day do Thou bless us!"

Ralph Waldo Emerson referred to the French expression: *"En peu d'heure Dieu labeure*—God works in moments." The New England philosopher stressed the importance of moments. "Moments of insight... what ample borrowers of eternity they are." We must treat each day respectfully, as a unique opportunity to be captured only once. "You must be a day yourself and not interrogate it like a college professor." Emerson had his own definition of the often enigmatic word "happiness." "Just to fill the hour, that is happiness." His great prayer was, "Fill my hour... so that I shall not say whilst I have done this, 'Behold, also, an hour of my life is gone' but rather, 'I have lived an hour!' "

Man must realize that time is the stuff of which our life is made. We must employ our time and allocate our days well. Prudently, Benjamin Franklin advised, "Since you are

303

not sure of a moment, throw not away an hour." No one knows the number of his days. We are all agitated by this uncertainty, consciously or subconsciously, as was Jean Jacques Rousseau when he felt he was going to pass away at a young age, believing himself to be affected with a fatal disease. Rousseau asked himself how he might make as much as possible of the brief interval of life that remained. All men have such an interval. Some spend this period in listlessness, others in high passion. Wisely our best chance is in expanding that interval by investing it with as much significance as is possible.

It was Walter Pater, the student of the Renaissance, who recommended that the best course for a man to take is, "To give nothing but the highest quality to your moments as they pass."

All of us who are so time-conscious suffer from modern man's disease—a shortage of time. It would be good to reflect on these words of a modern poet, Michael Quoist:

> *"I went out, Lord*
> *Everything was rushing . . .*
> *Men were rushing not to waste time*
> *They were rushing after time . . .*

> *"Good-bye, Sir, excuse me, I haven't time . . .*
> *I'll come back, I can't wait,*
> *I haven't time . . .*
> *I'd love to help you, but I haven't time . . .*
> *I'd like to pray, but I haven't time.*
> *You understand, Lord, they simply haven't time*
> *And so all men run after time, Lord.*

> *"Lord, You must have made a mistake,*
> *The hours are too short,*
> *The days are too short,*
> *Our lives are too short.*

"You who are beyond time, Lord,
You smile to see us fighting it,
And You know what You are doing.
You make no mistakes in Your
distribution of time and men.
You give each one time to do
What You want him to do.

"Lord, I have time
All the time that You give me.
The years of my life,
The days of my years,
The hours of my days.
They are all mine.
Mine to fill, quietly, calmly,
But to fill completely, up to the brim . . .

"I am not asking You tonight, Lord,
for time to do this and then that,
But Your grace to do conscientiously,
in the time
That You give me, what You want me to do."

The great challenge facing us is to understand the meaning of our days. The time to carry out our responsibility to life is *this day*. "Teach us," the Psalmist said, "to number our days so that we may apply our heart to wisdom."

Reflections on Repentance

WE ASSOCIATE the mood of repentance with the High Holiday season. We observe ten days of penitence and keep a special *Shabbat Shuvah*, a Sabbath of Return. Upon closer examination we realize that repentance is a constant theme in the prayer life of the Jew. It is accentuated, to be sure, during our High Holiday season, but it is with us at each of our daily services.

In the midst of our *tefillah,* we say,

> *"You graciously endow man with intelligence;*
> *You teach him knowledge and understanding.*
> *Grant us knowledge, discernment and wisdom.*
> *Praised art Thou, O Lord, for the gift of knowledge.*
>
> *Our Father, bring us back to Your Torah;*
> *Our King, draw us near to Your service;*
> *Lead us back to You, truly repentant.*
> *Praised art Thou, O Lord, who welcomes repentance.*
>
> *Our Father, forgive us, for we have sinned;*
> *Our King, pardon us, for we have transgressed;*
> *You forgive sin and pardon transgression.*
> *Praised art Thou, gracious and forgiving Lord."*

It might appear at first glance that these prayers are thrown together at random. However, their structure is significant. Like a well-built edifice, there is balance and design. We ask for wisdom, then we pray for repentance, and hope for forgiveness. We start from the base of wisdom. "If there is no understanding there can be no prayer," reads a code of

Jewish law. The medieval philosopher, Judah Halevi, explained, "First place is properly given to the prayer for intelligence ... wisdom, knowledge, moving in the path of the Torah ..." Without knowledge there can be no true repentance. Without comprehension there can be no meaningful prayer. That is why the order of our *Siddur* places wisdom before penitence.

Knowledge means more than the acquisition of facts and information. A knowledgeable person is not only a well informed person but an individual who is able to bring questions to life. The word *teshuva* means more than "repentance"; it means "an answer." An answer assumes a question. What is the question which we must be prepared to ask of life?

The decisive question which every man must ask himself can be stated in the simplest terms: "Am I related to something infinite or am I not?" This query is the most demanding one that we can ever make. It pierces to the very heart of our human situation. If we assume that our life is related to the infinite, we don't fix our concern upon the futile and the transitory. We don't content ourselves and our souls with the attainment of goals which are of no real significance. Our lives assume a more expansive character.

The Swiss psychoanalyst, C. G. Jung, wrote, "The more a man lays stress on false possessions and the less sensitivity he has for what is essential, the less satisfying is his life. He feels limited because he has limited aims, and the result is envy and jealousy."

Repentance means to retrace our steps back to God; to be blessed with the ability to ask the fundamental question and to pray for the strength to receive the correct answer. *Teshuva* means a return to the Source of our being. It means having proper concern for our personal salvation, not running away from asking questions about the individual self. "Great things begin in the tiny seed of the small change in the troubled individual heart."

If we will start with understanding, and pray for forgiveness, we may hope that a gracious and forgiving God will, in turn, pardon. "The erring in spirit shall come to understanding," is the promise of the prophet Isaiah. Let us take confidence from the promise that those who return to the Lord with understanding are pardoned by Him.

Unity in Diversity

"When the Most High gave to the nations
Their inheritance.
When He separated the children of men,
He set the borders of the peoples
According to the number of children of Israel."
(Deuteronomy 32: 8)

IN MOSES' FINAL ADDRESS to the children of Israel, the
law-giver sought to leave one final definitive message for his
people. He mentioned the fact that when God created the
peoples of the earth, He made them seventy in number. The
number seventy was highly symbolic in Jewish thought; the
seventy nations were comparable to the seventy members of
the family of Jacob, who went down to Egypt.

An ancient teacher observed that when the Bible speaks
of the seventy children of Jacob they are described as seventy
soul *(shivim nefesh)* rather than seventy souls *(shivim
n'fashot)*. As Jacob's children felt that, though they were
seventy different individuals, they shared one common soul,
aspiration, hope and destiny, so, too, the nations of the world,
though they were seventy in number, ought to feel that they
have one common purpose. The nations were to be separate
in culture, distinct in tradition, apart in language, possessing
a territory of their own, yet they were to feel as Jacob's sons
felt, that they were part of a greater world family.

It is difficult to learn how to live as a separate people, yet
united by the common bond of mankind. In our own nation,
we are undergoing one of the most difficult periods since the
Civil War. A tremendous tragedy has been unfolding in the
area of inter-group relations in the South. We feel a sense of

loss at our inability to comprehend Southern thinking attitudes. Psychiatrists tell us that there is little value in being
furious at people who behave wickedly. Instead of losing our
tempers and condemning the Southerners, we must understand the underlying causes for their behavior and try to
help them. We ought to attempt to bring them around to
the realization that though the peoples of the South ought to
be separate in matters of marriage, they can be united in
the improvement of the South. As Jews we know that it is
our duty to promote this harmony between the separate
peoples, for injustice in the arena of race relations is the
raw material of strife.

From the world scene, we must learn that each nation is
entitled to genuine nationalism. Though each is inherently
endowed with what President Woodrow Wilson called "self-
determination," this right is consistent with the process of
living together with all other nations, united in a world
organization.

Mankind must learn this basic lesson of variety within a
well organized international society—of diversity within the
framework of a family of nations. The world is moving
towards this goal and there can be no shortcut to world peace
until a world order is achieved. Let all the nations feel that
which the sons of Jacob realized—we have one soul.

Remembrance of Things Past

"Remember the days of old, Consider the years of the generations." (Deuteronomy 32: 7)

IN MOSES' FINAL ADDRESS to the Jewish people, he exhorts them to reflect on the events of distant history and to study the train of the generations. Our purpose in remembering the past is to gain proper perspective with which to comprehend the present. We reflect on our yesterdays to prepare properly for our tomorrows. Our generation's appoach to life is enriched when we consider what has happened to the successive ages of man. Startled by the tremendous forward strides of science, our reflections remind us of other impressive events in the annals of mankind.

We remember the changes, yet we realize, as the French express it, *plus ca change, plus c'est la meme chose,* the more change, the more of the same thing. With all that has transpired, man himself remains the same. His need for emotional security, his striving for recognition, his yearning to love and to be loved, has remained the same, unchanged since the birth of time.

Shortly after the pathetic early passing of Rabbi Milton Steinberg, I met his aged father in a book shop. I tried to give him some solace. A book shop, with its accumulation of the wisdom of the ages, is a wonderful locale for a man and his thoughts. Mr. Steinberg told me that his strength came from the words of the Psalm, "For the Lord is good, His mercy endures forever and His faithfulness unto all generations." "Yes," the old man said, "God is a good God, yet each generation has to recapture its faith, over and over again."

311

This profound insight of a grieving parent has remained with me. Every generation meets not only the challenge of outer change, but that of inner self-searching. We remember the test of centuries; we think of the generations; we are ever mindful of what has happened to them and what is happening to us. Those who had faith, persevered; and we who are their descendants are alive this day.

On Being a Friend

"And Jonathan said to David: 'Go in peace . . .'"
(I Samuel 20:42)

THE CLASSIC EXAMPLE in our heritage of selfless friendship is the case of David, a shepherd, and Jonathan, a king's child, bound together by loyalty and devotion.

Their friendship was an instance of what has been called "one soul and bodies twain." Their intimacy had no ulterior motive. Deep affection and common concern bound them together.

We moderns have a different approach to the total experience of companionship. So many of us, guided by a utilitarian concept of friendship, use the Dale Carnegie "How to Win Friends and Influence People" approach.

Why do we seek people out? To curry their favor? To win their confidence—so that we can influence and use them?

In Hebrew one has at least three alternate expressions for the word "friend." We can use *haver, reah,* or *ahuv.*

Haver literally means an associate who is bound together with us. His concerns are our concerns, his needs our needs. Ben Sira once said, "A true friend does not turn aside in the day of trouble." He is no fair weather comrade, but stands by us in our hour of need.

In the classic tradition it was said, "Friends are those who come to us in good fortune when they are called, and in adversity without waiting to be called."

Reah is close to the Hebrew word for shepherd. A friend is one who helps to guide us and is prepared to think through our problems with us. We are so intimate with him that he can help to correct, if need be.

313

Dr. Louis Finkelstein once spoke of the true friend as one who restores humility rather than feeds arrogance, who loves his friend's best self and does not cater to his worst. This type of colleague is surely the most creative of our associates.

Ahuv means an intimate one who is truly loved by us. This experience of friendship cannot always be explained by means of reason. It is a reflection of the mystery of human relations, the attraction which people feel for one another.

Essential to any real development of friendship is an understanding, not only for others, but of oneself. To have friends, one must be a friend, not only of others but of oneself.

I read this perceptive statement recently: "The art of getting along with others has deep roots. It comes from a deep conviction within oneself of the worth of oneself." To have proper respect and admiration for others we must assess ourselves correctly.

Getting along with people must include the ability to disagree with friends and still maintain a good companionship. Our friends are not to be expected to give up their earnest differences on crucial issues, their firm convictions on vital matters.

A Medieval Jewish philosopher captured the essence of this discussion: "A friend is someone outside yourself and, yet, in truth he is you; though the bodies of two friends are unique and distinct, their souls cling and cleave to each other."